ST/LIB/SER.B/E.87

# Index to the Proceedings of the Economic and Social Council

Organizational session – 2010
Substantive session – 2010

Dag Hammarskjöld Library      New York, 2011      United Nations

ST/LIB/SER.B/E.87

# DAG HAMMARSKJÖLD LIBRARY

Bibliographical Series, No. E.87

# UNITED NATIONS PUBLICATION

Sales No. 11.I.17

ISBN: 978-92-1-101254-5

ISSN: 0082-8084

# ANNOUNCEMENT

This is the last issue of the Index to Proceedings
in print format.

Future issues of the Index to Proceedings will be accessible
online.

To access the full-text versions of the Index to Proceedings,
please visit the **Dag Hammarskjöld Library's** website:

http://www.un.org/Depts/dhl/

Please send any comments you may have to:
unreference@un.org

# CONTENTS

## Organizational session

## Substantive session

# INTRODUCTION

The Economic and Social Council, under the authority of the General Assembly, is the United Nations organ which coordinates the economic and social work of the United Nations and its system of organizations. The Council has 54 members and until 1991 held the following sessions each year: a short organizational session in New York in January, the first regular session in New York in May, the second regular session in Geneva in July. The rules of procedure of the Council were amended by resolution 1992/2 and from 1992 on, the Council normally holds an organizational session in February in New York and one substantive session, with one "high-level segment" a year; the substantive session takes place in alternate years in New York and Geneva between May and July. Throughout the year there are meetings of the Council's committees, commissions and other subsidiary bodies.

The *Index to Proceedings of the Economic and Social Council* is an annual bibliographic guide to the proceedings and documentation of the Economic and Social Council. This issue covers the year 2010, which includes the documentation of the organizational and the substantive sessions. The *Index* is prepared by the Dag Hammarskjöld Library, Department of Public Information, as one of the products of the United Nations Bibliographic Information System (UNBIS).

## ARRANGEMENT OF THE INDEX

The *Index* consists of three sections.

The first section contains information relating to organizational matters:

**Sessional information**, listing member States and their terms of office as well as the officers of the Council and providing information on rules of procedure and resolutions and decisions;

**Subsidiary bodies and organs and programmes related to the Economic and Social Council to which members were elected or appointed during the 2010 sessions of the Council**, listing the members and terms of office.

The second section consists of two parts, one for each session which met during the year. Each part is subdivided as follows:

**Check-list of meetings**, listing the meetings of the Economic and Social Council;

**Agenda**, listing matters considered by and brought before the Council and the subject headings under which these items appear in the Subject index;

**Subject index**, providing topical access to Economic and Social Council documentation arranged alphabetically by subject and listing documents considered under each item, meetings at which the items were considered and the action taken by the Council;

**Index to speeches**, providing access to speeches that were made before the Council. The Index is divided into three sections: corporate names/countries, speakers and subjects.

*Speakers' names are based on information found in United Nations documents. To submit a name correction, please send an e-mail to unreference@un.org*

The third section contains consolidated information relating to resolutions, documents and reports:

**List of resolutions**, listing resolutions adopted by the Council and indicating for each session the resolution number, the subject and the meeting and date when the resolution was adopted;

**List of documents**, listing documents issued for the year 2010 and providing information on the republication of provisional documents in printed *Official Records*;

## SERIES SYMBOLS

In 1978 certain modifications were introduced in the citation and series symbols of the documents of the Economic and Social Council. They are as follows:

(a)    The sessions of the Council are formally identified as the organizational and substantive sessions of a particular calendar year, as prescribed in rule 1 of the rules of procedure of the Council;

(b)    Special sessions, including subject-oriented sessions, are numbered consecutively within each year, and are identified as the first special session (year), second special session (year), etc;

(c)    Ad hoc sessional committees may be established as required and are described as ad hoc sessional committees on particular subjects;

(d)    *Supplements* to the *Official Records* are numbered consecutively, with Supplements No. 1 and 1A containing the resolutions and decisions adopted during the year.

Symbols of documents of the Council and its ad hoc committees or other bodies consist of combinations as appropriate, of the following elements:

(a)    The parent body (i.e. the Economic and Social Council): E/- ;

(b)    The year of consideration.

## DOCUMENTATION OF THE ECONOMIC AND SOCIAL COUNCIL

Summary records of plenary meetings of the Economic and Social Council are first issued in provisional form for limited distribution. They are later combined in corrected form in a single printed volume of *Official Records* for the year.

All summary records may be identified by their symbol, which consists of the series symbol followed by SR. and then a number which corresponds to the number of the meeting. The 5th plenary meeting, for example, is cited as E/2010/SR.5.

Some documents may later be printed as *Supplements* to the *Official Records* (and are so indicated in this index); others are issued only in provisional form.

## HOW TO OBTAIN DOCUMENTS

Printed documentation of the Economic and Social Council for 2010 may be obtained or purchased from authorized sales agents by providing the following information:

*Official Records of the Economic and Social Council, 2010*:

**Meeting No.**    (specify meeting number) for summary record fascicles;

**Supplement No.**    (specify supplement number).

# ABBREVIATIONS

| | |
|---|---|
| Add. | addendum, addenda |
| A.I. | Agenda item |
| Corr. | corrigendum, corrigenda |
| ECA | Economic Commission for Africa |
| ECE | Economic Commission for Europe |
| ECLAC | Economic Commission for Latin America and the Caribbean |
| ECOSOC | Economic and Social Council |
| ESCAP | Economic and Social Commission for Asia and the Pacific |
| ESCOR | *Official Records of the Economic and Social Council* |
| ESCWA | Economic and Social Commission for Western Asia |
| FAO | Food and Agriculture Organization |
| GAOR | *Official Records of the General Assembly* |
| IAEA | International Atomic Energy Agency |
| IBRD | International Bank for Reconstruction and Development |
| ILO | International Labour Organization |
| IMF | International Monetary Fund |
| NGO | Non-governmental organizations |
| No. | Number |
| Rev. | Revision |
| sess. | session |
| Suppl. | Supplement |
| UN | United Nations |
| UNCTAD | United Nations Conference on Trade and Development |
| UNDP | United Nations Development Programme |
| UNEP | United Nations Environment Programme |
| Unesco | United Nations Educational, Scientific and Cultural Organization |
| UNFPA | United Nations Population Fund |
| UN-HABITAT | United Nations Settlement Programme |
| UNHCR | United Nations High Commissioner for Refugees |
| UNICEF | United Nations Children's Fund |
| WHO | World Health Organization |
| WMO | World Maritime Organization |
| WTO | World Trade Organization |

# SESSIONAL INFORMATION

## MEMBERS AND TERM OF OFFICE

| Members | Date of election by the General Assembly | Term of office (1 Jan.-31 Dec.) | Members | Date of election by the General Assembly | Term of office (1 Jan.-31 Dec.) |
|---|---|---|---|---|---|
| Argentina | 26 Oct. 2009 | 2010-2012 | Malta | 26 Oct. 2009 | 2010-2011 |
| Australia | 26 Oct. 2009 | 2010 | Mauritius | 22 Oct. 2008 | 2009-2011 |
| Bahamas | 26 Oct. 2009 | 2010-2012 | Mongolia | 26 Oct. 2009 | 2010-2012 |
| Bangladesh | 26 Oct. 2009 | 2010-2012 | Morocco | 22 Oct. 2008 | 2009-2011 |
| Belgium | 26 Oct. 2009 | 2010-2012 | Mozambique | 8 Nov. 2007 | 2008-2010 |
| Brazil | 8 Nov. 2007 | 2008-2010 | Namibia | 22 Oct. 2008 | 2009-2011 |
| Cameroon | 8 Nov. 2007 | 2008-2010 | Niger | 8 Nov. 2007 | 2008-2010 |
| Canada | 26 Oct. 2009 | 2010-2012 | Norway | 22 Oct. 2008 | 2008-2010 |
| Chile | 26 Oct. 2009 | 2010-2012 | Pakistan | 8 Nov. 2007 | 2008-2010 |
| China | 8 Nov. 2007 | 2008-2010 | Peru | 22 Oct. 2008 | 2009-2011 |
| Comoros | 26 Oct. 2009 | 2010-2012 | Philippines | 26 Oct. 2009 | 2010-2012 |
| Congo | 8 Nov. 2007 | 2008-2010 | Poland | 8 Nov. 2007 | 2008-2010 |
| Côte d'Ivoire | 22 Oct. 2008 | 2009-2011 | Republic of Korea | 8 Nov. 2007 | 2008-2010 |
| Egypt | 26 Oct. 2009 | 2010-2012 | Republic of Moldova | 8 Nov. 2007 | 2008-2010 |
| Estonia | 22 Oct. 2008 | 2009-2011 | Russian Federation | 8 Nov. 2007 | 2008-2010 |
| Finland | 26 Oct. 2009 | 2010 | Rwanda | 26 Oct. 2009 | 2010-2012 |
| France | 22 Oct. 2008 | 2009-2011 | Saint Kitts and Nevis | 22 Oct. 2008 | 2009-2011 |
| Germany | 22 Oct. 2008 | 2009-2011 | Saint Lucia | 8 Nov. 2007 | 2008-2010 |
| Ghana | 26 Oct. 2009 | 2010-2012 | Saudi Arabia | 22 Oct. 2008 | 2009-2011 |
| Guatemala | 22 Oct. 2008 | 2009-2011 | Slovakia | 26 Oct. 2009 | 2010-2012 |
| Guinea-Bissau | 22 Oct. 2008 | 2009-2011 | Turkey | 26 Oct. 2009 | 2010-2011 |
| India | 22 Oct. 2008 | 2009-2011 | Ukraine | 26 Oct. 2009 | 2010-2012 |
| Iraq | 26 Oct. 2009 | 2010-2012 | United Kingdom | 8 Nov. 2007 | 2008-2010 |
| Italy | 26 Oct. 2009 | 2010-2012 | United States | 26 Oct. 2009 | 2010-2012 |
| Japan | 22 Oct. 2008 | 2009-2011 | Uruguay | 8 Nov. 2007 | 2008-2010 |
| Liechtenstein | 22 Oct. 2008 | 2009-2011 | Venezuela (Bolivarian Republic of) | 22 Oct. 2008 | 2009-2011 |
| Malaysia | 8 Nov. 2007 | 2008-2010 | Zambia | 26 Oct. 2009 | 2010-2012 |

## OFFICERS

| | |
|---|---|
| President | Hamidon Ali (Malaysia) was elected by acclamation at the 1st plenary meeting (organizational session). |
| Vice-Presidents | Somduth Soborun (Mauritius), Alexandru Cujba (Republic of Moldova), Heraldo Muñoz (Chile) and Morten Wetland (Norway) were elected by acclamation at the 1st plenary meeting (organizational session). Octavio Errázuriz (Chile) was elected by acclamation at the 10st plenary meeting (organizational session) to serve the unexpired portion of the term of office of Heraldo Muñoz (Chile). |
| Secretaries | Jennifer De Laurentis<br>Otto Gustafik<br>Moncef Khane<br>Vivian Pliner |

## RULES OF PROCEDURE

The rules of procedure of the Economic and Social Council contained in document E/5715/Rev.2 (Sales No. E.92.I.22) were in effect during all 2010 sessions of the Council (organizational, high-level segment and substantive).

## RESOLUTIONS AND DECISIONS

Resolutions and decisions of the 2010 organizational and substantive sessions are collected in document E/2010/99 (ESCOR, 2010, Suppl. no. 1).

Resolutions are listed separately on pages 115-116 under the heading "List of resolutions".

# SUBSIDIARY BODIES AND ORGANS AND PROGRAMMES RELATED TO THE ECONOMIC AND SOCIAL COUNCIL TO WHICH MEMBERS WERE ELECTED OR APPOINTED DURING THE 2010 SESSIONS OF THE COUNCIL

## Commission for Social Development
### as of 1 Jan. 2011

| Members | Term of office (expires at close of session in the year) |
|---|---|
| Albania | 2013 |
| Andorra | 2015 |
| Argentina | 2012 |
| Armenia | 2012 |
| Benin | 2011 |
| Brazil | 2013 |
| Burkina Faso | 2015 |
| Cameroon | 2015 |
| China | 2013 |
| Cuba | 2015 |
| Egypt | 2015 |
| El Salvador | 2012 |
| Ethiopia | 2013 |
| France | 2012 |
| Gabon | 2013 |
| Germany | 2012 |
| Ghana | 2012 |
| Guatemala | 2012 |
| Haiti | 2013 |
| India | 2011 |
| Iran (Islamic Republic of) | 2013 |
| Italy | 2013 |
| Jamaica | 2011 |
| Japan | 2012 |
| Lesotho | 2013 |
| Mauritius | 2013 |
| Mexico | 2015 |
| Namibia | 2011 |
| Nepal | 2011 |
| Netherlands | 2013 |
| Nigeria | 2012 |
| Pakistan | 2012 |
| Peru | 2015 |
| Philippines | 2013 |
| Qatar | 2013 |
| Republic of Korea | 2012 |
| Russian Federation | 2012 |
| Senegal | 2012 |
| Slovakia | 2011 |
| Spain | 2015 |
| Sudan | 2012 |
| Sweden | 2013 |
| Switzerland | 2013 |
| Turkey | 2011 |
| United Arab Emirates | 2011 |
| United States | 2012 |
| Venezuela (Bolivarian Republic of) | 2013 |
| Zimbabwe | 2015 |

## Commission on Population and Development
### as of 1 Jan. 2011

| Members | Term of office (expires at close of session in the year) |
|---|---|
| Algeria | 2015 |
| Angola | 2014 |
| Bangladesh | 2013 |
| Belarus | 2013 |
| Belgium | 2013 |
| Benin | 2011 |
| Brazil | 2013 |
| China | 2014 |
| Colombia | 2012 |
| Côte d'Ivoire | 2013 |
| Croatia | 2012 |
| Cuba | 2013 |
| Democratic Republic of the Congo | 2013 |
| Equatorial Guinea | 2011 |
| Finland | 2012 |
| Gabon | 2015 |
| Georgia | 2015 |
| Germany | 2013 |
| Ghana | 2014 |
| Grenada | 2011 |
| Guatemala | 2014 |
| Haiti | 2013 |
| Honduras | 2011 |
| Hungary | 2014 |
| India | 2014 |
| Indonesia | 2013 |
| Iran (Islamic Republic of) | 2011 |
| Israel | 2013 |
| Jamaica | 2014 |
| Japan | 2012 |
| Kazakhstan | 2012 |
| Kenya | 2012 |
| Luxembourg | 2014 |
| Malawi | 2014 |
| Malaysia | 2014 |
| Netherlands | 2012 |
| Pakistan | 2013 |
| Philippines | 2014 |
| Poland | 2011 |
| Russian Federation | 2014 |
| Rwanda | 2013 |
| Saint Lucia | 2014 |
| Senegal | 2014 |
| Sri Lanka | 2011 |
| Spain | 2011 |
| Switzerland | 2013 |
| Tunisia | 2012 |
| Uganda | 2012 |
| United Kingdom | 2014 |
| United States | 2015 |

## Commission on Science and Technology for Development
as of 1 Jan. 2011

| Members | Term of office (expires 31 Dec.) |
|---|---|
| Austria | 2012 |
| Brazil | 2012 |
| Chile | 2012 |
| China | 2014 |
| Costa Rica | 2012 |
| Cuba | 2014 |
| Democratic Republic of the Congo | 2012 |
| Dominican Republic | 2014 |
| El Salvador | 2014 |
| Equatorial Guinea | 2012 |
| Finland | 2012 |
| France | 2014 |
| Ghana | 2012 |
| India | 2014 |
| Iran (Islamic Republic of) | 2014 |
| Israel | 2012 |
| Jamaica | 2012 |
| Jordan | 2012 |
| Latvia | 2014 |
| Lesotho | 2014 |
| Mali | 2012 |
| Mauritius | 2014 |
| Oman | 2012 |
| Pakistan | 2012 |
| Peru | 2014 |
| Philippines | 2014 |
| Portugal | 2012 |
| Russian Federation | 2012 |
| Rwanda | 2014 |
| Slovakia | 2012 |
| South Africa | 2012 |
| Sri Lanka | 2012 |
| Switzerland | 2012 |
| Togo | 2014 |
| Tunisia | 2014 |
| United Republic of Tanzania | 2014 |
| United States | 2014 |

## Commission on Sustainable Development
as of 1 Jan. 2011

| Members | Term of office (expires at close of session in the year) |
|---|---|
| Algeria | 2013 |
| Angola | 2014 |
| Antigua and Barbuda | 2012 |
| Argentina | 2011 |
| Armenia | 2014 |
| Australia | 2012 |
| Bahamas | 2013 |
| Bangladesh | 2011 |
| Belarus | 2013 |
| Belgium | 2014 |
| Benin | 2013 |
| Botswana | 2014 |

## Commission on Sustainable Development
as of 1 Jan. 2011
(continued)

| Members | Term of office (expires at close of session in the year) |
|---|---|
| Brazil | 2014 |
| Canada | 2011 |
| China | 2012 |
| Colombia | 2012 |
| Congo | 2014 |
| Côte d'Ivoire | 2013 |
| Cuba | 2012 |
| Democratic Republic of the Congo | 2011 |
| Denmark | 2013 |
| El Salvador | 2014 |
| Equatorial Guinea | 2014 |
| Eritrea | 2012 |
| Estonia | 2011 |
| Ethiopia | 2012 |
| France | 2013 |
| Gabon | 2011 |
| Germany | 2014 |
| Indonesia | 2014 |
| Israel | 2011 |
| Italy | 2014 |
| Japan | 2014 |
| Kazakhstan | 2013 |
| Kyrgyzstan | 2012 |
| Latvia | 2013 |
| Lebanon | 2014 |
| Lesotho | 2014 |
| Libyan Arab Jamahiriya | 2011 |
| Luxembourg | 2012 |
| Malawi | 2011 |
| Malaysia | 2013 |
| Mauritius | 2012 |
| Mexico | 2014 |
| Mongolia | 2013 |
| Montenegro | 2014 |
| Namibia | 2011 |
| Netherlands | 2013 |
| Nicaragua | 2014 |
| Nigeria | 2012 |
| Norway | 2013 |
| Pakistan | 2011 |
| Panama | 2013 |
| Peru | 2013 |
| Philippines | 2012 |
| Romania | 2011 |
| Russian Federation | 2012 |
| Saudi Arabia | 2014 |
| Spain | 2014 |
| Switzerland | 2011 |
| Thailand | 2013 |
| Togo | 2013 |
| Ukraine | 2012 |
| United Arab Emirates | 2011 |
| United Kingdom | 2012 |
| United States | 2012 |
| Uruguay | 2011 |
| Venezuela (Bolivarian Republic of) | 2011 |

## Commission on the Status of Women
as of 1 Jan. 2011

| Members | Term of office (expires at close of session in the year) |
| --- | --- |
| Armenia | 2011 |
| Argentina | 2014 |
| Azerbaijan | 2011 |
| Bangladesh | 2014 |
| Belarus | 2013 |
| Belgium | 2015 |
| Cambodia | 2011 |
| Central African Republic | 2014 |
| China | 2012 |
| Colombia | 2013 |
| Comoros | 2014 |
| Cuba | 2012 |
| Democratic Republic of the Congo | 2015 |
| Dominican Republic | 2012 |
| El Salvador | 2014 |
| Eritrea | 2012 |
| Estonia | 2015 |
| Gabon | 2011 |
| Gambia | 2014 |
| Georgia | 2015 |
| Germany | 2013 |
| Guinea | 2013 |
| Haiti | 2012 |
| India | 2012 |
| Iran (Islamic Republic of) | 2015 |
| Iraq | 2013 |
| Israel | 2013 |
| Italy | 2013 |
| Jamaica | 2015 |
| Japan | 2013 |
| Liberia | 2015 |
| Libyan Arab Jamahiriya | 2014 |
| Malaysia | 2014 |
| Mauritania | 2013 |
| Mongolia | 2014 |
| Namibia | 2011 |
| Netherlands | 2015 |
| Nicaragua | 2013 |
| Niger | 2011 |
| Pakistan | 2011 |
| Paraguay | 2011 |
| Philippines | 2014 |
| Republic of Korea | 2014 |
| Russian Federation | 2012 |
| Rwanda | 2013 |
| Senegal | 2012 |
| Spain | 2015 |
| Swaziland | 2014 |
| Sweden | 2012 |
| Thailand | 2015 |
| Turkey | 2011 |
| United States | 2012 |
| Uruguay | 2014 |
| Zimbabwe | 2015 |

## Committee for Development Policy
as of 1 Jan. 2011

| Members | Term of office (expires 31 Dec.) |
| --- | --- |
| Agarwal, Bina (India) | 2012 |
| Allegretti, Mary Helena (Brazil) | 2012 |
| Alonso, José Antonio (Spain) | 2012 |
| Amsden, Alice (United States) | 2012 |
| Arizpe, Lourdes (Mexico) | 2012 |
| Botchwey, Kwesi (Ghana) | 2012 |
| Cornia, Giovanni Andrea (Italy) | 2012 |
| Ffrench-Davis, Ricardo (Chile) | 2012 |
| Fukuda-Parr, Sakiko (Japan) | 2012 |
| Girvan, Norman (Jamaica) | 2012 |
| Hein, Philippe (Mauritius) | 2012 |
| Ketsela, Mulu (Ethiopia) | 2012 |
| Mahmud, Wahiduddin (Bangladesh) | 2012 |
| Mama, Amina (South Africa) | 2012 |
| Mkwandawire, Thandika (Sweden) | 2012 |
| Najam, Adil (Pakistan) | 2012 |
| Opschoor, Hans (Netherlands) | 2012 |
| Phongpaichit, Pasuk (Thailand) | 2012 |
| Plane, Patrick (France) | 2012 |
| Polterovich, Victor (Russian Federation) | 2012 |
| Sadiqi, Fatima (Morocco) | 2012 |
| Stewart, Frances (United Kingdom) | 2012 |
| Uvalic, Milica (Serbia) | 2012 |
| Yu, Yongding (China) | 2012 |

## Committee for Programme and Coordination
as of 1 Jan. 2011

| Members | Term of office (expires 31 Dec.) |
| --- | --- |
| Algeria | 2013 |
| Antigua and Barbuda | 2013 |
| Argentina | 2011 |
| Armenia | 2011 |
| Belarus | 2011 |
| Benin | 2013 |
| Brazil | 2011 |
| Central African Republic | 2011 |
| China | 2013 |
| Comoros | 2012 |
| Cuba | 2011 |
| Eritrea | 2013 |
| Guinea | 2011 |
| Haiti | 2012 |
| India | 2011 |
| Iran (Islamic Republic of) | 2011 |
| Israel | 2012 |
| Italy | 2011 |
| Kazakhstan | 2011 |
| Namibia | 2012 |
| Nigeria | 2011 |
| Pakistan | 2011 |
| Republic of Korea | 2013 |
| Russian Federation | 2012 |
| South Africa | 2011 |
| Spain | 2011 |
| Ukraine | 2011 |
| Uruguay | 2011 |
| Venezuela (Bolivarian Republic of) | 2012 |

## Committee for the United Nations Population Award
### as of 1 Jan. 2011

| Members | Term of office (expires 31 Dec.) |
|---|---|
| Bangladesh | 2012 |
| Czech Republic | 2012 |
| Egypt | 2012 |
| Ghana | 2012 |
| Guatemala | 2012 |
| Jamaica | 2012 |
| Malaysia | 2012 |
| Nicaragua | 2012 |
| Norway | 2012 |
| United Republic of Tanzania | 2012 |

## Committee of Experts on International Cooperation In Tax Matters
### as of 31 May 2011

| Members | Term of office (expires 30 June) |
|---|---|
| Adjei-Djan, Kwame (Ghana) | 2013 |
| Ahn, Sae Joon (Republic of Korea) | 2013 |
| Amjad, Farida (Pakistan) | 2013 |
| Aoyama, Keiji (Japan) | 2013 |
| Arrindell, Bernell L. (Barbados) | 2013 |
| Bensouda, Noureddine (Morocco) | 2013 |
| Devillet, Claudine (Belgium) | 2013 |
| Diop, El Hadj Ibrahima (Senegal) | 2013 |
| El Monayer, Amr (Egypt) | 2013 |
| Giraudi, Juerg (Switzerland) | 2013 |
| Hassan, Mansor (Malaysia) | 2013 |
| Kana, Liselott (Chile) | 2013 |
| Kapur, Anita (India) | 2013 |
| Lasars, Wolfgang Karl (Germany) | 2013 |
| Liao, Tizhong (China) | 2013 |
| Louie, Henry John (United States) | 2013 |
| Martínez Rico, Julia (Spain) | 2013 |
| Martino, Enrico (Italy) | 2013 |
| Oliver, Robin (New Zealand) | 2013 |
| Omoigui Okauru, Ifueko (Nigeria) | 2013 |
| Slavcheva, Iskra Georgieva (Bulgaria) | 2013 |
| Sollund, Stig B. (Norway) | 2013 |
| Valadao, Marcos Aurelio Pereira (Brazil) | 2013 |
| Van der Merwe, Ronald Peter (South Africa) | 2013 |
| Yaffar, Armando Lara (Mexico) | 2013 |

## Committee of Experts on the Transport of Dangerous Goods and on the Globally Harmonized System of Classification and Labelling of Chemicals. Subcommittee of Experts on the Globally Harmonized System of Classification and Labelling of Chemicals
### Membership in 2011

| Members | Members |
|---|---|
| Argentina | Belgium |
| Australia | Brazil |
| Austria | Canada |

## Committee of Experts on the Transport of Dangerous Goods and on the Globally Harmonized System of Classification and Labelling of Chemicals. Subcommittee of Experts on the Globally Harmonized System of Classification and Labelling of Chemicals
### Membership in 2011
### (continued)

| Members | Members |
|---|---|
| China | Norway |
| Czech Republic | Poland |
| Denmark | Portugal |
| Finland | Qatar |
| France | Republic of Korea |
| Germany | Russian Federation |
| Greece | Senegal |
| Iran (Islamic Republic of) | Serbia |
| Ireland | South Africa |
| Italy | Spain |
| Japan | Sweden |
| Kenya | Ukraine |
| Netherlands | United Kingdom |
| New Zealand | United States |
| Nigeria | Zambia |

## Committee of Experts on the Transport of Dangerous Goods and on the Globally Harmonized System of Classification and Labelling of Chemicals. Subcommittee of Experts on the Transport of Dangerous Goods
### Membership in 2011

| Members | Members |
|---|---|
| Argentina | Kenya |
| Australia | Netherlands |
| Austria | Norway |
| Belgium | Poland |
| Brazil | Portugal |
| Canada | Republic of Korea |
| China | Russian Federation |
| Czech Republic | Mexico |
| Finland | Morocco |
| France | South Africa |
| Germany | Spain |
| India | Sweden |
| Iran (Islamic Republic of) | Switzerland |
| Italy | United Kingdom |
| Japan | United States |

## Committee on Economic, Social and Cultural Rights
### as of 1 Jan. 2011

| Members | Term of office (expires 31 Dec.) |
|---|---|
| Abashidze, Aslan Khuseinovich (Russian Federation) | 2014 |
| Abdel-Moneim, Mohamed Ezzeldin (Egypt) | 2012 |
| Atangana, Clément (Cameroon) | 2014 |
| Barahona Riera, María del Rocío (Costa Rica) | 2012 |

## Committee on Economic, Social and Cultural Rights
### as of 1 Jan. 2011
### (continued)

| Members | Term of office (expires 31 Dec.) |
|---|---|
| Cong, Jun (China) | 2012 |
| Dasgupta, Chandrashekhar (India) | 2014 |
| Kedzia, Zdzislaw (Poland) | 2012 |
| Kerdoun, Azzouz (Algeria) | 2014 |
| Marchán Romero, Jaime (Ecuador) | 2014 |
| Martynov, Sergei N. (Belarus) | 2012 |
| Pillay, Ariranga Govindasamy (Mauritius) | 2012 |
| Ribeiro Leão, Renato Zerbini (Brazil) | 2014 |
| Riedel, Eibe (Germany) | 2014 |
| Sa'di, Waleed M. (Jordan) | 2012 |
| Schrijver, Nikolaas Jan (Netherlands) | 2012 |
| Shin, Heisoo (Republic of Korea) | 2014 |
| Texier, Philippe (France) | 2012 |
| Tirado Mejía, Alvaro (Colombia) | 2014 |

## Committee on Non-Governmental Organizations
### as 1 of Jan. 2011

| Members | Term of office (expires 31 Dec.) |
|---|---|
| Belgium | 2014 |
| Bulgaria | 2014 |
| Burundi | 2014 |
| China | 2014 |
| Cuba | 2014 |
| India | 2014 |
| Israel | 2014 |
| Kyrgyzstan | 2014 |
| Morocco | 2014 |
| Mozambique | 2014 |
| Nicaragua | 2014 |
| Pakistan | 2014 |
| Peru | 2014 |
| Russian Federation | 2014 |
| Senegal | 2014 |
| Sudan | 2014 |
| Turkey | 2014 |
| United States | 2014 |
| Venezuela (Bolivarian Republic of) | 2014 |

## Executive Committee of the UNHCR Programme
### Membership in 2011

| Members | Members |
|---|---|
| Algeria | Colombia |
| Argentina | Costa Rica |
| Australia | Côte d'Ivoire |
| Austria | Cyprus |
| Bangladesh | Democratic Republic of the Congo |
| Belgium | Denmark |
| Benin | Djibouti |
| Brazil | Ecuador |
| Canada | Egypt |
| Chile | Estonia |
| China | Ethiopia |

## Executive Committee of the UNHCR Programme
### Membership in 2011
### (continued)

| Members | Members |
|---|---|
| Finland | Pakistan |
| France | Philippines |
| Germany | Poland |
| Ghana | Portugal |
| Greece | Republic of Korea |
| Guinea | Republic of Moldova |
| Holy See | Romania |
| Hungary | Russian Federation |
| India | Serbia |
| Iran (Islamic Republic of) | Slovenia |
| Ireland | Somalia |
| Israel | South Africa |
| Italy | Spain |
| Japan | Sudan |
| Jordan | Sweden |
| Kenya | Switzerland |
| Lebanon | Thailand |
| Lesotho | The former Yugoslav Republic of Macedonia |
| Luxembourg | |
| Madagascar | Tunisia |
| Mexico | Turkey |
| Montenegro | Uganda |
| Morocco | United Kingdom |
| Mozambique | United Republic of Tanzania |
| Namibia | United States |
| Netherlands | Venezuela (Bolivarian Republic of) |
| New Zealand | |
| Nicaragua | Yemen |
| Nigeria | Zambia |
| Norway | |

## Intergovernmental Working Group of Experts on International Standards of Accounting and Reporting
### Membership in 2011

| Members | Term of office (expires 31 Dec.) |
|---|---|
| Benin | 2012 |
| Botswana | 2011 |
| Brazil | 2012 |
| Cameroon | 2012 |
| China | 2011 |
| Croatia | 2012 |
| Egypt | 2012 |
| Eritrea | 2011 |
| France | 2011 |
| Germany | 2011 |
| Kyrgyzstan | 2011 |
| Malta | 2011 |
| Namibia | 2011 |
| Niger | 2011 |
| Poland | 2012 |
| Portugal | 2011 |
| Russian Federation | 2011 |
| Saint Kitts and Nevis | 2012 |
| South Africa | 2011 |
| Sri Lanka | 2011 |
| Sweden | 2011 |
| United Republic of Tanzania | 2012 |

## International Narcotics Control Board
### as of 2 Mar. 2010

| Members | Term of office (expires 1 Mar.) |
|---|---|
| Ghodse, Hamid (Islamic Republic of Iran) | 2012 |
| Korchagina, Galina Aleksandrovna (Russian Federation) | 2015 |
| Lander, Carola (Germany) | 2012 |
| Levitsky, Melvyn (United States) | 2012 |
| Moinard, Marc (France) | 2015 |
| Montaño, Jorge (Mexico) | 2012 |
| Naidoo, Lochan (South Africa) | 2015 |
| Ray, Rajat (India) | 2015 |
| Sumyai, Viroj (Thailand) | 2015 |
| Suryawati, Sri (Indonesia) | 2012 |
| Uribe Granja, Camilo (Colombia) | 2015 |
| Yans, Raymond (Belgium) | 2012 |
| Yu, Xin (China) | 2012 |

## International Research and Training Institute for the Advancement of Women.
### Executive Board

| Members | Term of office (expires 31 Dec.) |
|---|---|
| Belarus | 2012 |
| Benin | 2012 |
| Djibouti | 2012 |
| Honduras | 2012 |
| Saint Vincent and the Grenadines | 2012 |
| Slovakia | 2012 |

## Joint United Nations Programme on HIV/AIS.
### Programme Coordination Board
#### Membership in 2011

| Members | Term of office (expires 31 Dec.) |
|---|---|
| Bangladesh | 2013 |
| Botswana | 2012 |
| Brazil | 2011 |
| Canada | 2011 |
| China | 2012 |
| Congo | 2011 |
| Djibouti | 2013 |
| Egypt | 2013 |
| El Salvador | 2012 |
| Finland | 2011 |
| India | 2013 |
| Japan | 2012 |
| Mexico | 2013 |
| Monaco | 2013 |
| Netherlands | 2012 |
| Poland | 2012 |
| Russian Federation | 2013 |
| Sweden | 2012 |
| Thailand | 2011 |
| Togo | 2012 |
| United Kingdom | 2012 |
| United States | 2013 |

## Peacebuilding Commission.
### Organizational Committee
#### as of 1 Jan. 2011

| Members | Term of office (expires 31 Dec.) |
|---|---|
| Australia | 2011 |
| Bangladesh | 2011 |
| Benin | 2011 |
| Brazil | 2011 |
| Canada | 2011 |
| Chile | 2011 |
| China | 2011 |
| Czech Republic | 2011 |
| Egypt | 2012 |
| France | 2011 |
| Gabon | 2011 |
| Germany | 2011 |
| Guatemala | 2012 |
| Guinea-Bissau | 2011 |
| India | 2011 |
| Japan | 2011 |
| Mexico | 2011 |
| Morocco | 2011 |
| Nepal | 2011 |
| Netherlands | 2011 |
| Nigeria | 2011 |
| Pakistan | 2011 |
| Peru | 2011 |
| Poland | 2011 |
| Republic of Korea | 2011 |
| Russian Federation | 2011 |
| Rwanda | 2012 |
| South Africa | 2011 |
| Spain | 2012 |
| Sweden | 2011 |
| Thailand | 2011 |
| Ukraine | 2012 |
| United Kingdom | 2011 |
| United States | 2011 |
| Uruguay | 2011 |
| Zambia | 2012 |

## Permanent Forum on Indigenous Issues
### as of 1 Jan. 2011

| Members | Term of office (1 Jan.-31 Dec.) |
|---|---|
| Biaudet, Eva (Finland) | 2011-2013 |
| Cunningham Kain, Mirna (Nicaragua) | 2011-2013 |
| Davis, Megan (Australia) | 2011-2013 |
| Devashish Roy, Raja (Bangladesh) | 2011-2013 |
| Dorough, Dalee Sambo (United States) | 2011-2013 |
| Hasteh, Paimaneh (Islamic Republic of Iran) | 2011-2013 |
| John, Edward (Canada) | 2011-2013 |
| Kaljuläte, Helen (Estonia) | 2011-2013 |
| M'Viboudoulou, Simon William (Congo) | 2011-2013 |
| Naikanchina, Anna (Russian Federation) | 2011-2013 |

## Permanent Forum on Indigenous Issues
### as of 1 Jan. 2011
### (continued)

| Members | Term of office (1 Jan.-31 Dec.) |
|---|---|
| Nikiforov, Andrey A. (Russian Federation) | 2011-2013 |
| Pop Ac, Alvaro Esteban (Guatemala) | 2011-2013 |
| Sena, Paul Kanyinke (Kenya) | 2011-2013 |
| Toki, Valmaine (New Zealand) | 2011-2013 |
| Vásquez, Saúl Vicente (Mexico) | 2011-2013 |
| Xavier, Bertie (Guyana) | 2011-2013 |

## United Nations Children's Fund.
### Executive Board
### as of 1 Jan. 2011

| Members | Term of office (expires 31 Dec.) |
|---|---|
| Antigua and Barbuda | 2013 |
| Bangladesh | 2011 |
| Belarus | 2012 |
| Belgium | 2011 |
| Cape Verde | 2012 |
| China | 2013 |
| Colombia | 2013 |
| Congo | 2012 |
| Cuba | 2011 |
| Denmark | 2012 |
| El Salvador | 2012 |
| Estonia | 2013 |
| France | 2012 |
| Germany | 2012 |
| Indonesia | 2013 |
| Italy | 2013 |
| Japan | 2011 |
| Kazakhstan | 2012 |
| Liberia | 2011 |
| Malawi | 2012 |
| Namibia | 2013 |
| Netherlands | 2013 |
| New Zealand | 2013 |
| Pakistan | 2012 |
| Qatar | 2012 |
| Republic of Korea | 2011 |
| Russian Federation | 2013 |
| Slovenia | 2011 |
| Somalia | 2012 |
| Spain | 2011 |
| Sudan | 2011 |
| Sweden | 2012 |
| Tunisia | 2012 |
| United Kingdom | 2013 |
| United States | 2011 |
| Uruguay | 2011 |

## United Nations Development Programme/ United Nations Population Fund.
### Executive Board
### as of 1 Jan. 2011

| Members | Term of office (expires 31 Dec.) |
|---|---|
| Antigua and Barbuda | 2012 |
| Argentina | 2013 |
| Bangladesh | 2013 |
| Belarus | 2013 |
| Burkina Faso | 2012 |
| Cameroon | 2012 |
| Canada | 2013 |
| China | 2013 |
| Cuba | 2011 |
| Czech Republic | 2013 |
| Democratic Republic of the Congo | 2012 |
| Denmark | 2011 |
| Djibouti | 2013 |
| El Salvador | 2013 |
| Estonia | 2012 |
| Finland | 2013 |
| Germany | 2011 |
| India | 2012 |
| Iran (Islamic Republic of) | 2011 |
| Ireland | 2012 |
| Italy | 2012 |
| Japan | 2012 |
| Luxembourg | 2013 |
| Mauritania | 2011 |
| Mexico | 2011 |
| Netherlands | 2012 |
| Pakistan | 2012 |
| Qatar | 2012 |
| Russian Federation | 2011 |
| Rwanda | 2012 |
| Sierra Leone | 2011 |
| South Africa | 2012 |
| Sweden | 2011 |
| United Kingdom | 2011 |
| United States | 2013 |
| Yemen | 2011 |

## United Nations Human Settlements Programme.
### Governing Council
### as of 1 Jan. 2011

| Members | Term of office (expires 31 Dec.) |
|---|---|
| Afghanistan | 2012 |
| Albania | 2014 |
| Algeria | 2014 |
| Antigua and Barbuda | 2012 |
| Argentina | 2014 |
| Armenia | 2012 |
| Bahrain | 2011 |
| Bangladesh | 2012 |
| Brazil | 2011 |
| Burkina Faso | 2011 |
| Central African Republic | 2014 |
| Chile | 2014 |

**United Nations Human Settlements Programme.**
**Governing Council**
as of 1 Jan. 2011
(continued)

| Members | Term of office (expires 31 Dec.) |
|---|---|
| China | 2012 |
| Congo | 2011 |
| Côte d'Ivoire | 2012 |
| Cuba | 2012 |
| Czech Republic | 2012 |
| Ethiopia | 2012 |
| France | 2012 |
| Gabon | 2014 |
| Germany | 2011 |
| Grenada | 2014 |
| Guatemala | 2012 |
| Honduras | 2011 |
| India | 2011 |
| Indonesia | 2014 |
| Iran (Islamic Republic of) | 2014 |
| Iraq | 2011 |
| Israel | 2011 |
| Jamaica | 2011 |
| Japan | 2014 |
| Kenya | 2011 |
| Mali | 2014 |
| Mozambique | 2014 |
| Nigeria | 2014 |
| Norway | 2012 |
| Pakistan | 2014 |
| Romania | 2011 |
| Republic of Korea | 2012 |
| Russian Federation | 2014 |
| Rwanda | 2012 |
| Saudi Arabia | 2011 |
| Serbia | 2011 |
| Spain | 2012 |
| Sri Lanka | 2011 |
| Sudan | 2012 |
| Swaziland | 2011 |
| Tunisia | 2012 |
| United States | 2014 |
| Venezuela (Bolivarian Republic of) | 2014 |
| Zambia | 2011 |

**UN-Women.**
**Executive Board**
as of 1 Jan. 2011

| Members | Term of office (expires 31 Dec.) |
|---|---|
| Angola | 2013 |
| Argentina | 2013 |
| Bangladesh | 2013 |
| Brazil | 2013 |
| Cape Verde | 2013 |
| China | 2013 |
| Congo | 2013 |
| Côte d'Ivoire | 2013 |
| Democratic Republic of the Congo | 2013 |
| Denmark | 2013 |
| Dominican Republic | 2013 |
| El Salvador | 2013 |
| Estonia | 2013 |
| Ethiopia | 2013 |
| France | 2013 |
| Grenada | 2013 |
| Hungary | 2013 |
| India | 2013 |
| Indonesia | 2013 |
| Italy | 2013 |
| Japan | 2013 |
| Kazakhstan | 2013 |
| Lesotho | 2013 |
| Libyan Arab Jamahiriya | 2013 |
| Luxembourg | 2013 |
| Malaysia | 2013 |
| Mexico | 2013 |
| Nigeria | 2013 |
| Norway | 2013 |
| Pakistan | 2013 |
| Peru | 2013 |
| Republic of Korea | 2013 |
| Russian Federation | 2013 |
| Saudi Arabia | 2013 |
| Spain | 2013 |
| Sweden | 2013 |
| Timor-Leste | 2013 |
| Ukraine | 2013 |
| United Kingdom | 2013 |
| United Republic of Tanzania | 2013 |
| United States | 2013 |

**World Food Programme.**
**Executive Board**
as of 1 Jan. 2011

| Members | Term of office (expires 31 Dec.) |
|---|---|
| Angola | 2011 |
| Australia | 2013 |
| Brazil | 2011 |
| Burkina Faso | 2012 |
| China | 2011 |
| Colombia | 2011 |
| Cuba | 2013 |
| Czech Republic | 2011 |
| Denmark | 2011 |
| Egypt | 2011 |
| France | 2012 |
| Guatemala | 2011 |
| India | 2012 |
| Iran (Islamic Republic of) | 2012 |
| Japan | 2011 |
| Jordan | 2012 |
| Kenya | 2012 |
| Mexico | 2012 |
| Morocco | 2013 |
| Netherlands | 2012 |
| Norway | 2013 |
| Philippines | 2012 |
| Republic of Korea | 2013 |
| Russian Federation | 2012 |
| Slovenia | 2011 |
| Spain | 2012 |
| Sudan | 2013 |
| Switzerland | 2011 |
| United Kingdom | 2011 |
| United States | 2012 |

# ORGANIZATIONAL SESSION OF THE COUNCIL

The organizational session for 2010 of the Economic and Social Council was held at United Nations Headquarters, New York on 19 Jan., 9 and 12 Feb. 2010. The organizational session was resumed on 28 Apr. and 21 May 2010.

## CHECK-LIST OF MEETINGS

### PLENARY
(Symbol E/2010/SR.-)

| Meeting | Date, 2010 |
|---------|------------|
| 1 | 19 Jan. |
| 2 | 9 Feb. |
| 3 | 12 Feb. |
| 4 | (*see* substantive session) |
| 5 | (*see* substantive session) |
| 6 | (*see* substantive session) |
| 7 | (*see* substantive session) |
| 8 | 28 Apr. |
| 9 | 28 Apr. |
| 10 | 21 May |

# AGENDA

1. Election of the Bureau.
   *See:* UN. ECONOMIC AND SOCIAL COUNCIL (2010 : NEW YORK)–OFFICERS

2. Adoption of the agenda and other organizational matters.
   *See:* UN. ECONOMIC AND SOCIAL COUNCIL (2010, ORGANIZATIONAL SESS.: NEW YORK)–AGENDA

3. Basic programme of work of the Council.
   *See:* UN. ECONOMIC AND SOCIAL COUNCIL–WORK PROGRAMME (2010-2011)

4. Elections, nominations, confirmations and appointments.
   *See:* INTERNATIONAL NARCOTICS CONTROL BOARD–MEMBERS
      JOINT UNITED NATIONS PROGRAMME ON HIV/AIDS. PROGRAMME COORDINATION BOARD–MEMBERS
      UN. COMMISSION FOR SOCIAL DEVELOPMENT–MEMBERS
      UN. COMMISSION ON CRIME PREVENTION AND CRIMINAL JUSTICE–MEMBERS
      UN. COMMISSION ON NARCOTIC DRUGS–MEMBERS
      UN. COMMISSION ON POPULATION AND DEVELOPMENT–MEMBERS
      UN. COMMISSION ON SCIENCE AND TECHNOLOGY FOR DEVELOPMENT–MEMBERS
      UN. COMMISSION ON SUSTAINABLE DEVELOPMENT–MEMBERS
      UN. COMMISSION ON THE STATUS OF WOMEN–MEMBERS
      UN. COMMITTEE FOR DEVELOPMENT POLICY–MEMBERS
      UN. COMMITTEE FOR PROGRAMME AND COORDINATION–MEMBERS
      UN. COMMITTEE FOR THE UNITED NATIONS POPULATION AWARD–MEMBERS
      UN. COMMITTEE OF EXPERTS ON INTERNATIONAL COOPERATION IN TAX MATTERS–MEMBERS
      UN. COMMITTEE ON ECONOMIC, SOCIAL AND CULTURAL RIGHTS–MEMBERS
      UN. COMMITTEE ON NON-GOVERNMENTAL ORGANIZATIONS–MEMBERS
      UN. EXECUTIVE COMMITTEE OF THE UNHCR PROGRAMME–MEMBERS
      UN. INTERGOVERNMENTAL WORKING GROUP OF EXPERTS ON INTERNATIONAL STANDARDS OF
         ACCOUNTING AND REPORTING–MEMBERS
      UN. INTERNATIONAL RESEARCH AND TRAINING INSTITUTE FOR THE ADVANCEMENT OF WOMEN.
         EXECUTIVE BOARD–MEMBERS
      UN. PEACEBUILDING COMMISSION. ORGANIZATIONAL COMMITTEE–MEMBERS
      UN. PERMANENT FORUM ON INDIGENOUS ISSUES–MEMBERS
      UN. STATISTICAL COMMISSION–MEMBERS
      UN. SUBCOMMITTEE OF EXPERTS ON THE GLOBALLY HARMONIZED SYSTEM OF CLASSIFICATION AND
         LABELLING OF CHEMICALS–MEMBERS
      UN. SUBCOMMITTEE OF EXPERTS ON THE TRANSPORT OF DANGEROUS GOODS–MEMBERS
      UN-HABITAT. GOVERNING COUNCIL–MEMBERS
      UN-WOMEN. EXECUTIVE BOARD–MEMBERS
      UNDP/UNFPA EXECUTIVE BOARD–MEMBERS
      UNICEF. EXECUTIVE BOARD–MEMBERS
      WORLD FOOD PROGRAMME. EXECUTIVE BOARD–MEMBERS

## JOINT UNITED NATIONS PROGRAMME ON HIV/AIDS. PROGRAMME COORDINATING BOARD–MEMBERS (Agenda item 4)

### General documents

**E/2010/2/Add.1** Agenda : Economic and Social Council, resumed organizational session for 2010, 28 and 29 April 2010 : addendum.

**E/2010/9/Add.6** Election of 8 members of the Programme Coordinating Board of the Joint United Nations Programme on HIV/AIDS (UNAIDS) : note : [addendum] / by the Secretary-General.

### Discussion in plenary

**E/2010/SR.8**  (28 Apr. 2010).

At the 8th meeting, the following 8 Member States were elected members of the Programme Coordinating of the Joint UN Programme on HIV/AIDS by acclamation for a 3-year term beginning 1 Jan. 2011: Bangladesh, Djibouti, Egypt, India, Mexico, Monaco, Russian Federation and United States; the Council also elected Togo to fill an outstanding vacancy on the Programme Coordinating Board for a term beginning on the date of election and expiring on 31 Dec. 2012; the Council also elected Canada for a term beginning on 1 Jan. 2011 and expiring on 31 Dec. 2011 to complete the term of office of Turkey, which was resigning its seat on the Programme Coordinating Board: decision 2010/201 B.

## UN. COMMISSION FOR SOCIAL DEVELOPMENT–MEMBERS (Agenda item 4)

### General documents

**E/2010/2/Add.1** Agenda : Economic and Social Council, resumed organizational session for 2010, 28 and 29 April 2010 : addendum.

**E/2010/9** Election of members of the functional commissions of the Council : note / by the Secretary-General.

### Discussion in plenary

**E/2010/SR.8**  (28 Apr. 2010).

At the 8th meeting, the following 8 Member States were elected members of the Commission on Social Development by acclamation for a 4-year term beginning at the 1st meeting of the Commission's 50th session in 2011 and expiring at the close of the Commission's 53rd session in 2015: Andorra, Burkina Faso, Cameroon, Cuba, Egypt, Mexico, Spain and Zimbabwe: decision 2010/201 B.

## UN. COMMISSION ON CRIME PREVENTION AND CRIMINAL JUSTICE–MEMBERS (Agenda item 4)

### General documents

**E/2010/9** Election of members of the functional commissions of the Council : note / by the Secretary-General.

## UN. COMMISSION ON NARCOTIC DRUGS–MEMBERS (Agenda item 4)

### General documents

**E/2010/9** Election of members of the functional commissions of the Council : note / by the Secretary-General.

## UN. COMMISSION ON POPULATION AND DEVELOPMENT–MEMBERS (Agenda item 4)

### General documents

**E/2010/2/Add.1** Agenda : Economic and Social Council, resumed organizational session for 2010, 28 and 29 April 2010 : addendum.

**E/2010/9** Election of members of the functional commissions of the Council : note / by the Secretary-General.

### Discussion in plenary

**E/2010/SR.8**  (28 Apr. 2010).

At the 8th meeting, the following 4 Member States were elected members of the Commission on Population and Development by acclamation for a 4-year term beginning at the 1st meeting of the Commission's 45th session in 2011 and expiring at the close of the Commission's 48th session in 2015: Algeria, Gabon, Georgia and United States: decision 2010/201 B.

## UN. COMMISSION ON SCIENCE AND TECHNOLOGY FOR DEVELOPMENT–MEMBERS (Agenda item 4)

### General documents

**E/2010/2/Add.1** Agenda : Economic and Social Council, resumed organizational session for 2010, 28 and 29 April 2010 : addendum.

**E/2010/9** Election of members of the functional commissions of the Council : note / by the Secretary-General.

### Discussion in plenary

**E/2010/SR.8**  (28 Apr. 2010).

At the 8th meeting, the following 16 Member States were elected members of the Commission on Science and Technology for Development by acclamation for a 4-year term beginning on 1 Jan. 2011: China, Cuba, Dominican Republic, El Salvador, India, Islamic Republic of Iran, Latvia, Lesotho, Mauritius, Peru, Philippines, Rwanda, Togo, Tunisia, United Republic of Tanzania and United States: decision 2010/201 B.

## UN. COMMISSION ON SUSTAINABLE DEVELOPMENT–MEMBERS (Agenda item 4)

### General documents

**E/2010/2/Add.1** Agenda : Economic and Social Council, resumed organizational session for 2010, 28 and 29 April 2010 : addendum.

**E/2010/9** Election of members of the functional commissions of the Council : note / by the Secretary-General.

## UN. COMMISSION ON SUSTAINABLE DEVELOPMENT–MEMBERS (Agenda item 4) (continued)

### Discussion in plenary

**E/2010/SR.8** (28 Apr. 2010).

At the 8th meeting, the following 19 Member States were elected members of the Commission on Sustainable Development by acclamation for a 3-year term beginning at the 1st meeting of the Commission's 20th session in 2010 and expiring at the close of the Commission's 21st session in 2014: Angola, Armenia, Belgium, Botswana, Brazil, Congo, El Salvador, Equatorial Guinea, Germany, Indonesia, Italy, Japan, Lebanon, Lesotho, Mexico, Montenegro, Nicaragua, Saudi Arabia and Spain: decision 2010/201 B.

## UN. COMMISSION ON THE STATUS OF WOMEN–MEMBERS (Agenda item 4)

### General documents

**E/2010/2/Add.1** Agenda : Economic and Social Council, resumed organizational session for 2010, 28 and 29 April 2010 : addendum.

**E/2010/9** Election of members of the functional commissions of the Council : note / by the Secretary-General.

### Discussion in plenary

**E/2010/SR.8** (28 Apr. 2010).

At the 8th meeting, the following 11 Member States were elected members of the Commission on Status of Women by acclamation for a 4-year term beginning at the 1st meeting of the Commission's 56th session in 2011 and expiring at the close of the Commission's 59th session in 2015: Belgium, Democratic Republic of the Congo, Estonia, Georgia, Islamic Republic of Iran, Jamaica, Liberia, Netherlands, Spain, Thailand and Zimbabwe: decision 2010/201 B.

## UN. COMMITTEE FOR PROGRAMME AND COORDINATION–MEMBERS (Agenda item 4)

### General documents

**E/2010/2/Add.1** Agenda : Economic and Social Council, resumed organizational session for 2010, 28 and 29 April 2010 : addendum.

**E/2010/9/Add.1** Nomination of 7 members of the Committee for Programme and Coordination : note / by the Secretary-General.

### Discussion in plenary

**E/2010/SR.8** (28 Apr. 2010).

At the 8th meeting, the following 6 Member States were nominated for election by the General Assembly to the Committee for Programme and Coordination for a 3-year term beginning 1 Jan. 2011: Algeria, Antigua and Barbuda, Benin, China, Eritrea and Republic of Korea: decision 2010/201 B.

## UN. COMMITTEE FOR THE UNITED NATIONS POPULATION AWARD–MEMBERS (Agenda item 4)

### Discussion in plenary

**E/2010/SR.2** (9 Feb. 2010).

At the 2nd meeting, the following 3 Member States were elected members of the Committee for the United Nations Population Award by acclamation for a term beginning on the date of the election and expiring on 31 Dec. 2012: Egypt, Ghana, Malaysia and Norway: decision 2010/201 A.

## UN. COMMITTEE ON ECONOMIC, SOCIAL AND CULTURAL RIGHTS–MEMBERS (Agenda item 4)

### General documents

**E/2010/2/Add.1** Agenda : Economic and Social Council, resumed organizational session for 2010, 28 and 29 April 2010 : addendum.

**E/2010/9/Add.10** Election of 9 members of the Committee on Economic, Social and Cultural Rights : note / by the Secretary-General.

**E/2010/9/Add.11** Election of 9 members of the Committee on Economic, Social and Cultural Rights : biographical information on candidates : note : addendum / by the Secretary-General.

### Discussion in plenary

**E/2010/SR.8** (28 Apr. 2010).

At the 8th meeting, the following representatives were elected members of the Committee on Economic, Social and Cultural Rights: Aslan Abashidze (Russian Federation), Clément Atangana (Cameroon), Azzouz Kerdoun (Algeria), Chandrashekhar Dasgupta (India) and Heisoo Shin (Republic of Korea): decision 2010/201 B.

**E/2010/SR.9** (28 Apr. 2010).

At the 9th meeting, the following representatives were elected members of the Committee on Economic, Social and Cultural Rights for a 4-year term beginning on 1 Jan. 2011: Jaime Marchan Romero (Ecuador), Renato Zerbini Ribeiro Leão (Brazil), Eibe Riedel (Germany) and Alvaro Tirado Mejia (Colombia): decision 2010/201 B.

## UN. COMMITTEE ON NON-GOVERNMENTAL ORGANIZATIONS–MEMBERS (Agenda item 4)

### General documents

**E/2010/2/Add.1** Agenda : Economic and Social Council, resumed organizational session for 2010, 28 and 29 April 2010 : addendum.

**E/2010/9/Add.2** Election of 19 members of the Committee on Non-Governmental Organizations : note : [addendum] / by the Secretary-General.

## UN. COMMITTEE ON NON-GOVERNMENTAL ORGANIZATIONS–MEMBERS (Agenda item 4) (continued)

### Discussion in plenary

**E/2010/SR.8** (28 Apr. 2010).

At the 8th meeting, the following 19 Member States were elected members of the Committee on Non-Governmental Organizations by acclamation for a 4-year term beginning on 1 Jan. 2011: Belgium, Bulgaria, Burundi, China, Cuba, India, Israel, Kyrgyzstan, Morocco, Mozambique, Nicaragua, Pakistan, Peru, Russian Federation, Senegal, Sudan, Turkey, United States and Bolivarian Republic of Venezuela: decision 2010/201 B.

## UN. ECONOMIC AND SOCIAL COUNCIL–WORK PROGRAMME (2010-2011) (Agenda item 3)

### General documents

**E/2010/1** Proposed basic programme of work of the Council for 2010 and 2011 : note / by the Secretary-General.

**E/2010/7** Single Convention on Narcotic Drugs, 1961, as amended by the Protocol amending the Single Convention on Narcotic Drugs, 1961 (New York, 8 August 1975) : proposal of amendments by the Plurinational State of Bolivia to article 49, paragraphs 1 (c) and 2 (e) : note / by the Secretary-General.

Transmits note verbale of 28 Jan. 2010 from Egypt informing the Office of Legal Affairs that Egypt withdraws its objection to the proposed amendment by the Government of Bolivia to the Convention.

### Draft resolutions/decisions

**E/2010/L.1** Draft proposals submitted by the President of the Council and members of the Bureau on the basis of informal consultations held pursuant to paragraph 2 (l) of Council decision 1988/77.

**E/2010/L.2** Theme for the item on regional cooperation of the 2010 substantive session of the Economic and Social Council : draft decision / submitted by the President of the Council, Hamidon Ali (Malaysia), on the basis of the proposal by the Executive Secretaries of the regional commissions.

**E/2010/L.3** Theme for the humanitarian affairs segment of the 2010 substantive session of the Economic and Social Council : draft decision / submitted by the Vice-President of the Council, Heraldo Muñoz (Chile), on the basis of informal consultations.

## UN. ECONOMIC AND SOCIAL COUNCIL–WORK PROGRAMME (2010-2011) (Agenda item 3) (continued)

### Discussion in plenary

**E/2010/SR.2** (9 Feb. 2010).

At the 2nd meeting, action on draft decisions contained in E/2010/L.1 was as follows: draft decision I entitled "Proposed date of the special high-level meeting of the Economic and Social Council with the Bretton Woods institutions, the World Trade Organization and the United Nations Conference on Trade and Development", adopted without vote: decision 2010/202; draft decision II entitled "Provisional agenda for the substantive session of 2010 of the Economic and Social Council", adopted without vote: decision 2010/203; draft decision III entitled "Basic programme of work of the Economic and Social Council for 2011", adopted without vote: decision 2010/204; draft decision IV entitled "Working arrangements for the substantive session of 2010 of the Economic and Social Council", adopted without vote: decision 2010/205; draft decision V entitled "Operational activities segment of the 2010 substantive session of the Economic and Social Council", adopted without vote: decision 2010/206.

**E/2010/SR.8** (28 Apr. 2010).

At the 8th meeting, action on draft decisions was as follows: draft decision E/2010/L.2, adopted without vote: decision 2010/207; draft decision E/2010/L.3, adopted without vote: decision 2010/208.

## UN. ECONOMIC AND SOCIAL COUNCIL (2010 : NEW YORK)–OFFICERS (Agenda item 1)

### Discussion in plenary

**E/2010/SR.1** (19 Jan. 2010).

At the 1st meeting, Hamidon Ali (Malaysia) was elected President by acclamation; Somduth Soborun (Mauritius), Alexandru Cujba (Republic of Moldova), Heraldo Muñoz (Chile) and Morten Wetland (Norway) were elected Vice-Presidents of the Council for 2010 by acclamation.

**E/2010/SR.10** (21 May 2010).

At the 10th meeting, Octavio Errázuriz (Chile) was elected, by acclamation, to serve the unexpired portion of Heraldo Muñoz (Chile) as Vice-President of the Council.

## UN. ECONOMIC AND SOCIAL COUNCIL (2010, ORGANIZATIONAL SESS. : NEW YORK)–AGENDA (Agenda item 2)

### General documents

**E/2010/2** Provisional agenda : Economic and Social Council, organizational session for 2010, 19 January, 9-12 February and 28 and 29 April 2010.

**E/2010/2/Corr.1** Provisional agenda : Economic and Social Council, organizational session for 2010, 19 January, 9-12 February and 28 and 29 April 2010 : corrigendum.

Replaces annex.

## UN. ECONOMIC AND SOCIAL COUNCIL (2010, ORGANIZATIONAL SESS. : NEW YORK)–AGENDA (Agenda item 2) (continued)

### Draft resolutions/decisions

**E/2010/L.1** Draft proposals submitted by the President of the Council and members of the Bureau on the basis of informal consultations held pursuant to paragraph 2 (I) of Council decision 1988/77.

**E/2010/L.2** Theme for the item on regional cooperation of the 2010 substantive session of the Economic and Social Council : draft decision / submitted by the President of the Council, Hamidon Ali (Malaysia), on the basis of the proposal by the Executive Secretaries of the regional commissions.

**E/2010/L.3** Theme for the humanitarian affairs segment of the 2010 substantive session of the Economic and Social Council : draft decision / submitted by the Vice-President of the Council, Heraldo Muñoz (Chile), on the basis of informal consultations.

**E/2010/L.4** Economic and Social Council event to discuss transition from relief to development : draft decision / submitted by Vice-President of the Council, Heraldo Muñoz (Chile), on the basis of informal consultations.

### Discussion in plenary

**E/2010/SR.1** (19 Jan. 2010).
At the 1st meeting, the provisional agenda for the 2010 organizational session of the Council (E/2010/2 and Corr.1) was adopted.

**E/2010/SR.2** (9 Feb. 2010).
At the 2nd meeting, action on draft decisions contained in E/2010/L.1 was as follows: draft decision I entitled "Proposed date of the special high-level meeting of the Economic and Social Council with the Bretton Woods institutions, the World Trade Organization and the United Nations Conference on Trade and Development", adopted without vote: decision 2010/202; draft decision II entitled "Provisional agenda for the substantive session of 2010 of the Economic and Social Council", adopted without vote: decision 2010/203; draft decision III entitled "Basic programme of work of the Economic and Social Council for 2011", adopted without vote: decision 2010/204; draft decision IV entitled "Working arrangements for the substantive session of 2010 of the Economic and Social Council", adopted without vote: decision 2010/205; draft decision V entitled "Operational activities segment of the 2010 substantive session of the Economic and Social Council", adopted without vote: decision 2010/206.

**E/2010/SR.3** (12 Feb. 2010).

**E/2010/SR.8** (28 Apr. 2010).
At the 8th meeting, action on draft decisions was as follows: draft decision E/2010/L.2, adopted without vote: 2010/207; draft decision E/2010/L.3, adopted without vote: decision 2010/208; draft decision E/2010/L.4, adopted without vote: 2010/209.

**E/2010/SR.10** (21 May 2010).

## UN. ECONOMIC AND SOCIAL COUNCIL (2010, ORGANIZATIONAL SESS. : NEW YORK)–RESOLUTIONS AND DECISIONS

### General documents

**E/2010/99** (ESCOR, 2010, Suppl. no. 1) Resolutions and decisions of the Economic and Social Council : organizational session for 2010, New York, 19 January, 9 and 12 February 2010; resumed organizational session for 2010, New York, 28 April and 21 May 2010; substantive session of 2010, New York, 28 June-23 July 2010; resumed substantive session of 2010, New York, 9 September, 25 October, 10 November and 14-15 December 2010.

**E/2010/INF/2** (To be issued in ESCOR, 2010, Suppl. no. 1.) Decisions adopted by the Economic and Social Council at its organizational and resumed organizational sessions for 2010 (19 January; 9 and 12 February; 28 April; and 21 May 2010).

## UN. EXECUTIVE COMMITTEE OF THE UNHCR PROGRAMME–MEMBERS (Agenda item 4)

### General documents

**E/2010/2/Add.1** Agenda : Economic and Social Council, resumed organizational session for 2010, 28 and 29 April 2010 : addendum.

### Discussion in plenary

**E/2010/SR.8** (28 Apr. 2010).
At the 8th meeting, Slovenia was elected member of the Executive Committee of the UNHCR Programme by acclamation: decision 2010/201 B.

## UN. INTERGOVERNMENTAL WORKING GROUP OF EXPERTS ON INTERNATIONAL STANDARDS OF ACCOUNTING AND REPORTING–MEMBERS (Agenda item 4)

### General documents

**E/2010/2/Add.1** Agenda : Economic and Social Council, resumed organizational session for 2010, 28 and 29 April 2010 : addendum.

## UN. INTERGOVERNMENTAL WORKING GROUP OF EXPERTS ON INTERNATIONAL STANDARDS OF ACCOUNTING AND REPORTING–MEMBERS (Agenda item 4) (continued)

### Discussion in plenary

**E/2010/SR.8** (28 Apr. 2010).

At the 8th meeting, the following Member States were elected members of the Intergovernmental Working Group of Experts on International Standards of Accounting and Reporting by acclamation: France, Niger and Portugal, for a term beginning on the date of election and expiring on 31 Dec. 2011; Poland and Saint Kitts and Nevis for a term beginning on the date of election and expiring on 31 Dec. 2012: decision 2010/201 B.

## UN. INTERNATIONAL RESEARCH AND TRAINING INSTITUTE FOR THE ADVANCEMENT OF WOMEN. EXECUTIVE BOARD–MEMBERS (Agenda item 4)

### General documents

**E/2010/2/Add.1** Agenda : Economic and Social Council, resumed organizational session for 2010, 28 and 29 April 2010 : addendum.

### Discussion in plenary

**E/2010/SR.8** (28 Apr. 2010).

At the 8th meeting, the following 4 Member States were elected members of the Executive Board of the International Research and Training Institute for the Advancement of Women by acclamation for a term beginning on the date of election and expiring on 31 Dec. 2012: Belarus, Benin, Djibouti and Slovakia: decision 2010/201 B.

## UN. PEACEBUILDING COMMISSION. ORGANIZATIONAL COMMITTEE–MEMBERS (Agenda item 4)

### General documents

**E/2010/2/Add.1** Agenda : Economic and Social Council, resumed organizational session for 2010, 28 and 29 April 2010 : addendum.

## UN. PERMANENT FORUM ON INDIGENOUS ISSUES–MEMBERS (Agenda item 4)

### General documents

**E/2010/2/Add.1** Agenda : Economic and Social Council, resumed organizational session for 2010, 28 and 29 April 2010 : addendum.

**E/2010/9/Add.8** Election of 8 members of the Permanent Forum on Indigenous Issues from among candidates nominated by Governments and appointment of 8 members by the President of the Economic and Social Council : note : [addendum] / by the Secretary-General.

**E/2010/9/Add.9** Election of 8 members of the Permanent Forum on Indigenous Issues from among candidates nominated by Governments : note : [addendum] / by the Secretary-General.

## UN. PERMANENT FORUM ON INDIGENOUS ISSUES–MEMBERS (Agenda item 4) (continued)

**E/2010/9/Add.12** Election of 8 members of the Permanent Forum on Indigenous Issues from among candidates nominated by Governments and appointment of 8 members by the President of the Economic and Social Council : note : [addendum] / by the Secretary-General. Includes biographical data on candidate.

### Discussion in plenary

**E/2010/SR.8** (28 Apr. 2010).

At the 8th meeting, the following representatives were elected members of the Permanent Forum on Indigenous Issues for a 3-year term beginning on 1 Jan. 2011: Simon William M'Viboudoulou (Congo), Paimaneh Hasteh (Islamic Republic of Iran), Helen Kaljuläte (Estonia), Andre Alexandrovich Nikiforov (Russian Federation), Alvaro Esteban Pop Ac (Guatemala), Mirian Masaquiza (Ecuador), Megan Davis (Australia) and Eva Biaudet (Finland): decision 2009/201 B.

**E/2010/SR.9** (28 Apr. 2010).

At the 9th meeting, the following representatives were elected members of the Permanent Forum on Indigenous Issues for a 3-year term beginning on 1 Jan. 2011: Mirna Cunningham Kain (Nicaragua), Dalee Sambo Dorough (United States), Edward John (Canada), Anna Naikanchina (Russian Federation), Raja Devashish Roy (Bangladesh), Paul Kanyinke Sena (Kenya), Valmaine Toki (New Zealand) and Saúl Vicente Vázquez (Mexico): decision 2010/201 B.

## UN. STATISTICAL COMMISSION–MEMBERS (Agenda item 4)

### General documents

**E/2010/9** Election of members of the functional commissions of the Council : note / by the Secretary-General.

## UN. SUBCOMMITTEE OF EXPERTS ON THE GLOBALLY HARMONIZED SYSTEM OF CLASSIFICATION AND LABELLING OF CHEMICALS–MEMBERS (Agenda item 4)

### General documents

**E/2010/9/Add.13** Committee of Experts on the Transport of Dangerous Goods and on the Globally Harmonized System of Classification and Labelling of Chemicals : Subcommittee of Experts on the Transport of Dangerous Goods : Subcommittee of Experts on the Globally Harmonized System of Classification and Labelling of Chemicals : note / by the Secretary-General.

### Discussion in plenary

**E/2010/SR.8** (28 Apr. 2010).

At the 8th meeting, the Council endorsed the Secretary General's decision to approve the application of the Russian Federation for membership to the Subcommittee of Experts on the Globally Harmonized System of Classification and Labelling of Chemicals: decision 2010/201 B.

## UN. SUBCOMMITTEE OF EXPERTS ON THE TRANSPORT OF DANGEROUS GOODS–MEMBERS (Agenda item 4)

### General documents

**E/2010/9/Add.13** Committee of Experts on the Transport of Dangerous Goods and on the Globally Harmonized System of Classification and Labelling of Chemicals : Subcommittee of Experts on the Transport of Dangerous Goods : Subcommittee of Experts on the Globally Harmonized System of Classification and Labelling of Chemicals : note / by the Secretary-General.

### Discussion in plenary

**E/2010/SR.8** (28 Apr. 2010).
At the 8th meeting, the Council endorsed the Secretary General's decision to approve the application of Switzerland for membership to the Subcommittee of Experts on the Transport of Dangerous Goods: decision 2010/201 B.

## UN-HABITAT. GOVERNING COUNCIL–MEMBERS (Agenda item 4)

### General documents

**E/2010/2/Add.1** Agenda : Economic and Social Council, resumed organizational session for 2010, 28 and 29 April 2010 : addendum.

**E/2010/9/Add.7** Election of 20 members of the Governing Council of the United Nations Human Settlements Programme : note : [addendum] / by the Secretary-General.

### Discussion in plenary

**E/2010/SR.8** (28 Apr. 2010).
At the 8th meeting, the following 20 Member States were elected members of the Governing Council of the UN-Habitat by acclamation for a 4-year term beginning 1 Jan. 2011: Albania, Algeria, Argentina, Central African Republic, Gabon, Indonesia, Islamic Republic of Iran, Japan, Mali, Mozambique, Nigeria, Pakistan, Russian Federation, United States and Bolivarian Republic of Venezuela: decision 2010/201 B.

## UNDP/UNFPA EXECUTIVE BOARD–MEMBERS (Agenda item 4)

### General documents

**E/2010/2/Add.1** Agenda : Economic and Social Council, resumed organizational session for 2010, 28 and 29 April 2010 : addendum.

**E/2010/9/Add.4** Election of 11 members of the Executive Board of the United Nations Development Programme/United Nations Population Fund : note : [addendum] / by the Secretary-General.

## UNDP/UNFPA EXECUTIVE BOARD–MEMBERS (Agenda item 4) (continued)

### Discussion in plenary

**E/2010/SR.8** (28 Apr. 2010).
At the 8th meeting, the following 11 Member States were elected members of the Executive Board of the UNDP/UNFPA by acclamation for a 3-year term beginning 1 Jan. 2011: Argentina, Bangladesh, Belarus, Canada, China, Czech Republic, Djibouti, El Salvador, Finland, Luxembourg and United States; the Council also elected the following Member States to replace members of the Executive Board who were resigning their seats effective 1 Jan. 2011: Denmark to complete the term of office of Austria (expiring 31 Dec. 2011), Germany to complete the term of office of Belgium (expiring 31 Dec. 2011), Italy to complete the term of office of France (expiring 31 Dec. 2012), Ireland to complete the term of office of Spain (expiring 31 Dec. 2012) and Estonia to complete the term of office of Slovenia (expiring 31 Dec. 2012): decision 2010/201 B.

## UNICEF. EXECUTIVE BOARD–MEMBERS (Agenda item 4)

### General documents

**E/2010/2/Add.1** Agenda : Economic and Social Council, resumed organizational session for 2010, 28 and 29 April 2010 : addendum.

**E/2010/9/Add.3** Election of 11 members of the Executive Board of the United Nations Children's Fund : note : [addendum] / by the Secretary-General.

### Discussion in plenary

**E/2010/SR.8** (28 Apr. 2010).
At the 8th meeting, the following 11 Member States were elected members of the Executive Board of the UN Children's Fund by acclamation for a 3-year term beginning 1 Jan. 2011: Antigua and Barbuda, China, Colombia, Estonia, Indonesia, Italy, Namibia, Netherlands, New Zealand, Russian Federation and United Kingdom; the Council also elected the following Member States to replace members of the Executive Board who were resigning their seats effective 1 Jan. 2011: Japan to complete the term of office of Iceland (expiring 31 Dec. 2011), Belgium to complete the term of office of Norway (expiring 31 Dec. 2011), Spain to complete the term of office of Switzerland (expiring 31 Dec. 2011), Germany to complete the term of office of Ireland (expiring 31 Dec. 2012) and Sweden to complete the term of office of Luxembourg (expiring 31 Dec. 2012): decision 2010/201 B.

## WORLD FOOD PROGRAMME. EXECUTIVE BOARD–MEMBERS (Agenda item 4)

### General documents

**E/2010/2/Add.1** Agenda : Economic and Social Council, resumed organizational session for 2010, 28 and 29 April 2010 : addendum.

**E/2010/9/Add.5** Election of 6 members of the Executive Board of the World Food Programme : note : [addendum] / by the Secretary-General.

**WORLD FOOD PROGRAMME. EXECUTIVE
BOARD–MEMBERS (Agenda item 4) (continued)**

<u>**Discussion in plenary**</u>

**E/2010/SR.8** (28 Apr. 2010).

At the 8th meeting, the following 6 Member States were elected members of the Executive Board of the World Food Progamme by acclamation for a 3-year term beginning on 1 Jan. 2011: Australia, Cuba, Morocco, Norway, Republic of Korea and Sudan; the Council also elected Spain for a term beginning on 1 Jan. 2011 and expiring on 31 Dec. 2012 to complete the term of office of Luxembourg, which was resigning its seat on the Executive Board: decision 2010/201 B.

# INDEX TO SPEECHES

## EXPLANATORY NOTE

Certain speakers are permitted to address the
*Economic and Social* Council in their personal capacity.
In such cases, a triple asterisk (***) appears in place of
the corporate name/country affiliation in each section
of the Index to speeches.

**Brazil**

HUMANITARIAN ASSISTANCE–HAITI
Patriota, Guilherme de Aguiar – E/2010/SR.2

**Caribbean Community**

HUMANITARIAN ASSISTANCE–HAITI
St. Aimee, Donatus Keith (Saint Lucia) –
E/2010/SR.1

**European Union**

HUMANITARIAN ASSISTANCE–HAITI
Yánez-Barnuevo, Juan Antonio (Spain) –
E/2010/SR.1
UN. ECONOMIC AND SOCIAL COUNCIL (2010 : NEW
YORK)–OFFICERS (Agenda item 1)
Yánez-Barnuevo, Juan Antonio (Spain) –
E/2010/SR.1

**Haiti**

HUMANITARIAN ASSISTANCE–HAITI
Mérorès, Léo – E/2010/SR.1

**IBRD**

HUMANITARIAN ASSISTANCE–HAITI
Meyer, Tania – E/2010/SR.2

**Indonesia**

UN. ECONOMIC AND SOCIAL COUNCIL (2010 : NEW
YORK)–OFFICERS (Agenda item 1)
Wahab, Dewi Savitri – E/2010/SR.1

**Pakistan**

HUMANITARIAN ASSISTANCE–HAITI
Khan, Asad Majeed – E/2010/SR.2

**Philippines**

UN. ECONOMIC AND SOCIAL COUNCIL (2010 : NEW
YORK)–OFFICERS (Agenda item 1)
Davide, Hilario G. – E/2010/SR.1

**Saint Lucia**

HUMANITARIAN ASSISTANCE–HAITI
St. Aimee, Donatus Keith – E/2010/SR.2

**UN. Deputy Secretary-General**

UN. ECONOMIC AND SOCIAL COUNCIL–WORK
PROGRAMME (2010-2011) (Agenda item 3)
Migiro, Asha-Rose Mtengeti – E/2010/SR.1

**UN. Economic and Social Council (2010 : New
York). President**

UN. COMMITTEE ON ECONOMIC, SOCIAL AND
CULTURAL RIGHTS–MEMBERS (Agenda item 4)
Ali, Hamidon (Malaysia) – E/2010/SR.9
UN. ECONOMIC AND SOCIAL COUNCIL–WORK
PROGRAMME (2010-2011) (Agenda item 3)
Ali, Hamidon (Malaysia) – E/2010/SR.1
UN. ECONOMIC AND SOCIAL COUNCIL (2010 : NEW
YORK)–OFFICERS (Agenda item 1)
Ali, Hamidon (Malaysia) – E/2010/SR.10

**UN. Economic and Social Council (2010 : New
York). President (continued)**

UN. ECONOMIC AND SOCIAL COUNCIL (2010,
ORGANIZATIONAL SESS. : NEW YORK)–AGENDA
(Agenda item 2)
Ali, Hamidon (Malaysia) – E/2010/SR.3;
E/2010/SR.10
UN. PERMANENT FORUM ON INDIGENOUS ISSUES–
MEMBERS (Agenda item 4)
Ali, Hamidon (Malaysia) – E/2010/SR.9

**UN. Economic and Social Council (2010 : New
York). Secretary**

JOINT UNITED NATIONS PROGRAMME ON HIV/AIDS.
PROGRAMME COORDINATING BOARD–MEMBERS
(Agenda item 4)
De Laurentis, Jennifer – E/2010/SR.8
UN. COMMISSION FOR SOCIAL DEVELOPMENT–
MEMBERS (Agenda item 4)
De Laurentis, Jennifer – E/2010/SR.8
UN. COMMISSION ON POPULATION AND
DEVELOPMENT–MEMBERS (Agenda item 4)
De Laurentis, Jennifer – E/2010/SR.8
UN. COMMISSION ON SCIENCE AND TECHNOLOGY
FOR DEVELOPMENT–MEMBERS (Agenda item 4)
De Laurentis, Jennifer – E/2010/SR.8
UN. COMMISSION ON SUSTAINABLE
DEVELOPMENT–MEMBERS (Agenda item 4)
De Laurentis, Jennifer – E/2010/SR.8
UN. COMMISSION ON THE STATUS OF WOMEN–
MEMBERS (Agenda item 4)
De Laurentis, Jennifer – E/2010/SR.8
UN. COMMITTEE FOR PROGRAMME AND
COORDINATION–MEMBERS (Agenda item 4)
De Laurentis, Jennifer – E/2010/SR.8
UN. COMMITTEE ON ECONOMIC, SOCIAL AND
CULTURAL RIGHTS–MEMBERS (Agenda item 4)
De Laurentis, Jennifer – E/2010/SR.9
UN. COMMITTEE ON NON-GOVERNMENTAL
ORGANIZATIONS–MEMBERS (Agenda item 4)
De Laurentis, Jennifer – E/2010/SR.8
UN. EXECUTIVE COMMITTEE OF THE UNHCR
PROGRAMME–MEMBERS (Agenda item 4)
De Laurentis, Jennifer – E/2010/SR.8
UN. INTERGOVERNMENTAL WORKING GROUP OF
EXPERTS ON INTERNATIONAL STANDARDS OF
ACCOUNTING AND REPORTING–MEMBERS (Agenda
item 4)
De Laurentis, Jennifer – E/2010/SR.8
UN. INTERNATIONAL RESEARCH AND TRAINING
INSTITUTE FOR THE ADVANCEMENT OF WOMEN.
EXECUTIVE BOARD–MEMBERS (Agenda item 4)
De Laurentis, Jennifer – E/2010/SR.8
UN. PERMANENT FORUM ON INDIGENOUS ISSUES–
MEMBERS (Agenda item 4)
De Laurentis, Jennifer – E/2010/SR.8
UN-HABITAT. GOVERNING COUNCIL–MEMBERS
(Agenda item 4)
De Laurentis, Jennifer – E/2010/SR.8
UNDP/UNFPA EXECUTIVE BOARD–MEMBERS
(Agenda item 4)
De Laurentis, Jennifer – E/2010/SR.8

**UN. Economic and Social Council (2010 : New York). Secretary (continued)**

UNICEF. EXECUTIVE BOARD–MEMBERS (Agenda item 4)
De Laurentis, Jennifer – E/2010/SR.8
WORLD FOOD PROGRAMME. EXECUTIVE BOARD–MEMBERS (Agenda item 4)
De Laurentis, Jennifer – E/2010/SR.8

**UN. Economic and Social Council (2010 : New York). Temporary President**

UN. ECONOMIC AND SOCIAL COUNCIL–WORK PROGRAMME (2010-2011) (Agenda item 3)
Lucas, Sylvie (Luxembourg) – E/2010/SR.1

**UN. Economic and Social Council. Ad Hoc Advisory Group on Haiti**

HUMANITARIAN ASSISTANCE–HAITI
McNee, John – E/2010/SR.1

**UN. Office for ECOSOC Support and Coordination. Director**

HUMANITARIAN ASSISTANCE–HAITI
Seth, Nikhil – E/2010/SR.2

**UN. Office for the Coordination of Humanitarian Affairs**

HUMANITARIAN ASSISTANCE–HAITI
Khalikov, Rashid – E/2010/SR.1

**Ali, Hamidon (Malaysia) (UN. Economic and Social Council (2010 : New York). President)**

UN. COMMITTEE ON ECONOMIC, SOCIAL AND CULTURAL RIGHTS–MEMBERS (Agenda item 4)
E/2010/SR.9
UN. ECONOMIC AND SOCIAL COUNCIL–WORK PROGRAMME (2010-2011) (Agenda item 3)
E/2010/SR.1
UN. ECONOMIC AND SOCIAL COUNCIL (2010 : NEW YORK)–OFFICERS (Agenda item 1)
E/2010/SR.10
UN. ECONOMIC AND SOCIAL COUNCIL (2010, ORGANIZATIONAL SESS. : NEW YORK)–AGENDA (Agenda item 2)
E/2010/SR.3; E/2010/SR.10
UN. PERMANENT FORUM ON INDIGENOUS ISSUES–MEMBERS (Agenda item 4)
E/2010/SR.9

**Davide, Hilario G. (Philippines)**

UN. ECONOMIC AND SOCIAL COUNCIL (2010 : NEW YORK)–OFFICERS (Agenda item 1)
E/2010/SR.1

**De Laurentis, Jennifer (UN. Economic and Social Council (2010 : New York). Secretary)**

JOINT UNITED NATIONS PROGRAMME ON HIV/AIDS. PROGRAMME COORDINATING BOARD–MEMBERS (Agenda item 4)
E/2010/SR.8
UN. COMMISSION FOR SOCIAL DEVELOPMENT–MEMBERS (Agenda item 4)
E/2010/SR.8
UN. COMMISSION ON POPULATION AND DEVELOPMENT–MEMBERS (Agenda item 4)
E/2010/SR.8
UN. COMMISSION ON SCIENCE AND TECHNOLOGY FOR DEVELOPMENT–MEMBERS (Agenda item 4)
E/2010/SR.8
UN. COMMISSION ON SUSTAINABLE DEVELOPMENT–MEMBERS (Agenda item 4)
E/2010/SR.8
UN. COMMISSION ON THE STATUS OF WOMEN–MEMBERS (Agenda item 4)
E/2010/SR.8
UN. COMMITTEE FOR PROGRAMME AND COORDINATION–MEMBERS (Agenda item 4)
E/2010/SR.8
UN. COMMITTEE ON ECONOMIC, SOCIAL AND CULTURAL RIGHTS–MEMBERS (Agenda item 4)
E/2010/SR.9
UN. COMMITTEE ON NON-GOVERNMENTAL ORGANIZATIONS–MEMBERS (Agenda item 4)
E/2010/SR.8
UN. EXECUTIVE COMMITTEE OF THE UNHCR PROGRAMME–MEMBERS (Agenda item 4)
E/2010/SR.8
UN. INTERGOVERNMENTAL WORKING GROUP OF EXPERTS ON INTERNATIONAL STANDARDS OF ACCOUNTING AND REPORTING–MEMBERS (Agenda item 4)
E/2010/SR.8

**De Laurentis, Jennifer (UN. Economic and Social Council (2010 : New York). Secretary) (continued)**

UN. INTERNATIONAL RESEARCH AND TRAINING INSTITUTE FOR THE ADVANCEMENT OF WOMEN. EXECUTIVE BOARD–MEMBERS (Agenda item 4)
E/2010/SR.8
UN. PERMANENT FORUM ON INDIGENOUS ISSUES–MEMBERS (Agenda item 4)
E/2010/SR.8
UN-HABITAT. GOVERNING COUNCIL–MEMBERS (Agenda item 4)
E/2010/SR.8
UNDP/UNFPA EXECUTIVE BOARD–MEMBERS (Agenda item 4)
E/2010/SR.8
UNICEF. EXECUTIVE BOARD–MEMBERS (Agenda item 4)
E/2010/SR.8
WORLD FOOD PROGRAMME. EXECUTIVE BOARD–MEMBERS (Agenda item 4)
E/2010/SR.8

**Khalikov, Rashid (UN. Office for the Coordination of Humanitarian Affairs)**

HUMANITARIAN ASSISTANCE–HAITI
E/2010/SR.1

**Khan, Asad Majeed (Pakistan)**

HUMANITARIAN ASSISTANCE–HAITI
E/2010/SR.2

**Lucas, Sylvie (Luxembourg) (UN. Economic and Social Council (2010 : New York). Temporary President)**

UN. ECONOMIC AND SOCIAL COUNCIL–WORK PROGRAMME (2010-2011) (Agenda item 3)
E/2010/SR.1

**McNee, John (UN. Economic and Social Council. Ad Hoc Advisory Group on Haiti)**

HUMANITARIAN ASSISTANCE–HAITI
E/2010/SR.1

**Mérorès, Léo (Haiti)**

HUMANITARIAN ASSISTANCE–HAITI
E/2010/SR.1

**Meyer, Tania (IBRD)**

HUMANITARIAN ASSISTANCE–HAITI
E/2010/SR.2

**Migiro, Asha-Rose Mtengeti (UN. Deputy Secretary-General)**

UN. ECONOMIC AND SOCIAL COUNCIL–WORK PROGRAMME (2010-2011) (Agenda item 3)
E/2010/SR.1

**Patriota, Guilherme de Aguiar (Brazil)**

HUMANITARIAN ASSISTANCE–HAITI
E/2010/SR.2

**Seth, Nikhil (UN. Office for ECOSOC Support and Coordination. Director)**

    HUMANITARIAN ASSISTANCE–HAITI
        E/2010/SR.2

**St. Aimee, Donatus Keith (Saint Lucia)**

    HUMANITARIAN ASSISTANCE–HAITI
        E/2010/SR.2

**St. Aimee, Donatus Keith (Saint Lucia) (Caribbean Community)**

    HUMANITARIAN ASSISTANCE–HAITI
        E/2010/SR.1

**Wahab, Dewi Savitri (Indonesia)**

    UN. ECONOMIC AND SOCIAL COUNCIL (2010 : NEW YORK)–OFFICERS (Agenda item 1)
        E/2010/SR.1

**Yánez-Barnuevo, Juan Antonio (Spain) (European Union)**

    HUMANITARIAN ASSISTANCE–HAITI
        E/2010/SR.1
    UN. ECONOMIC AND SOCIAL COUNCIL (2010 : NEW YORK)–OFFICERS (Agenda item 1)
        E/2010/SR.1

## HUMANITARIAN ASSISTANCE–HAITI

Brazil
    Patriota, Guilherme de Aguiar – E/2010/SR.2
Caribbean Community
    St. Aimee, Donatus Keith (Saint Lucia) –
      E/2010/SR.1
European Union
    Yánez-Barnuevo, Juan Antonio (Spain) –
      E/2010/SR.1
Haiti
    Mérorès, Léo – E/2010/SR.1
IBRD
    Meyer, Tania – E/2010/SR.2
Pakistan
    Khan, Asad Majeed – E/2010/SR.2
Saint Lucia
    St. Aimee, Donatus Keith – E/2010/SR.2
UN. Economic and Social Council. Ad Hoc Advisory
Group on Haiti
    McNee, John – E/2010/SR.1
UN. Office for ECOSOC Support and Coordination.
Director
    Seth, Nikhil – E/2010/SR.2
UN. Office for the Coordination of Humanitarian Affairs
    Khalikov, Rashid – E/2010/SR.1

## JOINT UNITED NATIONS PROGRAMME ON HIV/AIDS. PROGRAMME COORDINATING BOARD–MEMBERS (Agenda item 4)

UN. Economic and Social Council (2010 : New York).
Secretary
    De Laurentis, Jennifer – E/2010/SR.8

## UN. COMMISSION FOR SOCIAL DEVELOPMENT–MEMBERS (Agenda item 4)

UN. Economic and Social Council (2010 : New York).
Secretary
    De Laurentis, Jennifer – E/2010/SR.8

## UN. COMMISSION ON POPULATION AND DEVELOPMENT–MEMBERS (Agenda item 4)

UN. Economic and Social Council (2010 : New York).
Secretary
    De Laurentis, Jennifer – E/2010/SR.8

## UN. COMMISSION ON SCIENCE AND TECHNOLOGY FOR DEVELOPMENT–MEMBERS (Agenda item 4)

UN. Economic and Social Council (2010 : New York).
Secretary
    De Laurentis, Jennifer – E/2010/SR.8

## UN. COMMISSION ON SUSTAINABLE DEVELOPMENT–MEMBERS (Agenda item 4)

UN. Economic and Social Council (2010 : New York).
Secretary
    De Laurentis, Jennifer – E/2010/SR.8

## UN. COMMISSION ON THE STATUS OF WOMEN–MEMBERS (Agenda item 4)

UN. Economic and Social Council (2010 : New York).
Secretary
    De Laurentis, Jennifer – E/2010/SR.8

## UN. COMMITTEE FOR PROGRAMME AND COORDINATION–MEMBERS (Agenda item 4)

UN. Economic and Social Council (2010 : New York).
Secretary
    De Laurentis, Jennifer – E/2010/SR.8

## UN. COMMITTEE ON ECONOMIC, SOCIAL AND CULTURAL RIGHTS–MEMBERS (Agenda item 4)

UN. Economic and Social Council (2010 : New York).
President
    Ali, Hamidon (Malaysia) – E/2010/SR.9
UN. Economic and Social Council (2010 : New York).
Secretary
    De Laurentis, Jennifer – E/2010/SR.9

## UN. COMMITTEE ON NON-GOVERNMENTAL ORGANIZATIONS–MEMBERS (Agenda item 4)

UN. Economic and Social Council (2010 : New York).
Secretary
    De Laurentis, Jennifer – E/2010/SR.8

## UN. ECONOMIC AND SOCIAL COUNCIL–WORK PROGRAMME (2010-2011) (Agenda item 3)

UN. Deputy Secretary-General
    Migiro, Asha-Rose Mtengeti – E/2010/SR.1
UN. Economic and Social Council (2010 : New York).
President
    Ali, Hamidon (Malaysia) – E/2010/SR.1
UN. Economic and Social Council (2010 : New York).
Temporary President
    Lucas, Sylvie (Luxembourg) – E/2010/SR.1

## UN. ECONOMIC AND SOCIAL COUNCIL (2010 : NEW YORK)–OFFICERS (Agenda item 1)

European Union
    Yánez-Barnuevo, Juan Antonio (Spain) –
      E/2010/SR.1
Indonesia
    Wahab, Dewi Savitri – E/2010/SR.1
Philippines
    Davide, Hilario G. – E/2010/SR.1
UN. Economic and Social Council (2010 : New York).
President
    Ali, Hamidon (Malaysia) – E/2010/SR.10

## UN. ECONOMIC AND SOCIAL COUNCIL (2010, ORGANIZATIONAL SESS. : NEW YORK)–AGENDA (Agenda item 2)

UN. Economic and Social Council (2010 : New York).
President
    Ali, Hamidon (Malaysia) – E/2010/SR.3;
      E/2010/SR.10

## UN. EXECUTIVE COMMITTEE OF THE UNHCR PROGRAMME–MEMBERS (Agenda item 4)

UN. Economic and Social Council (2010 : New York).
Secretary
De Laurentis, Jennifer – E/2010/SR.8

## UN. INTERGOVERNMENTAL WORKING GROUP OF EXPERTS ON INTERNATIONAL STANDARDS OF ACCOUNTING AND REPORTING–MEMBERS (Agenda item 4)

UN. Economic and Social Council (2010 : New York).
Secretary
De Laurentis, Jennifer – E/2010/SR.8

## UN. INTERNATIONAL RESEARCH AND TRAINING INSTITUTE FOR THE ADVANCEMENT OF WOMEN. EXECUTIVE BOARD–MEMBERS (Agenda item 4)

UN. Economic and Social Council (2010 : New York).
Secretary
De Laurentis, Jennifer – E/2010/SR.8

## UN. PERMANENT FORUM ON INDIGENOUS ISSUES–MEMBERS (Agenda item 4)

UN. Economic and Social Council (2010 : New York).
President
Ali, Hamidon (Malaysia) – E/2010/SR.9
UN. Economic and Social Council (2010 : New York).
Secretary
De Laurentis, Jennifer – E/2010/SR.8

## UN-HABITAT. GOVERNING COUNCIL–MEMBERS (Agenda item 4)

UN. Economic and Social Council (2010 : New York).
Secretary
De Laurentis, Jennifer – E/2010/SR.8

## UNDP/UNFPA EXECUTIVE BOARD–MEMBERS (Agenda item 4)

UN. Economic and Social Council (2010 : New York).
Secretary
De Laurentis, Jennifer – E/2010/SR.8

## UNICEF. EXECUTIVE BOARD–MEMBERS (Agenda item 4)

UN. Economic and Social Council (2010 : New York).
Secretary
De Laurentis, Jennifer – E/2010/SR.8

## WORLD FOOD PROGRAMME. EXECUTIVE BOARD–MEMBERS (Agenda item 4)

UN. Economic and Social Council (2010 : New York).
Secretary
De Laurentis, Jennifer – E/2010/SR.8

# SUBSTANTIVE SESSION OF THE COUNCIL

The substantive session for 2010 of the Economic and Social Council was held at United Nations Headquarters 28 June-23 July 2010. The substantive session was resumed at United Nations Headquarters on 9 Sept.-15 Dec. 2010. A high-level meeting with Bretton Woods Institutions was held on 18-19 Mar. 2010 at the United Nations Headquarters. A list of participants in the session is contained in documents E/2010/INF/1 and E/2010/INF/3.

## CHECK-LIST OF MEETINGS

### Plenary
(Symbol: E/2010/SR.-)

| Meeting | Date, 2010 | Meeting | Date, 2010 | Meeting | Date, 2010 |
|---|---|---|---|---|---|
| 1 | (*see* organizational session) | 17(B) | 1 July | 34 | 14 July |
| 2 | (*see* organizational session) | 18(A) | 1 July | 35 | 15 July |
| 3 | (*see* organizational session) | 18(B) | 1 July | 36 | 15 July |
| 4 | 18 Mar. | 19(A) | 2 July | 37 | 16 July |
| 5 | 18 Mar. | 19(B) | 2 July | 38 | 16 July |
| 6 | 19 Mar. | 20 | 2 July | 39 | 19 July |
| 7 | 19 Mar. | 21 | 6 July | 40 | 19 July |
| 8 | (*see* organizational session) | 22 | 6 July | 41 | 20 July |
| 9 | (*see* organizational session) | 23 | 7 July | 42 | 20 July |
| 10 | (*see* organizational session) | 24 | 7 July | 43 | 21 July |
| 11 | 28 June | 25 | 8 July | 44 | 22 July |
| 12 | 28 June | 26 | 8 July | 45 | 22 July |
| 13 | 29 June | 27 | 9 July | 46 | 23 July |
| 14 | 29 June | 28 | 9 July | 47 | 23 July |
| 15(A) | 30 June | 29 | 12 July | 48 | 9 Sept. |
| 15(B) | 30 June | 30 | 12 July | 49 | 25 Oct. |
| 16 | 30 June | 31 | 13 July | 50 | 10 Nov. |
| 17(A) | 1 July | 32 | 13 July | 51 | 14 Dec. |
| | | 33 | 14 July | 52 | 15 Dec. |

# AGENDA

1. Adoption of the agenda and other organizational matters.

   *See:* UN. ECONOMIC AND SOCIAL COUNCIL (2010, SUBSTANTIVE SESS. : NEW YORK)–AGENDA

2. High-level segment.

   (a) High-level policy dialogue with international financial and trade institutions.

   *See:* INTERNATIONAL FINANCIAL INSTITUTIONS

   (b) Development Cooperation Forum.

   *See:* DEVELOPMENT COOPERATION FORUM

   (c) Annual ministerial review : implementing the internationally agreed goals and commitments in regard to gender equality and empowerment of women.

   *See:* GENDER EQUALITY

   (d) Thematic discussion : current global and national trends and challenges and their impact on gender equality and empowerment of women.

   *See:* EMPOWERMENT OF WOMEN

3. Operational activities of the United Nations for international development cooperation.

   *See:* OPERATIONAL ACTIVITIES – UN

   (a) Follow-up to policy recommendations of the General Assembly and the Council.

   *See:* UN POLICY RECOMMENDATIONS – FOLLOW-UP

   (b) Reports of the Executive Boards of the United Nations Development Programme/United Nations Population Fund, the United Nations Children's Fund and the World Food Programme.

   *See:* UNDP/UNFPA
   UNICEF
   WORLD FOOD PROGRAMME

4. The role of the United Nations system in implementing the ministerial declaration of the high level segment of the 2009 substantive session of the Economic and Social Council.

   *See:* POVERTY MITIGATION

5. Special economic, humanitarian and disaster relief assistance.

   *See:* HUMANITARIAN ASSISTANCE

6. Implementation of and follow up to major United Nations conferences and summits.

   *See:* UN CONFERENCES–FOLLOW-UP

   (a) Follow-up to the International Conference on Financing for Development.

   *See:* DEVELOPMENT FINANCE– CONFERENCE (2002 : MONTERREY, MEXICO)–FOLLOW-UP

   (b) Review and coordination of the implementation of the Programme of Action for the Least Developed Countries for the Decade 2001-2010.

   *See:* LEAST DEVELOPED COUNTRIES– INTERNATIONAL DECADE (2001-2010)

7. Coordination, programme and other questions.

   *See:* COORDINATION AND PROGRAMMES

   (a) Reports of coordination bodies.

   *See:* COORDINATION–REPORTS

   (b) Proposed strategic framework for the period 2012-2013.

   *See:* UN–BUDGET (2012-2013)

   (c) International cooperation in the field of informatics.

   *See:* INFORMATICS–INTERNATIONAL COOPERATION

   (d) Long-term programme of support for Haiti.

   *See:* ECONOMIC ASSISTANCE–HAITI

   (e) Mainstreaming a gender perspective into all policies and programmes in the United Nations system.

   *See:* GENDER MAINSTREAMING–UN SYSTEM

   (f) African countries emerging from conflict.

   *See:* POST-CONFLICT RECONSTRUCTION– AFRICA

   (g) Tobacco or health.

   *See:* TOBACCO–HEALTH

8. Implementation of General Assembly resolutions 50/227, 52/12 B, 57/270 B and 60/265.

   *See:* RESOLUTIONS–UN. GENERAL ASSEMBLY– IMPLEMENTATION

9. Implementation of the Declaration on the Granting of Independence to Colonial Countries and Peoples by the specialized agencies and the international institutions associated with the United Nations.

   *See:* DECOLONIZATION

10. Regional cooperation.

    *See:* REGIONAL COOPERATION

11. Economic and social repercussions of the Israeli occupation on the living conditions of the Palestinian people in the Occupies Palestinian Territory, including East Jerusalem, and the Arab population in the occupied Syrian Golan.

    *See:* PALESTINIANS–TERRITORIES OCCUPIED BY ISRAEL–LIVING CONDITIONS

12. Non-governmental organizations.

    *See:* NON-GOVERNMENTAL ORGANIZATIONS

# AGENDA

13. Economic and environmental questions.
    *See:* ENVIRONMENT–ECONOMIC ASPECTS
    (a) Sustainable development.
        *See:* SUSTAINABLE DEVELOPMENT
    (b) Science and technology for development.
        *See:* SCIENCE AND TECHNOLOGY–
              DEVELOPMENT
    (c) Statistics.
        *See:* STATISTICS
    (d) Human settlements.
        *See:* HUMAN SETTLEMENTS
    (e) Environment.
        *See:* ENVIRONMENT
    (f) Population and development.
        *See:* POPULATION–DEVELOPMENT
    (g) Public administration and development.
        *See:* PUBLIC ADMINISTRATION
    (h) International cooperation in tax matters.
        *See:* TAXATION
    (i) Assistance to 3rd States affected by the
        application of sanctions.
        *See:* SANCTIONS COMPLIANCE–ECONOMIC
              ASSISTANCE
    (j) Cartography.
        *See:* CARTOGRAPHY
    (k) Women and development.
        *See:* WOMEN IN DEVELOPMENT

14. Social and human rights questions.
    (a) Advancement of women.
        *See:* WOMEN'S ADVANCEMENT
    (b) Social development.
        *See:* SOCIAL DEVELOPMENT
    (c) Crime and prevention and criminal justice.
        *See:* CRIME PREVENTION
    (d) Narcotic drugs.
        *See:* NARCOTIC DRUGS
    (e) United Nations High Commissioner for
        Refugees.
        *See:* REFUGEES
    (f) Comprehensive implementation of the Durban
        Declaration and Programme of Action.
        *See:* RACIAL DISCRIMINATION–
              PROGRAMME OF ACTION
    (g) Human rights.
        *See:* HUMAN RIGHTS
    (h) Permanent Forum on Indigenous Issues.
        *See:* UN. PERMANENT FORUM ON
              INDIGENOUS ISSUES
    (i) Genetic privacy and non-discrimination.
        *See:* GENETIC PRIVACY–DISCRIMINATION

## BRETTON WOODS INSTITUTIONS

### General documents

**E/2010/11** Building on Monterrey and Doha : towards achieving the internationally agreed development goals, including the Millennium Development Goals : note / by the Secretary-General.

**E/2010/83** (A/65/81) Summary by the President of the Economic and Social Council of the Special High-Level Meeting of the Council with the Bretton Woods Institutions, the World Trade Organization and the United Nations Conference on Trade and Development (New York, 18 and 19 March 2010).

**E/2010/INF/1** List of delegations : Special High-Level Meeting with the Bretton Woods institutions, the World Trade Organization and the United Nations Conference on Trade and Development, New York, 18-19 March 2010 = Liste des délégations = Lista de las delegaciones.

### Discussion in plenary

**E/2010/SR.4** (18 Mar. 2010).

**E/2010/SR.5** (18 Mar. 2010).

**E/2010/SR.6** (19 Mar. 2010).

**E/2010/SR.7** (19 Mar. 2010).

## CARTOGRAPHY (Agenda item 13j)

**E/CONF.99/3** Ninth United Nations Regional Cartographic Conference for the Americas, New York, 10-14 August 2009 : report of the Conference.

**E/CONF.100/9** Eighteenth United Nations Regional Cartographic Conference for Asia and the Pacific, Bangkok, 26-29 October 2009 : report of the conference.

### Draft resolutions/decisions

**E/2010/L.23** Global geographic information management : draft decision / submitted by the Vice-President of the Council, Somduth Soborun (Mauritius), on the basis of informal consultations.

### Discussion in plenary

**E/2010/SR.43** (21 July 2010).
At the 43rd meeting, the Council took note of the report of the 9th UN Regional Cartographic Conference of the Americas (E/CONF.99/3) and of the report of the 18th UN Regional Cartographic Conference for Asia and the Pacific (E/CONF.100/9): decision 2010/241; at the same meeting, draft decision E/2010/L.23 was adopted without vote: decision 2010/240.

## COORDINATION–REPORTS (Agenda item 7a)

### Reports

**A/65/16** (GAOR, 65th sess., Suppl. no. 16) Report of the Committee for Programme and Coordination, 50th session (7 June-2 July 2010).
Issued: 2010.

## COORDINATION–REPORTS (Agenda item 7a) (continued)

**E/2010/69** Annual overview report of the United Nations System Chief Executives Board for Coordination for 2009/10.
Issued: 7 May 2010.

### Discussion in plenary

**E/2010/SR.23** (7 July 2010).

**E/2010/SR.26** (8 July 2010).

**E/2010/SR.37** (16 July 2010).
At the 37th meeting, the Council took note of the Report of the Committee for Programme and Coordination on its 50th session and of the Annual overview report of the UN System Chief Executives Board for Coordination for 2009/2010: decision 2010/211.

## CRIME PREVENTION (Agenda item 14c)

### Reports

**E/2009/30/Add.1** (E/CN.15/2009/20/Add.1) (ESCOR, 2009, Suppl. no. 10A) Commission on Crime Prevention and Criminal Justice : report on the reconvened 18th session (3-4 December 2009).
Issued: 2009.

**E/2010/10** Capital punishment and implementation of the safeguards guaranteeing protection of the rights of those facing the death penalty : report of the Secretary-General.
Issued: 18 Dec. 2009.

**E/2010/30** (E/CN.15/2010/20) (ESCOR, 2010, Suppl. no. 10) Commission on Crime Prevention and Criminal Justice : report on the 19th session (4 December 2009 and 17-21 May 2010).
Issued: 2010.

**E/2010/30/Add.1** (E/CN.15/2010/20/Add.1) (ESCOR, 2010, Suppl. no. 10A) Commission on Crime Prevention and Criminal Justice : report on the reconvened 19th session (3 December 2010).
Issued: 2010.

### Discussion in plenary

**E/2010/SR.44** (22 July 2010).

## CRIME PREVENTION (Agenda item 14c) (continued)

**E/2010/SR.45**  (22 July 2010).

At the 45th meeting, action on draft resolutions and decisions in E/2010/30 was as follows: draft resolution I in section A entitled "Strengthening crime prevention and criminal justice responses to violence against women", adopted without vote: resolution 2010/15; draft resolution II in section A entitled "United Nations Rules for the Treatment of Women Prisoners and Non-custodial Measures for Women Offenders (the Bangkok Rules)", adopted without vote: resolution 2010/16; draft resolution III in section A entitled "Realignment of the functions of the United Nations Office on Drugs and Crime and changes to the strategic framework", adopted without vote: resolution 2010/17; draft resolution IV in section A entitled "12th United Nations Congress on Crime Prevention and Criminal Justice", adopted without vote: resolution 2010/18; draft resolution I in section B entitled "Crime prevention and criminal justice responses to protect cultural property, especially with regard to its trafficking", adopted without vote: resolution 2010/19; draft resolution II in section B entitled "Support for the development and implementation of an integrated approach to programme development at the United Nations Office on Drugs and Crime", adopted without vote: resolution 2010/20; draft decision in section C entitled "Report of the Commission on Crime Prevention and Criminal Justice on its 19th session and provisional agenda for its 20th session", adopted without vote: decision 2010/243.

**E/2010/SR.46**  (23 July 2010).

At the 46th meeting, the Council took note of the following documents: Report of the Secretary-General on capital punishment and implementation of the safeguards guaranteeing protection of the rights of those facing the death penalty (E/2010/10) and Report of the Commission on Crime Prevention and Criminal Justice on its reconvened 18th session (E/2009/30/Add.1): decision 2010/258.

## Resolutions

**E/RES/2010/15**  (E/2010/INF/2/Add.1)  Strengthening crime prevention and criminal justice responses to violence against women.

Strongly condemns all acts of violence against women; also urges Member States to take into account the special needs and vulnerabilities of women within the criminal justice system; urges Member States to provide appropriate assistance to women victims of violence; urges the UN Office on Drugs and Crime and Member States and invites the institutes of the UN Crime Prevention and Criminal Justice Programme network to continue to offer training and capacity-building opportunities; requests the UN Office on Drugs and Crime to intensify its efforts to ensure the widest possible use and dissemination of the updated Model Strategies and Practical Measures; invites the UN Office on Drugs and Crime to strengthen coordination in its activities in the area of violence against women with other relevant entities of the UN system. (Adopted without vote, 45th plenary meeting, 22 July 2010)

## CRIME PREVENTION (Agenda item 14c) (continued)

**E/RES/2010/16**  (E/2010/INF/2/Add.1)  United Nations Rules for the Treatment of Women Prisoners and Non-custodial Measures for Women Offenders (the Bangkok Rules).

Expresses its gratitude to the Government of Thailand for having acted as host to the meeting of the expert group and for the financial support provided for the organization of the meeting; adopts the UN Rules for the Treatment of Women Prisoners and Non-custodial Measures for Women Offenders and approves the recommendation of the 12th UN Congress on Crime Prevention and Criminal Justice that the Rules should be known as 'the Bangkok Rules'; invites Member States to take into consideration the specific needs and realities of women as prisoners when developing relevant legislation, procedures; requests the UN Office on Drugs and Crime to provide technical assistance and advisory services to Member States; also requests the UN Office on Drugs and Crime to take steps to ensure broad dissemination of the Bangkok Rules; further requests the UN Office on Drugs and Crime to increase its cooperation with other relevant UN entities; invites specialized agencies of the UN system and relevant regional and international intergovernmental and non-governmental organizations to engage in the implementation of the Bangkok Rules. (Adopted without vote, 45th plenary meeting, 22 July 2010)

**E/RES/2010/17**  (E/2010/INF/2/Add.1)  Realignment of the functions of the United Nations Office on Drugs and Crime and changes to the strategic framework.

Requests the Executive Director of the UN Office on Drugs and Crime to ensure the sustainability of the Strategic Planning Unit, consistent with the importance of its functions; urges the Executive Director of the UN Office on Drugs and Crime to ensure that the Office submits to the Secretary-General a proposed programme budget for the biennium 2012-2013 that appropriately reflects the financial needs of the Office; requests the Secretary-General to devote due attention to the resource requirements for meeting the mandates entrusted to the UN Office on Drugs and Crime. (Adopted without vote, 45th plenary meeting, 22 July 2010)

## CRIME PREVENTION (Agenda item 14c) (continued)

**E/RES/2010/18** (E/2010/INF/2/Add.1) Twelfth United Nations Congress on Crime Prevention and Criminal Justice.

Invites Governments to take into consideration the Salvador Declaration and the recommendations adopted by the 12th Congress; invites Member States to identify areas covered in the Salvador Declaration where further tools and training manuals based on international standards and best practices are needed and to submit that information to the Commission; requests the Commission to establish an open-ended intergovernmental expert group, to be convened prior to the twentieth session of the Commission; also requests the Commission to establish to be convened between the 20th and 21st sessions of the Commission; requests the open-ended intergovernmental expert groups to report to the Commission on progress in their work; requests the UN Office on Drugs and Crime to continue to provide technical assistance to facilitate the ratification and implementation of the Convention against Corruption, the Convention against Transnational Organized Crime and the international instruments related to the prevention and suppression of terrorism; requests the Commission to consider at its 20th session options to improve the efficiency of the process involved in the UN congresses on crime prevention and criminal justice; requests the Secretary-General to distribute the report of the 12th Congress. (Adopted without vote, 45th plenary meeting, 22 July 2010)

**E/RES/2010/19** (E/2010/INF/2/Add.1) Crime prevention and criminal justice responses to protect cultural property, especially with regard to its trafficking.

Welcomes the report of the meeting of the expert group on protection against trafficking in cultural property, held in Vienna from 24 to 26 Nov. 2009; requests the UN Office on Drugs and Crime to provide appropriate follow-up to the recommendations of the expert group on protection against trafficking in cultural property; invites Member States to take appropriate measures to prevent cultural property from being trafficked; requests the UN Office on Drugs and Crime to join the UN Educational, Scientific and Cultural Organization and other relevant international organizations in promoting and organizing meetings, seminars and similar events to which the Office can contribute as regards the crime prevention and criminal justice aspects of protection against trafficking in cultural property; requests the UN Office on Drugs and Crime to further explore the development of specific guidelines for crime prevention with respect to trafficking in cultural property; requests the UN Office on Drugs and Crime to explore possibilities for the collection, analysis and dissemination of relevant data, specifically addressing the relevant aspects of trafficking in cultural property. (Adopted without vote, 45th plenary meeting, 22 July 2010)

## CRIME PREVENTION (Agenda item 14c) (continued)

**E/RES/2010/20** (E/2010/INF/2/Add.1) Support for the development and implementation of an integrated approach to programme development at the United Nations Office on Drugs and Crime.

Encourages Member States to support the regional and thematic programmes of the UN Office on Drugs and Crime through unearmarked voluntary contributions; welcomes the advances in the implementation of the Santo Domingo Pact and Managua Mechanism interregional initiative; welcomes the holding in Cairo, from 27-29 Apr. 2010, of the regional expert meeting organized by the League of Arab States in partnership with the UN Office on Drugs and Crime, and with the support of the Government of Egypt, on drug control, crime prevention and criminal justice reform in the Arab States, in order to prepare a regional programme for the period 2011-2015; requests the UN Office on Drugs and Crime to continue with the development of regional programmes in 2010; supports the work of the UN Office on Drugs and Crime in leading the development of the integrated programme approach; requests the Executive Director of the UN Office on Drugs and Crime to continue giving high priority and support to the implementation of the integrated programme approach through the promotion of the regional and thematic programmes. (Adopted without vote, 45th plenary meeting, 22 July 2010)

## DECOLONIZATION (Agenda item 9)

### Reports

**A/65/61** Implementation of the Declaration on the Granting of Independence to Colonial Countries and Peoples by the specialized agencies and the international institutions associated with the United Nations : report of the Secretary-General.
Issued: 24 Feb. 2010.

**A/65/61/Corr.1** Implementation of the Declaration on the Granting of Independence to Colonial Countries and Peoples by the specialized agencies and the international institutions associated with the United Nations : report of the Secretary-General : corrigendum.
Issued: 17 June 2010. - Corrects text.

**E/2010/54** Report of the President of the Council on consultations with the Special Committee on the Situation with regard to the Implementation of the Declaration on the Granting of Independence to Colonial Countries and Peoples : information submitted by the specialized agencies and other organizations of the United Nations System on their activities with regard to the implementation of the Declaration.
Issued: 4 May 2010.

## DECOLONIZATION (Agenda item 9) (continued)

**E/2010/54/Add.1** Report of the President of the Council on consultations with the Special Committee on the Situation with regard to the Implementation of the Declaration on the Granting of Independence to Colonial Countries and Peoples : information submitted by the specialized agencies and other organizations of the United Nations System on their activities with regard to the implementation of the Declaration : addendum.
Issued: 16 June 2010.

**E/2010/56** (A/65/77) Assistance to the Palestinian people : report of the Secretary-General.
Issued: 5 May 2010.

### Draft resolutions/decisions

**E/2010/L.22** Support to Non-Self-Governing Territories by the specialized agencies and international institutions associated with the United Nations : draft decision / China, Cuba, Ecuador, Grenada, Nicaragua, Papua New Guinea, Saint Lucia, Sierra Leone and Syrian Arab Republic.
Additional sponsors: Bolivarian Republic of Venezuela, Saint Kitts and Nevis and Timor-Leste (E/2010/SR.41).

### Discussion in plenary

**E/2010/SR.41** (20 July 2010).

**E/2010/SR.46** (23 July 2010).
At the 46th meeting, draft resolution E/2010/L.22 was adopted (26-0-26): resolution 2010/30.

### Resolutions

**E/RES/2010/30** (E/2010/INF/2/Add.1) Support to Non-Self-Governing Territories by the specialized agencies and international institutions associated with the United Nations.
Recommends that all States intensify their efforts within the specialized agencies and other organizations of the UN system of which they are members to ensure the full and effective implementation of the Declaration on the Granting of Independence to Colonial Countries and Peoples. (Adopted 26-0-26, 46th plenary meeting, 23 July 2010)

## DEVELOPMENT COOPERATION FORUM (Agenda item 2b)

### Reports

**E/2010/93** Trends and progress in international development cooperation : report of the Secretary-General.
Issued: 10 June 2010.

### General documents

**E/2010/47** Letter, 10 Mar. 2010, from Ghana. Transmits Chair's summary of the discussion at the 48th session of the Commission for Social Development on "Emerging issues: policy responses on employment and the social consequences of the financial and economic crisis, including its gender dimension".

## DEVELOPMENT COOPERATION FORUM (Agenda item 2b) (continued)

**E/2010/92** Summary by the Chair of the panel discussion on the theme "Gender and science and technology", held at the 13th session of the Commission on Science and Technology for Development : note / by the Secretariat.

**E/2010/98** Note verbale, 23 June 2010, from Austria. Transmits report of the High-level Symposium on the Theme "Accountable and Transparent Development Cooperation : Towards a More Inclusive Framework", held in Vienna on 12 and 13 Nov. 2009.

**E/2010/104** Letter, 15 Nov. 2010, from Finland. Transmits report of the Development Cooperation Forum High-level Symposium on the theme "Coherent development cooperation: maximizing impact in a changing environment", held in Helsinki, 3-4 June 2010.

**E/2010/CRP.2** Review of progress in international and national mutual accountability and transparency on development cooperation : background paper for Development Cooperation Forum High-Level Symposium.

**E/2010/NGO/1** Statement / submitted by International Peace Research Association.
Transmits statement entitled "Integrating financing for development and climate justice".

**E/2010/NGO/4** Statement / submitted by Comité français pour l'Afrique du Sud.
Transmits statement entitled "Developing public services in the areas of education, housing and health during a crisis".

**E/2010/NGO/7** Statement / submitted by All India Shah Behram Baug Society for Scientific and Educational Research.
Transmits statement entitled "Recommendation for an action plan for the Millennium Development Goals in the coming decade".

**E/2010/NGO/8** Statement / submitted by Company of the Daughters of Charity of St. Vincent de Paul.
Transmits statement entitled "Development cooperation in times of crisis: debt relief".

**E/2010/NGO/9** Statement / submitted by Salesian Missions.
Transmits statement entitled "Financial transaction tax: development cooperation in times of crises".

**E/2010/NGO/21** Statement / submitted by Institute of International Social Development.
Transmits recommendations regarding the achievement of the Millennium Development Goals.

**E/2010/NGO/39** Statement / submitted by Nord-Sud XXI.
Transmits statement on achieving the Millennium Development Goals.

**E/2010/NGO/60** Statement / submitted by Christian Blind Mission International.
Transmits statement on the rights of persons with disabilities in relation to Millennium Development Goals.

## DEVELOPMENT COOPERATION FORUM (Agenda item 2b) (continued)

**E/2010/NGO/82** Statement / submitted by the Centre de Formation aux Techniques Informatiques.
  Transmits statement on the impact of the economic crisis on Africa, the African Peer Review Mechanism and tax revenues of developing countries.

### Discussion in plenary

**E/2010/SR.13** (29 June 2010).

**E/2010/SR.14** (29 June 2010).

**E/2010/SR.16** (30 June 2010).

## DEVELOPMENT FINANCE–CONFERENCE (2002 : MONTERREY, MEXICO)–FOLLOW-UP (Agenda item 6a)

### Reports

**E/2010/64** Recovering from the crisis: a Global Jobs Pact : report of the Secretary-General.
  Issued: 6 May 2010.

### General documents

**E/2010/83** (A/65/81) Summary by the President of the Economic and Social Council of the Special High-Level Meeting of the Council with the Bretton Woods Institutions, the World Trade Organization and the United Nations Conference on Trade and Development (New York, 18 and 19 March 2010).

### Draft resolutions/decisions

**E/2010/L.9** Recovering from the world financial and economic crisis : a Global Jobs Pact : draft resolution / Yemen [on behalf of the Group of 77 and China].

**E/2010/L.9/Rev.1** Recovering from the world financial and economic crisis : a Global Jobs Pact : revised draft resolution / Belgium, Canada, Finland, France, Germany, Italy, Japan, Netherlands, Portugal, Russian Federation, Sweden, Turkey, United States of America and Yemen [on behalf of the Group of 77 and China].

**E/2010/L.12** Follow-up to the International Conference on Financing for Development : draft resolution / Mexico.

**E/2010/L.12/Rev.1** Follow-up to the International Conference on Financing for Development and the 2008 review conference: draft resolution / Mexico.

**E/2010/L.37** Establishment of an ad hoc panel of experts on the world financial and economic crisis and its impact on development : draft resolution / Yemen [on behalf of the Group of 77 and China].

### Discussion in plenary

**E/2010/SR.23** (7 July 2010).

**E/2010/SR.24** (7 July 2010).

**E/2010/SR.25** (8 July 2010).

**E/2010/SR.26** (8 July 2010).

## DEVELOPMENT FINANCE–CONFERENCE (2002 : MONTERREY, MEXICO)–FOLLOW-UP (Agenda item 6a) (continued)

**E/2010/SR.46** (23 July 2010).
  At the 46th meeting, action on draft resolutions was as follows: draft resolution E/2010/L.9/Rev.1, as orally revised, adopted without vote: resolution 2010/25; draft resolution E/2010/L.12/Rev.1, adopted without vote: resolution 2010/26.

**E/2010/SR.47** (23 July 2010).
  At the 47th meeting, the Council decided to defer the consideration of draft resolution E/2010/L.37 until its resumed 2010 substantive session: decision 2010/260.

**E/2010/SR.52** (15 Dec. 2010).
  At the 52nd meeting, the Council decided to continue its consideration of draft resolution E/2010/L.37, with a view to making final recommendations to the General Assembly, in accordance with the mandate of para. 56 (e) of the Outcome of the Conference on the World Financial and Economic Crisis and Its Impact on Development, during its substantive session of 2011: decision 2010/264.

### Resolutions

**E/RES/2010/25** (E/2010/INF/2/Add.1) Recovering from the world financial and economic crisis : a Global Jobs Pact.
  Welcomes the Global Jobs Pact as a general framework within which each country can formulate policy packages specific to its situation and priorities; underlines the fact that countries can harness the Global Jobs Pact to accelerate recovery and place the goals of full and productive employment and decent work for all in national and international policy frameworks; requests the UN funds and programmes and the specialized agencies to take further into account the Global Jobs Pact in their policies and programmes through their appropriate decision-making processes; reiterates that giving effect to the recommendations and policy options of the Global Jobs Pact requires consideration of financing and capacity-building; requests the Secretary-General to report to the Economic and Social Council at its substantive session of 2011 on progress made in implementing the present resolution. (Adopted without vote, 46th plenary meeting, 23 July 2010)

## DEVELOPMENT FINANCE–CONFERENCE (2002 : MONTERREY, MEXICO)–FOLLOW-UP (Agenda item 6a) (continued)

### Resolutions

**E/RES/2010/26** (E/2010/INF/2/Add.1) Follow-up to the International Conference on Financing for Development and the 2008 Review Conference.

Reaffirms the importance of staying fully engaged in ensuring proper and effective follow-up to the implementation of the Monterrey Consensus as reaffirmed in the Doha Declaration on Financing for Development; emphasizes that the financing for development follow-up process should constitute a continuum of events; welcomes the new modalities of the special high-level meeting of the Council with the Bretton Woods institutions, the World Trade Organization and the UN Conference on Trade and Development; further welcomes the increased interaction and coordination at the staff level with the institutions involved prior to the Council's high-level meeting; encourages all relevant stakeholders to consider organizing seminars, panel discussions and briefings; encourages the Department of Economic and Social Affairs of the Secretariat, and especially the Financing for Development Office, to maintain regular interaction at the staff level with the World Bank, the International Monetary Fund, the World Trade Organization and the UN Conference on Trade and Development in the interest of greater coherence, coordination and cooperation, each acting in accordance with its respective intergovernmental mandates. (Adopted without vote, 46th plenary meeting, 23 July 2010)

## ECONOMIC ASSISTANCE–HAITI (Agenda item 7d)

### Reports

**E/2010/102** Report of the Ad Hoc Advisory Group on Haiti.
Issued: 14 July 2010.

**E/2010/102/Corr.1** Report of the Ad Hoc Advisory Group on Haiti : corrigendum.
Issued: 27 July 2010. - Replaces text.

**E/2010/CRP.5** Report of the ECOSOC Ad Hoc Advisory Group on Haiti (New York, 13 July 2010).
Issued: 12 July 2010.

### Draft resolutions/decisions

**E/2010/L.27** Ad Hoc Advisory Group on Haiti : draft resolution / Benin, Brazil, Canada, Chile, El Salvador, Guatemala, Haiti, Luxembourg, Peru, Poland, Spain, Trinidad and Tobago.
Additional sponsors: Australia, Bahamas, Bangladesh, Cameroon, Republic of Korea, Saint Kitts and Nevis, Saint Lucia and United States (E/2010/SR.46).

### Discussion in plenary

**E/2010/SR.32** (13 July 2010).

**E/2010/SR.44** (22 July 2010).

**E/2010/SR.46** (23 July 2010).
At the 46th meeting, draft resolution E/2010/L.27 was adopted without vote: resolution 2010/28.

## ECONOMIC ASSISTANCE–HAITI (Agenda item 7d) (continued)

### Resolutions

**E/RES/2010/28** (E/2010/INF/2/Add.1) Ad Hoc Advisory Group on Haiti.

Expresses its deepest sympathy and solidarity to all those affected by the devastating earthquake of 12 Jan. 2010 in Haiti and to their families; affirms the leading role of the Government of Haiti in all aspects of the recovery, reconstruction and development plans for the country; commends the creation of the Interim Haiti Recovery Commission; decides to extend the mandate of the Ad Hoc Advisory Group on Haiti until the substantive session of the Economic and Social Council in 2012; recommends that full use continue to be made of the UN capacity to mobilize international efforts and aid, and that the leadership role of the UN in this respect be recognized and promoted on the ground; requests the Ad Hoc Advisory Group on Haiti to continue to cooperate with the Secretary-General; invites additional members to participate in the work of the Ad Hoc Advisory Group. (Adopted without vote, 46th plenary meeting, 23 July 2010)

## ECONOMIC SURVEYS

### Reports

**E/2010/50** World economic and social survey. 2010, Retooling global development : overview.
Issued: 19 Apr. 2010.

**E/2010/50/Rev.1** (ST/ESA/330) World economic and social survey. 2010, Retooling global development.
Issued: 2010.

**E/2010/73** World economic situation and prospects as of mid-2010.
Issued: 11 May 2010.

## ECONOMIC, SOCIAL AND CULTURAL RIGHTS–TREATY (1966) (Agenda item 14g)

### Reports

**E/2010/22** (E/C.12/2009/3) (ESCOR, 2010, Suppl. no. 2) Committee on Economic, Social and Cultural Rights : report on the 42nd and 43rd sessions, 4-22 May 2009, 2-20 November 2009.
Issued: 2010.

### Draft resolutions/decisions

**E/2010/L.43** Report of the Committee on Economic, Social and Cultural Rights at its 42nd and 43rd sessions : draft resolution / submitted by the President of the Council on the basis of informal consultations.

### Discussion in plenary

**E/2010/SR.51** (14 Dec. 2010).
At the 51st meeting, draft resolution E/2010/L.43 was adopted without vote: resolution 2010/37.

## ECONOMIC, SOCIAL AND CULTURAL RIGHTS– TREATY (1966) (Agenda item 14g) (continued)

### Resolutions

**E/RES/2010/37** (E/2010/INF/2/Add.2) Report of the Committee on Economic, Social and Cultural Rights on its 42nd and 43rd sessions.

Requests the Committee on Economic, Social and Cultural Rights to improve the efficiency of its working methods; requests the Secretary-General to include in the report to be submitted to the General Assembly at its 66th session concrete and tailored proposals on the human rights treaty bodies. (Adopted without vote, 51st plenary meeting, 14 Dec. 2010)

## EMPOWERMENT OF WOMEN (Agenda item 2d)

### Discussion in plenary

**E/2010/SR.15(B)** (30 June 2010).

**E/2010/SR.17(B)** (1 July 2010).

**E/2010/SR.18(B)** (1 July 2010).

**E/2010/SR.19(B)** (2 July 2010).

## ENVIRONMENT (Agenda item 13e)

### Reports

**A/65/25** (GAOR, 65th sess., Suppl. no. 25) United Nations Environment Programme : report of the Governing Council/Global Ministerial Environment Forum on the work of its 11th special session (Bali, Indonesia, 24-26 February 2010).
Issued: 2010.

### General documents

**E/2010/79** Chemicals volume of the Consolidated List of Products Whose Consumption and/or Sale have been Banned, Withdrawn, Severely Restricted or Not Approved by Governments : note / by the Secretary-General.
Transmits the contribution by UNEP covering pesticides and industrial chemicals of the Consolidated List.

**E/2010/84** Note [of transmittal only; concerns the updating of the pharmaceuticals volume of the Consolidated List by WHO] / by the Secretary-General.

### Draft resolutions/decisions

**E/2010/L.38** Consolidated List of Products Whose Consumption and/or Sale have been Banned, Withdrawn, Severely Restricted or Not Approved by Governments : draft resolution / submitted by the Vice-President of the Council, Somduth Soborun (Mauritius), on the basis of informal consultations.

### Discussion in plenary

**E/2010/SR.43** (21 July 2010).
At the 43rd meeting, the Council took note of the report of the Governing Council of the UN Environment Programme on its 11th special session (A/65/25): decision 2010/237.

## ENVIRONMENT (Agenda item 13e) (continued)

**E/2010/SR.46** (23 July 2010).
At the 46th meeting, draft resolution E/2010/L.38 was adopted without vote: resolution 2010/32.

### Resolutions

**E/RES/2010/32** (E/2010/INF/2/Add.1) Consolidated List of Products Whose Consumption and / or Sale Have Been Banned, Withdrawn, Severely Restricted or Not Approved by Governments.
Decides to discontinue consideration of the Consolidated List of Products Whose Consumption and/or Sale Have Been Banned, Withdrawn, Severely Restricted or Not Approved by Governments at its future substantive sessions. (Adopted without vote, 46th plenary meeting, 23 July 2010)

## ENVIRONMENT–ECONOMIC ASPECTS (Agenda item 13)

### Reports

**E/2010/90** (A/65/84) Role of the Economic and Social Council in the integrated and coordinated implementation of the outcomes of and follow-up to major United Nations conferences and summits, in the light of relevant General Assembly resolutions, including resolution 61/16 : report of the Secretary-General.
Issued: 3 June 2010.

### General documents

**E/2010/91** (A/64/803) Letter, 25 May 2010, from Spain. Transmits Madrid Declaration entitled "Towards a new stage in the biregional partnership: innovation and technology for sustainable development and social inclusion", adopted by the Heads of State and Government meeting at the 6th summit of the European Union and the Latin American and Caribbean States, which was held in Madrid on 18 May 2010.

## GENDER EQUALITY (Agenda item 2c)

### Reports

**E/2010/49** Current global and national trends and challenges and their impact on gender equality and empowerment of women : report of the Secretary-General.
Issued: 14 Apr. 2010.

### General documents

**E/2010/47** Letter, 10 Mar. 2010, from Ghana. Transmits Chair's summary of the discussion at the 48th session of the Commission for Social Development on "Emerging issues: policy responses on employment and the social consequences of the financial and economic crisis, including its gender dimension".

## GENDER EQUALITY (Agenda item 2c) (continued)

**E/2010/58**  Letter, 4 May 2010, from the United States. Transmits document entitled "Voluntary national presentation of the United States of America: implementing the internationally agreed goals and commitments in regard to gender equality and empowerment of women", for the annual ministerial review to be held during the high-level segment of the substantive session of 2010 of the Economic and Social Council.

**E/2010/59**  Letter, 5 May 2010, from Portugal. Transmits national report of Portugal on gender equality and empowerment of women for the annual ministerial review to be held during the High-level Segment of the 2010 substantive session of the Economic and Social Council.

**E/2010/60**  Letter, 5 May 2010, from Guatemala. Transmits national report of Guatemala entitled "Gender Equality and Empowerment of Women in the Context of the Implementation of the Millennium Development Goals" which will be presented during the high-level segment of the 2010 substantive session of the Economic and Social Council.

**E/2010/61**  Letter, 30 Apr. 2010, from Namibia. Transmits national report of Namibia on implementation of national strategies to achieve the internationally agreed goals, including the Millennium Development Goals, with a focus on health, education, poverty, gender equality and empowerment of women, for the annual ministerial review to be held during the high-level segment of the 2010 substantive session of the Economic and Social Council.

**E/2010/62**  Letter, 6 May 2010, from the Netherlands. Transmits national report of the Netherlands on progress towards the achievement of the internationally agreed goals, including the Millennium Development Goals, for the annual ministerial review to be held during the high-level segment of the 2010 substantive session of the Economic and Social Council.

**E/2010/63**  Letter, 5 May 2010, from Australia. Transmits document entitled "Voluntary national presentation of Australia: implementing the internationally agreed goals and commitments in regard to gender equality and the empowerment of women" for the annual ministerial review to be held during the high-level segment of the substantive session of 2010 of the Economic and Social Council.

**E/2010/66**  Letter, 5 May 2010, from Norway. Transmits document entitled "National report of Norway on gender equality and the empowerment of women for the annual ministerial review of the Economic and Social Council".

**E/2010/67**  Letter, 5 May 2010, from the Republic of Moldova. Transmits the national report of Moldova on the implementation of the Millennium Development Goals, with a special focus on Goal 3, on gender equality and the empowerment of women, prepared for the Annual Ministerial Review Meeting to be held during the high-level segment of the 2010 substantive session of the Economic and Social Council.

## GENDER EQUALITY (Agenda item 2c) (continued)

**E/2010/71**  Letter, 10 May 2010, from the Republic of Korea. Transmits report entitled "Implementing the internationally agreed goals and commitments in regard to gender equality and empowerment of women" for the Annual Ministerial Review to be held during the high-level segment of the 2010 substantive session of the Economic and Social Council.

**E/2010/75**  Letter, 14 May 2010, from Senegal. Transmits report of the African Regional Preparatory Meeting on Women and Health, held in Dakar on 12-13 Jan. 2010.

**E/2010/78**  Letter, 20 May 2010, from Congo. Transmits the national report of the Republic of the Congo on gender equality and the empowerment of women, for the Annual Ministerial Review to be held during the high-level segment of the 2010 substantive session of the Economic and Social Council.

**E/2010/80**  Letter, 25 May 2010, from Mongolia. Transmits national report of Mongolia on gender equality and women's empowerment, for the annual ministerial review to be held during the high-level segment of the substantive session of 2010 of the Economic and Social Council.

**E/2010/81**  Letter, 20 May 2010, from France. Transmits the national report of France entitled "Policies implemented by France with a view to achievement of the internationally agreed goals and commitments in regard to the promotion of women's rights and gender equality",.

**E/2010/92**  Summary by the Chair of the panel discussion on the theme "Gender and science and technology", held at the 13th session of the Commission on Science and Technology for Development : note / by the Secretariat.

**E/2010/NGO/3**  Statement / submitted by Fondation Ostad Elahi: éthique et solidarité humaine.
Reports that a panel met on 26 Mar. 2010 on the premises of the French Economic, Social and Environmental Council, at the initiative of the Fondation Ostad Elahi: éthique et solidarité humaine under the auspices of the International Association of Economic and Social Councils and Similar Institutions and that the panel considered the topic "How to achieve professional equality".

**E/2010/NGO/5**  Statement / submitted by World for World Organization.
Recommends innovative approaches, which identify key elements to women's economic empowerment.

**E/2010/NGO/6**  Statement / submitted by Fondation Surgir.
Transmits statement entitled "Strengthening the fight against crimes of honour".

**E/2010/NGO/10**  Statement / submitted by IPAS.
Transmits statement entitled "Gender equality and women's empowerment through improved maternal health".

## GENDER EQUALITY (Agenda item 2c) (continued)

**E/2010/NGO/11**  Statement / submitted by African Citizens Development Foundation.
Transmits statement entitled "Gender stability: the catalyst to world peace".

**E/2010/NGO/12**  Statement / submitted by Alulbayt Foundation.
Transmits statement entitled "Promoting women's education and employment as a means for promoting gender equality and empowerment".

**E/2010/NGO/13**  Statement / submitted by Fédération européenne des femmes actives au foyer.
Concerns recognition and support for unpaid caregiving and related work; promotes women's economic independence.

**E/2010/NGO/14**  Statement / submitted by Federation of Women Lawyers in Kenya.
Transmits statement entitled "Gender equality and women's empowerment: where is Kenya 15 years after Beijing?".

**E/2010/NGO/15**  Statement / submitted by International Alliance of Women.
Transmits statement entitled "Tobacco free is a woman's rights issue".

**E/2010/NGO/16**  Statement / submitted by International Association of Applied Psychology.
Transmits statement entitled "Grass-roots preparation for women's right to work".

**E/2010/NGO/18**  Statement / submitted by School Sisters of Notre Dame.
Transmits statement entitled "Remember the girls".

**E/2010/NGO/20**  Statement / submitted by Gray Panthers.
Transmits statement on the importance of gender equality and the empowerment of women in implementing the Millennium Development Goals.

**E/2010/NGO/22**  Statement / submitted by International Planned Parenthood Federation.
Recognizes that sexual and reproductive health and rights are central to addressing obstacles related to women's advancement worldwide and to reaching the internationally agreed goals and commitments in regard to gender equality and equity and to equitable and sustainable development.

**E/2010/NGO/23**  Statement / submitted by Equality Now.
Transmits statement on discrimination against women in law and practice.

**E/2010/NGO/24**  Statement / submitted by Forum of Women's NGOs of Kyrgyzstan.
Transmits statement entitled "Women's empowerment is a key to successful development".

**E/2010/NGO/25**  Statement / submitted by Women's International League for Peace and Freedom.
Transmits statement on the financing of the implementation of universal gender equality.

## GENDER EQUALITY (Agenda item 2c) (continued)

**E/2010/NGO/26**  Statement / submitted by Soroptimist International.
Transmits statement on gender barriers to achieving the Millennium Development Goals.

**E/2010/NGO/27**  Statement / submitted by Misión Mujer.
Transmits statement on the cross-cutting issues which affect development.

**E/2010/NGO/28**  Statement / submitted by China NGO Network for International Exchanges.
Transmits statement on the 5th Conference of the UN Non-Governmental Organizations Informal Regional Network/Asia-Pacific on women empowerment in the development of outlying regions, Xining City, Qinghai Province, China, 2 Apr. 2010; includes recommendations to the annual ministerial review of the Economic and Social Council in 2010.

**E/2010/NGO/30**  Statement / submitted by Israel Women's Network.
Transmits statement on the Women of Valour programme.

**E/2010/NGO/31**  Statement / submitted by Peace Boat.
Transmits statement on the centrality of women in relations to Millennium Development Goals.

**E/2010/NGO/32**  Statement / submitted by Sisters of Charity Federation.
Transmits statement concerning water, sanitation and women and the implementation of the Millennium Development Goals.

**E/2010/NGO/33**  Statement / submitted by Society of Catholic Social Scientists.
Transmits statement on the implementation of Goal 5 of the Millennium Development Goals and reducing maternal mortality.

**E/2010/NGO/34**  Statement / submitted by Women in Europe for a Common Future.
Transmits statement on the right to water for all and the gender-related issues in relation to water.

**E/2010/NGO/35**  Statement / submitted by Association for World Education.
Transmits statement on the promotion of gender equality.

**E/2010/NGO/36**  Statement / submitted by World Society for the Protection of Animals.
Transmits statement on the importance of women's role as caregivers of farm animals and their use to their family.

**E/2010/NGO/37**  Statement / submitted by S.M. Sehgal Foundation.
Transmits statement on the importance of women's role in rural society.

**E/2010/NGO/38**  Statement / submitted by Radin Institute for Family Health Education and Promotion.
Transmits statement on the importance of youth in achieving Millennium Development Goals.

## GENDER EQUALITY (Agenda item 2c) (continued)

**E/2010/NGO/40** Statement / submitted by Tides Center.
Transmits statement on the achievement of the Millennium Development Goals and women's human rights.

**E/2010/NGO/42** Statement / submitted by Priests for Life.
Transmits statement on gender equality and empowerment of women.

**E/2010/NGO/43** Statement / submitted by Association tunisienne des mères.
Transmits statement on the empowerment of women and girls in Tunisia.

**E/2010/NGO/44** Statement / submitted by World Association of Girl Guides and Girl Scouts.
Concerns education and empowerment of girls and young women.

**E/2010/NGO/45** Statement / submitted by Center for Health and Gender Equity.
Transmits statement on the achievement of the Millennium Development Goals and gender equality for women.

**E/2010/NGO/46** Statement / submitted by Center for Reproductive Rights.
Transmits statement on improving maternal health, Goal 5 of the Millennium Development Goals, focussing on maternal mortality in Brazil.

**E/2010/NGO/47** Statement / submitted by Women's Board Educational Cooperation Society.
Transmits statement on the achievement of the Millennium Development Goals and empowerment based on the education of girls.

**E/2010/NGO/48** Statement / submitted by Centre for Social Research.
Concerns the importance of taking affirmative steps towards the inclusion of women in political processes.

**E/2010/NGO/49** Statement / submitted by Korea Institute of Brain Science.
Transmits statement entitled "Empowering women through brain education".

**E/2010/NGO/50** Statement / submitted by Northern Ireland Women's European Platform.
Presents recommendations in regards to gender equality and empowerment of women.

**E/2010/NGO/51** Statement / submitted by Salesian Missions.
Transmits statement entitled "Legal empowerment of those living in poverty: an important protection for women".

**E/2010/NGO/53** Statement / submitted by Agency for Cooperation and Research in Development.
Transmits statement entitled "End impunity for sexual and gender-based violence".

**E/2010/NGO/54** Statement / submitted by Loretto Community.
Transmits statement entitled "The need for a recommitment to girls' education".

## GENDER EQUALITY (Agenda item 2c) (continued)

**E/2010/NGO/55** Statement / submitted by Concerned Women for America.
Transmits statement entitled "Goal 5, target 1, of the Millennium Development Goals: reducing maternal mortality".

**E/2010/NGO/56** Statement / submitted by Congregation of Our Lady of Charity of the Good Shepherd.
Transmits statement entitled "Vision, investment, implementation: gender equality and the empowerment of women".

**E/2010/NGO/57** Statement / submitted by Equidad de Genero: Ciudadania, Trabajo y Familia.
Transmits statement entitled "Gender mainstreaming as a strategy of actions".

**E/2010/NGO/58** Statement / submitted by Family Care International.
Tranamits statement concerning family planning and reproductive health care.

**E/2010/NGO/59** Statement / submitted by Family Research Council.
Transmits statement entitled "Scientific, peer-reviewed studies on the psychological impact of abortion".

**E/2010/NGO/61** Statement / submitted by Imamia Medics International.
Transmits statement on gender equality and reproductive health in relation to Millennium Development Goals.

**E/2010/NGO/63** Statement / submitted by Legião da Boa Vontade.
Transmits proposals and recommendations from the participants of the 7th Solidary Society Network Multi-stakeholder Forum: 4th Innovation Fair, stemming from their own practical experience, as well as proposals for a series of innovative social technologies experienced by the Legion of Good Will.

**E/2010/NGO/64** Statement / submitted by Life Ethics Educational Association.
Concerns sex-selected abortion.

**E/2010/NGO/65** Statement / submitted by National Right to Life Educational Trust Fund.
Transmits statement on whether to legalize abortion to protect women's health.

**E/2010/NGO/67** Statement / submitted by Women's Environment and Development Organization.
Transmits statement on advancing women's empowerment and gender equality.

**E/2010/NGO/68** Statement / submitted by World Family Organization.
Transmits statement on entitled "Families in balance".

**E/2010/NGO/69** Statement / submitted by VIVAT International.
Transmits statement on entitled "Empowerment of women".

## GENDER EQUALITY (Agenda item 2c) (continued)

**E/2010/NGO/70**  Statement / submitted by World Federation of Khoja Shi'a Ithna- Asheri Muslim Communities.
Transmits statement on implementing the internationally agreed goals and commitments in regard to gender equality and empowerment of women.

**E/2010/NGO/71**  Statement / submitted by ISHA Foundation.
Transmits statement entitled "Gender mainstreaming through sport".

**E/2010/NGO/73**  Statement / submitted by Coalition Against Trafficking in Women.
Transmits statement on elimination of violence against women and the realization of gender equality.

**E/2010/NGO/74**  Statement / submitted by Commission of the Churches on International Affairs of the World Council of Churches.
Transmits statement affirming the promotion of gender equality and justice from a theological and human rights perspective.

**E/2010/NGO/75**  Statement / submitted by Family Welfare in Brazil Civil Society.
Transmits statement on social development as means to reduce inequalities among the most vulnerable members of society.

**E/2010/NGO/76**  Statement / submitted by Foundation for the Social Promotion of Culture.
Transmits statement entitled "Gender equality and environmental sustainability in the development agenda of the Middle East".

**E/2010/NGO/77**  Statement / submitted by Friends of Africa International.
Transmits statement entitled "Keeping our promises to future generations: achieving gender equality in the midst of a global economic crisis".

**E/2010/NGO/78**  Statement / submitted by Global Alliance for Women's Health.
Transmits statement on women and non-communicable diseases.

**E/2010/NGO/79**  Statement / submitted by Mulchand and Parpati Thadhani Foundation.
Transmits statement on gender empowerment to achieve the Millennium Development Goals.

**E/2010/NGO/80**  Statement / submitted by Hope for the Nations.
Transmits statement including recommendations on the topic "Implementing the internationally agreed goals and commitments in regard to gender equality and empowerment of women", discussed at a forum and workshop held in Kelowna, British Columbia, Canada in Apr. 2010.

**E/2010/NGO/81**  Statement / submitted by International Federation of Family Associations of Missing Persons from Armed Conflicts.
Transmits statement on families with members missing as a result of armed conflicts.

## GENDER EQUALITY (Agenda item 2c) (continued)

**E/2010/NGO/83**  Statement / submitted by Marangopoulos Foundation for Human Rights.
Transmits statement with proposals on the topic "Implementing the internationally agreed goals and commitments in regard to gender equality and empowerment of women".

**E/2010/NGO/84**  Statement / submitted by Christian Blind Mission International.
Transmits statement on women with disabilities, highlighting the forms of discrimination faced by women with disabilities in low- and middle-income countries.

**E/2010/NGO/85**  Statement / submitted by International Peace Research Association.
Transmits statement entitled "Towards gender-responsive and equitable climate change financing".

**E/2010/NGO/86**  Statement / submitted by Presbyterian Church USA and World Federation of Methodist and Uniting Church Women.
Transmits statement entitled "Partners for change: faith-based engagement in achieving gender equality and empowerment of women".

**E/2010/NGO/87**  Statement / submitted by World Federation of Ukrainian Women's Organizations.
Transmits statement on the achievement of equal rights for women.

**E/2010/NGO/88**  Statement / submitted by Center for Women's Global Leadership, Amnesty International, Development Alternatives with Women for a New Era, Fundación para Estudio e Investigación de la Mujer and Women's Environment and Development Organization.
Transmits statement on commitments to advance gender equality and empowerment of women and the proposed establishment of the UN entity for women.

**E/2010/NGO/89**  Statement / submitted by HelpAge International, AARP, International Council of Psychologists, International Federation on Ageing, European Federation for the Welfare of the Elderly and International Network for the Prevention of Elder Abuse.
Transmits statement entitled "Implementation of key international commitments and goals on gender inequality in relation to older women".

**E/2010/NGO/90**  Statement / submitted by the Women's Federation for World Peace International.
Transmits statement on gender equality and empowerment of women.

### Draft resolutions/decisions

**E/2010/L.8**  Draft ministerial declaration of the 2009 high-level segment of the Economic and Social Council : implementing the internationally agreed goals and commitments in regard to gender equality and empowerment of women / submitted by the President of the Council.

### Discussion in plenary

**E/2010/SR.11**  (28 June 2010).

**E/2010/SR.12**  (28 June 2010).

## GENDER EQUALITY (Agenda item 2c) (continued)

**E/2010/SR.15(A)** (30 June 2010).

**E/2010/SR.15(B)** (30 June 2010).

**E/2010/SR.17(A)** (1 July 2010).

**E/2010/SR.17(B)** (1 July 2010).

**E/2010/SR.18(A)** (1 July 2010).

**E/2010/SR.19(A)** (2 July 2010).
At the 19th meeting, the ministerial declaration (E/2010/L.8), as orally corrected, was adopted.

**E/2010/SR.19(B)** (2 July 2010).

## GENDER MAINSTREAMING–UN SYSTEM (Agenda item 7e)

### Reports

**E/2010/57** Mainstreaming a gender perspective into all policies and programmes in the United Nations system : report of the Secretary-General.
Issued: 5 May 2010.

### Draft resolutions/decisions

**E/2010/L.35** Mainstreaming a gender perspective into all policies and programmes in the United Nations system : draft resolution / submitted by the Vice-President of the Council, Somduth Soborun (Mauritius), on the basis of informal consultations.

### Discussion in plenary

**E/2010/SR.19(B)** (2 July 2010).

**E/2010/SR.46** (23 July 2010).
At the 46th meeting, draft resolution E/2010/L.35 was adopted without vote: resolution 2010/29.

### Resolutions

**E/RES/2010/29** (E/2010/INF/2/Add.1) Mainstreaming a gender perspective into all policies and programmes in the United Nations system.
Requests the UN system funds and programmes, within their respective mandates, to continue mainstreaming the issue of gender in accordance with previous Council resolutions. (Adopted without vote, 46th plenary meeting, 23 July 2010)

## GENETIC PRIVACY–DISCRIMINATION (Agenda item 14i)

### General documents

**E/2010/82** Genetic privacy and non-discrimination : note / by the Secretary-General.
Transmits note on genetic privacy and non-discrimination by the Director-General of the Unesco, submitted in response to Economic and Social Council decision 2008/233.

### Draft resolutions/decisions

**E/2010/L.34** Genetic privacy and non-discrimination : draft decision / submitted by the Vice-President of the Council, Somduth Soborun (Mauritius), on the basis of informal consultations.

## GENETIC PRIVACY–DISCRIMINATION (Agenda item 14i) (continued)

### Discussion in plenary

**E/2010/SR.37** (16 July 2010).

**E/2010/SR.46** (23 July 2010).
At the 46th meeting, draft decision E/2010/L.34 was adopted without vote: decision 2010/259.

## HUMAN RIGHTS (Agenda item 14g)

### Reports

**A/65/41** (GAOR, 65th sess., Suppl. no. 41) Report of the Committee on the Rights of the Child.
Issued: 2010.

**E/2010/89** Report of the United Nations High Commissioner for Human Rights.
Issued: 1 June 2010.

### General documents

**E/2010/L.16** Programme budget implications of the recommendations contained in the report of the Committee on Economic, Social and Cultural Rights on its 42nd and 43rd sessions : statement / submitted by the Secretary-General in accordance with rule 31 of the rules of procedure of the Economic and Social Council.

**E/2010/NGO/19** Statement / submitted by International Presentation Association of the Sisters of the Presentation of the Blessed Virgin Mary.
Transmits statement entitled "Human rights-based approach: a way to achieve the Millennium Development Goals".

### Discussion in plenary

**E/2010/SR.44** (22 July 2010).

**E/2010/SR.45** (22 July 2010).

**E/2010/SR.46** (23 July 2010).
At the 46th meeting, the Council took note of the following documents: Report of the UN High Commissioner for Human Rights (E/2010/89); Report of the Committee on the Rights of the Child on its 53rd session (A/65/41): decision 2010/258.

## HUMAN SETTLEMENTS (Agenda item 13d)

### Reports

**E/2010/72** Coordinated implementation of the Habitat Agenda : report of the Secretary-General.
Issued: 11 May 2010.

### Draft resolutions/decisions

**E/2010/L.25** Human settlements : draft decision / submitted by the Vice-President of the Council, Somduth Soborun (Mauritius), on the basis of informal consultations.

### Discussion in plenary

**E/2010/SR.43** (21 July 2010).
At the 43rd meeting, draft decision E/2010/L.25 entitled was adopted without vote: decision 2010/236.

## HUMANITARIAN ASSISTANCE (Agenda item 5)

### Reports

**E/2010/88** (A/65/82) Strengthening of the coordination of emergency humanitarian assistance of the United Nations : report of the Secretary-General.
Issued: 25 May 2010.

### General documents

**E/2010/101** (A/64/852) Letter, 19 Jan. 2010, from Spain. Transmits conclusions by the Council of the European Union at an extraordinary meeting on the humanitarian crisis in Haiti.

### Draft resolutions/decisions

**E/2010/L.15** Strengthening of the coordination of emergency humanitarian assistance of the United Nations : draft resolution / Chile.

### Discussion in plenary

**E/2010/SR.33** (14 July 2010).

**E/2010/SR.34** (14 July 2010).

**E/2010/SR.35** (15 July 2010).

**E/2010/SR.36** (15 July 2010).
At the 36th meeting, draft resolution E/2010/L.15 was adopted without vote: resolution 2010/1.

### Resolutions

**E/RES/2010/1** (E/2010/INF/2/Add.1) Strengthening of the coordination of emergency humanitarian assistance of the United Nations.
Stresses that the UN system should make efforts to enhance existing humanitarian capacities; urges Member States to develop, update and strengthen disaster preparedness and risk reduction measures at all levels, in accordance with the Hyogo Framework for Action. (Adopted without vote, 36th plenary meeting, 15 July 2010)

## INFORMATICS–INTERNATIONAL COOPERATION (Agenda item 7c)

### Reports

**E/2010/48** International cooperation in the field of informatics : report of the Secretary-General.
Issued: 29 Mar. 2010.

## INFORMATICS–INTERNATIONAL COOPERATION (Agenda item 7c) (continued)

### Draft resolutions/decisions

**E/2010/L.44** The need to harmonize and improve United Nations informatics systems for optimal utilization and accessibility by all States : draft resolution / submitted by the Vice-President of the Council, Somduth Soborun (Mauritius), on the basis of informal consultations.

### Discussion in plenary

**E/2010/SR.38** (16 July 2010).

**E/2010/SR.39** (19 July 2010).
At the 39th meeting, the Council decided to defer its consideration of agenda item 7 (c) until its resumed substantive session of 2010: decision 2010/212.

**E/2010/SR.52** (15 Dec. 2010).
At the 52nd meeting, draft resolution E/2010/L.44 was adopted without vote: resolution 2010/38.

### Resolutions

**E/RES/2010/38** (E/2010/INF/2/Add.2) The need to harmonize and improve United Nations informatics systems for optimal utilization and accessibility by all States.
Requests the President of the Economic and Social Council to convene the Ad Hoc Open-ended Working Group on Informatics for one more year to enable it to carry out to facilitate the successful implementation of the initiatives being taken by the Secretary-General with regard to the use of information technology and to continue the implementation of measures required to achieve its objectives; requests the Secretary-General to extend full cooperation to the Working Group and to give priority to implementing its recommendations and guidance. (Adopted without vote, 52nd plenary meeting, 15 Dec. 2010)

## INTERNATIONAL FINANCIAL INSTITUTIONS (Agenda item 2a)

### Reports

**E/2010/50** World economic and social survey. 2010, Retooling global development : overview.
Issued: 19 Apr. 2010.

**E/2010/50/Rev.1** (ST/ESA/330) World economic and social survey. 2010, Retooling global development.
Issued: 2010.

**E/2010/73** World economic situation and prospects as of mid-2010.
Issued: 11 May 2010.

### General documents

**E/2010/NGO/66** Statement / submitted by UNANIMA International.
Transmits statement on the impact of the global economic crisis on civil society organizations.

## INTERNATIONAL FINANCIAL INSTITUTIONS (Agenda item 2a) (continued)

**E/2010/NGO/72** Statement / submitted by International Presentation Association of the Sisters of the Presentation of the Blessed Virgin Mary.
Transmits statement on the creation of an international insolvency framework.

### Discussion in plenary

**E/2010/SR.19(A)** (2 July 2010).

## INTERNATIONAL NARCOTICS CONTROL BOARD– MEMBERS (Agenda item 1)

### General documents

**E/2010/9/Add.15** Election of 1 member of the International Narcotics Control Board from among candidates nominated by Governments : note : [addendum] / by the Secretary-General.

**E/2010/9/Add.16** Election of 1 member of the International Narcotics Control Board from among candidates nominated by Governments : note : / by the Secretary-General.

**E/2010/9/Add.17** Election of 1 member of the International Narcotics Control Board from among candidates nominated by Governments : note : addendum / by the Secretary-General.

**E/2010/9/Add.18** Election of 1 member of the International Narcotics Control Board from among candidates nominated by Governments : note : addendum / by the Secretary-General.

### Discussion in plenary

**E/2010/SR.42** (20 July 2010).

**E/2010/SR.45** (22 July 2010).
At the 45th meeting, Galina Aleksandrovna Korchagina (Russian Federation) was elected a member of the International Narcotics Control Board for a term beginning on 22 July 2010 and expiring on 1 Mar. 2015: decision 2010/201 D.

## LEAST DEVELOPED COUNTRIES– INTERNATIONAL DECADE (2001-2010) (Agenda item 6b)

### Reports

**E/2010/77** (A/65/80) Implementation of the Programme of Action for the Least Developed Countries for the Decade 2001-2010 : report of the Secretary-General.
Issued: 17 May 2010.

### Draft resolutions/decisions

**E/2010/L.20** Implementation of the Programme of Action for the Least Developed Countries for the Decade 2001-2010 : draft decision / Yemen [On behalf of the Group of 77 and China].
The draft resolution was withdrawn (E/2010/SR.46).

### Discussion in plenary

**E/2010/SR.37** (16 July 2010).

## LEAST DEVELOPED COUNTRIES– INTERNATIONAL DECADE (2001-2010) (Agenda item 6b) (continued)

**E/2010/SR.41** (20 July 2010).

**E/2010/SR.46** (23 July 2010).
At the 46th meeting, action on draft resolutions was as follows: draft resolution entitled "Implementation of the Programme of Action for the Least Developed Countries for the Decade 2001-2010", as orally amended, adopted without vote: resolution 2010/27; draft resolution E/2010/L.20, withdrawn.

### Resolutions

**E/RES/2010/27** (E/2010/INF/2/Add.1) Implementation of the Programme of Action for the Least Developed Countries for the Decade 2001-2010.
Remains concerned about the uneven and insufficient progress achieved in the implementation of the Programme of Action for the Least Developed Countries for the Decade 2001-2010; urges the least developed countries to strengthen country ownership in the implementation of the Programme of Action; expresses concern that the severity and persistence of poverty remains a serious challenge for the least developed countries; notes with appreciation the efforts made to address the debt problem of the least developed countries; calls for an effective implementation of the outcome of the 2005 Hong Kong Ministerial Meeting concerning least developed countries; also calls for an early, ambitious, successful, balanced and development oriented conclusion of the Doha Round of trade negotiations; emphasizes the critical importance of the 4th UN Conference on the Least Developed Countries, to be convened in Istanbul, Turkey, in 2011; expresses its concern about the insufficiency of resources in the trust fund for the least developed countries; requests the Secretary-General to submit a 10-year comprehensive report on the implementation of the Programme of Action for the Least Developed Countries for the Decade 2001-2010 to the 4th UN Conference on the Least Developed Countries. (Adopted without vote, 46th plenary meeting, 23 July 2010). - Resolution based on an "Informal paper submitted on the basis of informal consultations held on draft resolution E/2010/L.20 and E/2010/SR.46" (E/2010/INF/2/Add.1).

## NARCOTIC DRUGS (Agenda item 14d)

**E/INCB/2009/1** Report of the International Narcotics Control Board for 2009.

### Reports

**E/2009/28/Add.1** (E/CN.7/2009/12/Add.1) (ESCOR, 2009, Suppl. no. 8A) Commission on Narcotic Drugs : report on the reconvened 52nd session (1-2 December 2009).
Issued: 2009.

**E/2010/28** (E/CN.7/2010/18) (ESCOR, 2010, Suppl. no. 8) Commission on Narcotic Drugs : report on the 53rd session (2 December 2009 and 8-12 March 2010).
Issued: 2010.

## NARCOTIC DRUGS (Agenda item 14d) (continued)

**E/2010/28/Add.1** (E/CN.7/2010/18/Add.1) (ESCOR, 2010, Suppl. no. 8A) Commission on Narcotic Drugs : report on the reconvened 53rd session (2 December 2010).
Issued: 2010.

### Discussion in plenary

**E/2010/SR.44** (22 July 2010).

**E/2010/SR.45** (22 July 2010).
At the 45th meeting, action on draft resolution and decisions in E/2010/28 was as follows: draft resolution entitled "Realignment of the functions of the United Nations Office on Drugs and Crime and changes to the strategic framework", adopted without vote: resolution 2010/21; draft decision I entitled "Report of the Commission on Narcotic Drugs on its 53rd session and provisional agenda and documentation for its 54th session", adopted without vote: decision 2010/244; draft decision II entitled "Report of the International Narcotics Control Board", adopted without vote: decision 2010/245.

**E/2010/SR.46** (23 July 2010).
At the 46th meeting, the Council took note of the report of the Commission on Narcotic Drugs on its reconvened 52nd session (E/2009/28/Add.1): decision 2010/258.

### Resolutions

**E/RES/2010/21** (E/2010/INF/2/Add.1) Realignment of the functions of the United Nations Office on Drugs and Crime and changes to the strategic framework.
Requests the Executive Director of the UN Office on Drugs and Crime to ensure the sustainability of the Strategic Planning Unit, consistent with the importance of its functions; urges the Executive Director of the UN Office on Drugs and Crime to ensure that the Office submits to the Secretary-General a proposed programme budget for the biennium 2012-2013 that appropriately reflects the financial needs of the Office; requests the Secretary-General to devote due attention to the resource requirements for meeting the mandates entrusted to the UN Office on Drugs and Crime. (Adopted without vote, 45th plenary meeting, 22 July 2010)

## NON-GOVERNMENTAL ORGANIZATIONS (Agenda item 12)

### Reports

**E/2010/32(PartI)** Report of the Committee on Non-Governmental Organizations on its 2010 regular session (New York, 25 January to 3 February 2010).
Issued: 3 Mar. 2010.

**E/2010/32(PartII)** Report of the Committee on Non-Governmental Organizations on its 2010 resumed session (New York, 26 May-4 June and 18 June 2010).
Issued: 21 June 2010.

### General documents

**E/2010/INF/4** List of non-governmental organizations in consultative status with the Economic and Social Council as of 1 September 2010 : note / by the Secretary-General.

## NON-GOVERNMENTAL ORGANIZATIONS (Agenda item 12) (continued)

### Draft resolutions/decisions

**E/2010/L.19** Application of the non-governmental organization International Gay and Lesbian Human Rights Commission for consultative status with the Economic and Social Council : draft decision / United States.

### Discussion in plenary

**E/2010/SR.39** (19 July 2010).
At the 39th meeting, action on draft decisions in E/2010/32 (Part I) was as follows: draft decision I entitled "Applications for consultative status and requests for reclassification received from non-governmental organizations", adopted without vote: decision 2010/213; draft decision II entitled "Withdrawal of consultative status of the non-governmental organization General Federation of Iraqi Women", adopted without vote: decision 2010/214; draft decision III entitled "Suspension of consultative status of the non-governmental organization Interfaith International", adopted without vote: decision 2010/215; draft decision IV entitled "Report of the Committee on Non-Governmental Organizations on its 2010 regular session", adopted without vote: decision 2010/216; at the same meeting, action on draft decisions in E/2010/32 (Part II) was as follows: draft decision I entitled "Applications for consultative status and requests for reclassification received from non-governmental organizations", adopted without vote: decision 2010/217; draft decision II entitled "Suspension of consultative status of non-governmental organizations with outstanding quadrennial reports, pursuant to Council resolution 2008/4", adopted without vote: decision 2010/218; draft decision III entitled "Reinstatement of consultative status of non-governmental organizations that submitted outstanding quadrennial reports, pursuant to Council resolution 2008/4", adopted without vote: decision 2010/219; draft decision IV entitled "Withdrawal of consultative status of non-governmental organizations, pursuant to Council resolution 2008/4", adopted without vote: decision 2010/220; draft decision V entitled "Suspension of consultative status of the Centre Europe-tiers monde", adopted without vote: decision 2010/221; draft decision VI entitled "Modification of the agenda of the Committee on Non-Governmental Organizations at its 2011 session", adopted without vote: decision 2010/222; draft decision VII entitled "Dates of and provisional agenda for the 2011 session of the Committee on Non-Governmental Organizations", adopted without vote: decision 2010/223; draft decision VIII entitled "Report of the Committee on Non-Governmental Organizations on its 2010 resumed session", adopted without vote: decision 2010/224; at the same meeting, draft decision E/2010/L.19 was adopted (23-13-13): decision 2010/225.

## OPERATIONAL ACTIVITIES–UN (Agenda item 3)

### Reports

**E/2010/52** Actions taken by the executive boards and governing bodies of the United Nations funds, programmes and specialized agencies in the area of simplification and harmonization of the United Nations development system : report of the Secretary-General.
Issued: 28 Apr. 2010.

**E/2010/53** Functioning of the resident coordinator system, including costs and benefits : report of the Secretary-General.
Issued: 30 Apr. 2010.

**E/2010/70** Results achieved and measures and processes implemented in follow-up to General Assembly resolution 62/208 on the triennial comprehensive policy review of operational activities for development of the United Nations system : report of the Secretary-General.
Issued: 19 May 2010.

**E/2010/76** (A/65/79) Analysis of the funding of operational activities for development of the United Nations system for 2008 : report of the Secretary-General.
Issued: 14 May 2010.

### Discussion in plenary

**E/2010/SR.27** (9 July 2010).

**E/2010/SR.28** (9 July 2010).

**E/2010/SR.29** (12 July 2010).

**E/2010/SR.30** (12 July 2010).

**E/2010/SR.31** (13 July 2010).

## PALESTINIANS–TERRITORIES OCCUPIED BY ISRAEL–LIVING CONDITIONS (Agenda item 11)

### Reports

**E/2010/13** (A/65/72) Economic and social repercussions of the Israeli occupation on the living conditions of the Palestinian people in the Occupied Palestinian Territory, including East Jerusalem, and of the Arab population in the occupied Syrian Golan : note / by the Secretary-General.
Issued: 20 Apr. 2010. - Transmits report prepared by the Economic and Social Commission for Western Asia, submitted in response to the Economic and Social Council resolution 2009/34 and General Assembly resolution 64/185.

### Draft resolutions/decisions

**E/2010/L.31** Economic and social repercussions of the Israeli occupation on the living conditions of the Palestinian people in the Occupied Palestinian Territory, including East Jerusalem, and the Arab population in the occupied Syrian Golan : [draft resolution] / Bangladesh, Comoros, Cuba, Ecuador, Egypt, Jordan, Morocco, Namibia, Palestine, Saudi Arabia, Senegal and Venezuela (Bolivarian Republic of).

## PALESTINIANS–TERRITORIES OCCUPIED BY ISRAEL–LIVING CONDITIONS (Agenda item 11) (continued)

### Discussion in plenary

**E/2010/SR.41** (20 July 2010).

**E/2010/SR.45** (22 July 2010).

**E/2010/SR.46** (23 July 2010).
At the 46th meeting, draft resolution E/2010/L.31 was adopted (45-3-3): resolution 2010/31.

### Resolutions

**E/RES/2010/31** (E/2010/INF/2/Add.1) Economic and social repercussions of the Israeli occupation on the living conditions of the Palestinian people in the Occupied Palestinian Territory, including East Jerusalem, and the Arab population in the occupied Syrian Golan.
Calls for the full opening of the border crossings of the Gaza Strip; stresses the need to preserve the territorial contiguity, unity and integrity of the Occupied Palestinian Territory; demands that Israel comply with the Protocol on Economic Relations between the Government of Israel and the Palestine Liberation Organization signed in Paris on 29 Apr. 1994; calls upon Israel to cease its destruction of homes and properties; also calls upon Israel to end immediately its exploitation of natural resources; calls upon Israel to comply with the provisions of the Geneva Convention relative to the Protection of Civilian Persons in Time of War; decides to include the item entitled "Economic and social repercussions of the Israeli occupation on the living conditions of the Palestinian people in the Occupied Palestinian Territory, including East Jerusalem, and the Arab population in the occupied Syrian Golan" in the agenda of its substantive session of 2011. (Adopted 45-3-3, 46th plenary meeting, 23 July 2010)

## POPULATION–DEVELOPMENT (Agenda item 13f)

### Reports

**E/2010/25** (E/CN.9/2010/9) (ESCOR, 2010, Suppl. no. 5) Commission on Population and Development : report on the 43rd session (3 April 2009 and 12-16 April 2010).
Issued: 2010.

### Discussion in plenary

**E/2010/SR.43** (21 July 2010).
At the 43rd meeting, draft decision in E/2010/25 entitled "Report of the Commission on Population and Development on its 43rd session and provisional agenda for its 44th session" was adopted without vote: decision 2010/238.

## POST-CONFLICT RECONSTRUCTION–AFRICA (Agenda item 7f)

### Discussion in plenary

**E/2010/SR.40** (19 July 2010).
At the 40th meeting, the Council adopted draft oral decision entitled "African countries emerging from conflict": decision 2010/231.

## POVERTY MITIGATION (Agenda item 4)

### Reports

**E/2010/85** Theme of the coordination segment : implementing the internationally agreed development goals and commitments in regard to global public health : report of the Secretary-General.
Issued: 24 May 2010.

**E/2010/90** (A/65/84) Role of the Economic and Social Council in the integrated and coordinated implementation of the outcomes of and follow-up to major United Nations conferences and summits, in the light of relevant General Assembly resolutions, including resolution 61/16 : report of the Secretary-General.
Issued: 3 June 2010.

### General documents

**E/2010/CRP.3** Theme of the Coordination Segment : implementing the internationally agreed development goals and commitments in regard to global public health : conference room paper.

### Draft resolutions/decisions

**E/2010/L.11** Role of the Council in the integrated and coordinated implementation of the outcomes of and follow-up to major United Nations conferences and summits, in the light of relevant General Assembly resolutions, including resolution 61/16 : draft decision / submitted by Vice-President of the Council, Morten Wetland (Norway), on the basis of informal consultations.

**E/2010/L.13** The role of the United Nations System in implementing the Ministerial Declaration on the Internationally Agreed Development Goals and Commitments in Regard to Global Public Health adopted at the high-level segment of the 2009 substantive session of the Economic and Social Council : draft resolution / submitted by the Vice-President of the Council, Morten Wetland (Norway), on the basis of informal consultations.

### Discussion in plenary

**E/2010/SR.21** (6 July 2010).

**E/2010/SR.22** (6 July 2010).

**E/2010/SR.23** (7 July 2010).

**E/2010/SR.26** (8 July 2010).

**E/2010/SR.46** (23 July 2010).
At the 46th meeting, action on draft resolution and draft decision was as follows: draft resolution E/2010/L.13, adopted without vote: resolution 2010/24; draft decision E/2010/L.11, as orally revised, adopted without vote: decision 2010/252.

## POVERTY MITIGATION (Agenda item 4) (continued)

### Resolutions

**E/RES/2010/24** (E/2010/INF/2/Add.1) The role of the United Nations system in implementing the ministerial declaration on the internationally agreed goals and commitments in regard to global public health adopted at the high-level segment of the 2009 substantive session of the Economic and Social Council.
Welcomes the increasing focus on advancing maternal and child health; invites the World Health Organization, the UN Population Fund, the UN Children's Fund and the Joint UN Programme on HIV/AIDS to make special efforts to invest in family planning and maternal and child health; requests the UN system to continue coordinated action to respond to communicable diseases, in particular HIV/AIDS, malaria and tuberculosis; urges the UN system to support the efforts made by Member States to build national capacity to ensure compliance with their obligations and their right to utilize, to the full, the provisions contained in the World Trade Organization Agreement on Trade-Related Aspects of Intellectual Property Rights (TRIPS Agreement); stresses the need for international cooperation and assistance. (Adopted without vote, 46th plenary meeting, 23 July 2010)

## PUBLIC ADMINISTRATION (Agenda item 13g)

### Reports

**E/2010/44** (E/C.16/2010/5) (ESCOR, 2010, Suppl. no. 24) Committee of Experts on Public Administration : report on the 9th session (19-23 April 2010).
Issued: 2010.

### Draft resolutions/decisions

**E/2010/L.29** Provisional agenda for 10th session of the Committee of Experts on Public Administration : draft decision / submitted by the Vice-President of the Council, Somduth Soborun (Mauritius), on the basis of informal consultations.

### Discussion in plenary

**E/2010/SR.43** (21 July 2010).
At the 43rd meeting, the Council drew attention to the draft decision in E/2010/44 entitled "Report of the Committee of Experts on Public Administration on its 9th session"; at the same meeting, draft decision E/2010/L.29 was adopted without vote: decision 2010/239.

**E/2010/SR.46** (23 July 2010).
At the 46th meeting, the Council decided to defer its consideration of the report of the Committee of Experts on Public Administration on its 9th session (E/2010/44) until a later stage but before its substantive session of 2011: decision 2010/256.

## PUBLIC ADMINISTRATION (Agenda item 13g) (continued)

**E/2010/SR.52**  (15 Dec. 2010).

At the 52nd meeting, the Council recalled that, in its decision 2010/256, the Council had decided to defer consideration of the report of the Committee of Experts on Public Administration on its 9th session (E/2010/44) to a later stage and before its 2011 substantive session; having been informed that no action was required, the Council would revert to the matter at a later stage and before its 2011 substantive session.

## RACIAL DISCRIMINATION–PROGRAMME OF ACTION (Agenda item 14f)

### Discussion in plenary

**E/2010/SR.44**  (22 July 2010).

## REFUGEES (Agenda item 14e)

### General documents

**E/2010/86**  Note verbale, 27 Oct. 2009, from Bulgaria. Presents the application of the Government of Bulgaria for admission to the Executive Committee of the Programme of the UN High Commissioner for Refugees.

**E/2010/87**  Letter, 19 May 2010, from Croatia. Reports Croatia's wish to become a member of the Executive Committee of the Programme of the UN High Commissioner for Refugees and provides information on Croatia's involvement in the field of protection and promotion of the rights of refugees.

**E/2010/94**  Note verbale, 9 Sept. 2009, from Cameroon. Concerns Cameroon's application for admission to the Executive Committee of the Programme of the UN High Commissioner for Refugees.

**E/2010/95**  Note verbale, 23 Oct. 2009, from Togo. Presents the application of the Government of Togo for membership in the Executive Committee of the Programme of the UN High Commissioner for Refugees.

**E/2010/96**  Letter, 9 Feb. 2010, from Turkmenistan. Concerns the desire of Turkmenistan to become a member of the Executive Committee of the Programme of the United Nations High Commissioner for Refugees.

**E/2010/103**  Note verbale, 12 July 2010, from Congo. Reports the decision of the Government of the Congo to present its candidature for membership in the Executive Committee of the Programme of the UN High Commissioner for Refugees.

### Draft resolutions/decisions

**E/2010/L.18**  Enlargement of the Executive Committee of the Programme of the United Nations High Commissioner for Refugees : draft decision / Bulgaria, Cameroon, Croatia and Togo.

**E/2010/L.41**  Enlargement of the Executive Committee of the Programme of the United Nations High Commissioner for Refugees : draft decision / Congo.

### Discussion in plenary

**E/2010/SR.44**  (22 July 2010).

## REFUGEES (Agenda item 14e) (continued)

**E/2010/SR.45**  (22 July 2010).

At the 45th meeting, draft decision E/2010/L.18 was adopted without vote: decision 2010/246.

**E/2010/SR.50**  (10 Nov. 2010).

At the 50th meeting, draft decision E/2010/L.41 was adopted without vote: decision 2010/263.

## REGIONAL COOPERATION (Agenda item 10)

### Reports

**E/2010/15**  Regional cooperation in the economic, social and related fields : report of the Secretary-General. Issued: 7 June 2010.

**E/2010/15/Add.1**  Regional cooperation in the economic, social and related fields : report of the Secretary-General : addendum. Issued: 11 June 2010.

**E/2010/16**  The economic situation in the Economic Commission for Europe region : Europe, North America and the Commonwealth of Independent States in 2009-2010. Issued: 20 Apr. 2010.

**E/2010/19**  Latin America and the Caribbean : economic situation and outlook, 2009-2010. Issued: 22 Apr. 2010.

### Discussion in plenary

**E/2010/SR.20**  (2 July 2010).

**E/2010/SR.41**  (20 July 2010).

**E/2010/SR.42**  (20 July 2010).

**E/2010/SR.46**  (23 July 2010).

At the 46th meeting, the Council decided to defer action on draft resolutions in E/2010/15/Add.1, entitled respectively, "Upgrading the Economic and Social Commission for Western Asia Section for Emerging and Conflict-Related Issues to the level of a division and establishing a governmental committee on emerging issues and development in conflict settings" and "Upgrading the Economic and Social Commission for Western Asia Centre for Women to the level of a division and follow-up to the implementation of the Beijing Platform for Action in the Arab countries after 15 years: Beijing+15", until its resumed 2010 substantive session: decision 2010/253.

**E/2010/SR.52**  (15 Dec. 2010).

At the 52nd meeting, the Council decided to defer action on draft resolutions in E/2010/15/Add.1 entitled "Upgrading the Economic and Social Commission for Western Asia Section for Emerging and Conflict-Related Issues to the level of a division and establishing a governmental committee on emerging issues and development in conflict settings" and "Upgrading the Economic and Social Commission for Western Asia Centre for Women to the level of a division and follow-up to the implementation of the Beijing Platform for Action in the Arab countries after 15 years: Beijing+15", until its 2011 substantive session: decision 2010/265.

## REGIONAL COOPERATION–AFRICA (Agenda item 10)

### Reports

**E/2010/15** Regional cooperation in the economic, social and related fields : report of the Secretary-General.
Issued: 7 June 2010.

**E/2010/15/Add.1** Regional cooperation in the economic, social and related fields : report of the Secretary-General : addendum.
Issued: 11 June 2010.

**E/2010/17** Overview of the economic and social conditions in Africa 2010.
Issued: 4 May 2010.

### Discussion in plenary

**E/2010/SR.20** (2 July 2010).

## REGIONAL COOPERATION–ASIA AND THE PACIFIC (Agenda item 10)

### Reports

**E/2010/15** Regional cooperation in the economic, social and related fields : report of the Secretary-General.
Issued: 7 June 2010.

**E/2010/15/Add.1** Regional cooperation in the economic, social and related fields : report of the Secretary-General : addendum.
Issued: 11 June 2010.

**E/2010/18** Summary of the economic and social survey of Asia and the Pacific 2010.
Issued: 4 May 2010.

**E/2010/39** (E/ESCAP/66/27) (ESCOR, 2010, Suppl. no. 19) Economic and Social Commission for Asia and the Pacific : annual report, 30 April 2009-19 May 2010.
Issued: 2010.

### Discussion in plenary

**E/2010/SR.20** (2 July 2010).

## REGIONAL COOPERATION–EUROPE (Agenda item 10)

### Reports

**E/2010/15** Regional cooperation in the economic, social and related fields : report of the Secretary-General.
Issued: 7 June 2010.

**E/2010/16** The economic situation in the Economic Commission for Europe region : Europe, North America and the Commonwealth of Independent States in 2009-2010.
Issued: 20 Apr. 2010.

### Discussion in plenary

**E/2010/SR.20** (2 July 2010).

## REGIONAL COOPERATION–LATIN AMERICA AND THE CARIBBEAN (Agenda item 10)

### Reports

**E/2010/15** Regional cooperation in the economic, social and related fields : report of the Secretary-General.
Issued: 7 June 2010.

**E/2010/15/Add.1** Regional cooperation in the economic, social and related fields : report of the Secretary-General : addendum.
Issued: 11 June 2010.

**E/2010/19** Latin America and the Caribbean : economic situation and outlook, 2009-2010.
Issued: 22 Apr. 2010.

### Discussion in plenary

**E/2010/SR.20** (2 July 2010).

**E/2010/SR.42** (20 July 2010).
At the 42nd meeting, draft resolution in E/2010/15/Add.1 entitled "Venue of the 34th session of the Economic Commission for Latin America and the Caribbean" was adopted without vote: resolution 2010/4.

### Resolutions

**E/RES/2010/4** (E/2010/INF/2/Add.1) Venue of the 34th session of the Economic Commission for Latin America and the Caribbean.
Expresses its gratitude to the Government of El Salvador for its generous invitation; notes the acceptance by the Economic Commission for Latin America and the Caribbean of this invitation with pleasure; endorses the decision of the Commission to hold its 34th session in El Salvador in the first half of 2012. (Adopted without vote, 42nd plenary meeting, 20 July 2010)

## REGIONAL COOPERATION–WESTERN ASIA (Agenda item 10)

### Reports

**E/2010/15** Regional cooperation in the economic, social and related fields : report of the Secretary-General.
Issued: 7 June 2010.

**E/2010/15/Add.1** Regional cooperation in the economic, social and related fields : report of the Secretary-General : addendum.
Issued: 11 June 2010.

**E/2010/20** Summary of the survey of economic and social developments in the Economic and Social Commission for Western Asia region, 2009-2010.
Issued: 30 Apr. 2010.

**E/2010/41** (E/ESCWA/26/9/Report) (ESCOR, 2010, Suppl. no. 21) Economic and Social Commission for Western Asia : report on the 26th session, 17-20 May 2010.
Issued: 2010.

### Discussion in plenary

**E/2010/SR.20** (2 July 2010).

## REGIONAL COOPERATION–WESTERN ASIA (Agenda item 10) (continued)

**E/2010/SR.42**  (20 July 2010).

At the 42nd meeting, draft resolution in E/2010/15/Add.1 entitled "Establishment of the Economic and Social Commission for Western Asia Technology Centre" was adopted without vote: resolution 2010/5.

**E/2010/SR.46**  (23 July 2010).

At the 46th meeting, the Council decided to defer action on draft resolutions in E/2010/15/Add.1, entitled respectively, "Upgrading the Economic and Social Commission for Western Asia Section for Emerging and Conflict-Related Issues to the level of a division and establishing a governmental committee on emerging issues and development in conflict settings" and "Upgrading the Economic and Social Commission for Western Asia Centre for Women to the level of a division and follow-up to the implementation of the Beijing Platform for Action in the Arab countries after 15 years: Beijing+15", until its resumed 2010 substantive session: decision 2010/253.

**E/2010/SR.52**  (15 Dec. 2010).

At the 52nd meeting, the Council decided to defer action on draft resolutions in E/2010/15/Add.1 entitled "Upgrading the Economic and Social Commission for Western Asia Section for Emerging and Conflict-Related Issues to the level of a division and establishing a governmental committee on emerging issues and development in conflict settings" and "Upgrading the Economic and Social Commission for Western Asia Centre for Women to the level of a division and follow-up to the implementation of the Beijing Platform for Action in the Arab countries after 15 years: Beijing+15", until its 2011 substantive session: decision 2010/265.

### Resolutions

**E/RES/2010/5**  (E/2010/INF/2/Add.1)  Establishment of the Economic and Social Commission for Western Asia Technology Centre.

Endorses the resolution on the establishment of the Economic and Social Commission for Western Asia Technology Centre and the statute of the Centre, as set out in annexes I and II to the present resolution. (Adopted without vote, 42nd plenary meeting, 20 July 2010)

## RESOLUTIONS–UN. GENERAL ASSEMBLY– IMPLEMENTATION (Agenda item 8)

### Reports

**E/2010/90**  (A/65/84)  Role of the Economic and Social Council in the integrated and coordinated implementation of the outcomes of and follow-up to major United Nations conferences and summits, in the light of relevant General Assembly resolutions, including resolution 61/16 : report of the Secretary-General.

Issued: 3 June 2010.

## RESOLUTIONS–UN. GENERAL ASSEMBLY– IMPLEMENTATION (Agenda item 8) (continued)

### Draft resolutions/decisions

**E/2010/L.11**  Role of the Council in the integrated and coordinated implementation of the outcomes of and follow-up to major United Nations conferences and summits, in the light of relevant General Assembly resolutions, including resolution 61/16 : draft decision / submitted by Vice-President of the Council, Morten Wetland (Norway), on the basis of informal consultations.

### Discussion in plenary

**E/2010/SR.22**  (6 July 2010).

**E/2010/SR.23**  (7 July 2010).

**E/2010/SR.26**  (8 July 2010).

**E/2010/SR.46**  (23 July 2010).

At the 46th meeting, draft decision E/2010/L.11 as orally revised, was adopted without vote: decision 2010/252.

## SANCTIONS COMPLIANCE–ECONOMIC ASSISTANCE (Agenda item 13i)

### Discussion in plenary

**E/2010/SR.43**  (21 July 2010).

## SCIENCE AND TECHNOLOGY–DEVELOPMENT (Agenda item 13b)

### Reports

**E/2009/92**  Enhanced cooperation on public policy issues pertaining to the Internet : report of the Secretary-General.

Issued: 10 June 2009.

**E/2010/12**  (A/65/64)  Progress made in the implementation of and follow-up to the outcomes of the World Summit on the Information Society at the regional and international levels : report of the Secretary-General.

Issued: 8 Mar. 2010.

**E/2010/31**  (E/CN.16/2010/5)  (ESCOR, 2010, Suppl. no. 11)  Commission on Science and Technology for Development : report on the 13th session (17-21 May 2010).

Issued: 2010.

### General documents

**E/2010/68**  (A/65/78)  Continuation of the Internet Governance Forum : note / by the Secretary-General.

Transmits recommendations regarding the extension of the mandate of the Internet Governance Forum.

**E/2010/CRP.4**  Update on enhanced cooperation on public policy issues pertaining to the Internet : conference room paper / prepared by the Division for Public Administration and Development Management (DPADM) of the United Nations Department of Economic and Social Affairs (DESA).

## SCIENCE AND TECHNOLOGY–DEVELOPMENT (Agenda item 13b) (continued)

### Discussion in plenary

**E/2010/SR.38** (16 July 2010).

**E/2010/SR.39** (19 July 2010).
At the 39th meeting, action on draft resolutions and decisions in E/2010/31 was as follows: draft resolution I entitled "Assessment of the progress made in the implementation of and follow-up to the outcomes of the World Summit on the Information Society", adopted without vote: resolution 2010/2; draft resolution II entitled "Science and Technology for Development", adopted without vote: resolution 2010/3; draft decision I entitled "Participation of non-governmental organizations and civil society entities in the work of the Commission on Science and Technology for Development", adopted without vote: decision 2010/226; draft decision II entitled "Participation of academic entities in the work of the Commission on Science and Technology for Development", adopted without vote: decision 2010/227; draft decision III entitled "Participation of business sector entities, including the private sector, in the work of the Commission on Science and Technology for Development", adopted without vote: decision 2010/228; draft decision IV entitled "Report of the Commission on Science and Technology for Development at its 13th session and provisional agenda and documentation for the 14th session of the Commission", adopted without vote: decision 2010/229 ; at the same meeting, the Council took note of the note by the Secretary-General on the Internet Governance Forum: decision 2010/230.

## SCIENCE AND TECHNOLOGY–DEVELOPMENT (Agenda item 13b) (continued)

### Resolutions

**E/RES/2010/2** (E/2010/INF/2/Add.1) Assessment of the progress made in the implementation of and follow-up to the outcomes of the World Summit on the Information Society.
Expresses concern regarding the widening gap in broadband connectivity among countries at different levels of development; welcomes the recent establishment of the Broadband Commission for Digital Development at the initiative of the International Telecommunication Union and the UN Educational, Scientific and Cultural Organization; reaffirms the principles enunciated at the World Summit that the Internet has evolved into a global facility available to the public, that its governance should constitute a core issue of the information society agenda and that the international management of the Internet should be multilateral, transparent and democratic; expresses its appreciation for the work done by the Chair, the secretariat and the host Governments of the meetings of the Internet Governance Forum and looks forward to the results of the 5th meeting, to be held in Vilnius from 14 to 17 Sept. 2010; urges UN entities to take the necessary steps and commit to a people-centred, inclusive and development-oriented information society; urges all countries to make concrete efforts to fulfil their commitments under the Monterrey Consensus of the International Conference on Financing for Development; invites the international community to make voluntary contributions to the special trust fund established by the UN Conference on Trade and Development. (Adopted without vote, 39th plenary meeting, 19 July 2010)

**E/RES/2010/3** (E/2010/INF/2/Add.1) Science and technology for development.
Decides to make recommendations for consideration by Governments, the Commission on Science and Technology for Development and the UN Conference on Trade and Development. (Adopted without vote, 39th plenary meeting, 19 July 2010)

## SOCIAL DEVELOPMENT (Agenda item 14b)

### Reports

**E/2010/26** (E/CN.5/2010/9) (ESCOR, 2010, Suppl. no. 6) Commission for Social Development : report on the 48th session (13 February 2009 and 3-12 and 19 February 2010).
Issued: 2010.

### General documents

**E/2010/91** (A/64/803) Letter, 25 May 2010, from Spain. Transmits Madrid Declaration entitled "Towards a new stage in the biregional partnership: innovation and technology for sustainable development and social inclusion", adopted by the Heads of State and Government meeting at the 6th summit of the European Union and the Latin American and Caribbean States, which was held in Madrid on 18 May 2010.

## SOCIAL DEVELOPMENT (Agenda item 14b) (continued)

**E/2010/NGO/17**  Statement / submitted by International Presentation Association of the Sisters of the Presentation of the Blessed Virgin Mary.
Transmits statement entitled "Participation of people living in poverty".

**E/2010/NGO/41**  Statement / submitted by Associazione Amici dei Bambini.
Transmits statement concerning the Millennium Development Goals; includes recommendations with regard to young people without a stable family who are leaving or have recently left alternative care or residential placements after reaching a legally set age (usually 18 years of age).

**E/2010/NGO/52**  Statement / submitted by Brothers of Charity.
Transmits statement entitled "No health without mental health".

### Discussion in plenary

**E/2010/SR.44**  (22 July 2010).

**E/2010/SR.45**  (22 July 2010).
At the 45th meeting, action on draft resolutions and decisions in E/2010/26 was as follows: draft resolution I entitled "Future organization and methods of work of the Commission for Social Development", adopted without vote: resolution 2010/10; draft resolution II entitled "Social dimensions of the New Partnership for Africa's Development", adopted without vote: resolution 2010/11; draft resolution III entitled "Promoting social integration", adopted without vote: resolution 2010/12; draft resolution IV entitled "Mainstreaming disability in the development agenda", adopted without vote: resolution 2010/13; draft resolution V entitled "Future implementation of the Madrid International Plan of Action on Ageing, 2002", adopted without vote: resolution 2010/14; draft decision entitled "Report of the Commission for Social Development on its 48th session and provisional agenda and documentation for the 49th session", adopted without vote: decision 2010/242.

### Resolutions

**E/RES/2010/10**  (E/2010/INF/2/Add.1)  Future organization and methods of work of the Commission for Social Development.
Decides that the priority theme for the 2011-2012 review and policy cycle should be poverty eradication; recommends that the officers elected to the Bureau of the Commission serve for a term of office of 2 years, in parallel with the review and policy cycle; decides that the Commission for Social Development should keep its methods of work under review. (Adopted without vote, 45th plenary meeting, 22 July 2010)

## SOCIAL DEVELOPMENT (Agenda item 14b) (continued)

**E/RES/2010/11**  (E/2010/INF/2/Add.1)  Social dimensions of the New Partnership for Africa's Development.
Welcomes the organization of the 1st session of the African Union Conference of Ministers in Charge of Social Development; requests the Secretary-General to continue to take measures to strengthen the Office of the Special Adviser on Africa, and requests the Office to collaborate with the Department of Economic and Social Affairs of the Secretariat; requests the Commission for Social Development to discuss in its annual programme of work those regional programmes that promote social development so as to enable all regions to share experiences and best practices; decides that the Commission for Social Development should continue to give prominence to and raise awareness of the social dimensions of the New Partnership during its 49th session. (Adopted without vote, 45th plenary meeting, 22 July 2010)

**E/RES/2010/12**  (E/2010/INF/2/Add.1)  Promoting social integration.
Stresses that the benefits of economic growth should be distributed more equitably; recognizes that empowerment of the poor is essential for the effective eradication of poverty and hunger; recognizes that sustainable social integration requires creating short and long-term policies that are comprehensive; stresses the importance of eradicating illiteracy and promoting for all equal access to and opportunities for quality education; requests the UN system to support national efforts to achieve social development. (Adopted without vote, 45th plenary meeting, 22 July 2010)

**E/RES/2010/13**  (E/2010/INF/2/Add.1)  Mainstreaming disability in the development agenda.
Calls upon those States that have not yet done so to consider signing and ratifying the Convention on the Rights of Persons with Disabilities and the Optional Protocol thereto as a matter of priority; encourages all Member States to engage in cooperative arrangements that aim at providing the necessary technical and expert assistance to enhance capacities in mainstreaming disability; stresses the need to enhance accountability in the work of mainstreaming disability into the development agenda; welcomes the appointment of a new Special Rapporteur on disability of the Commission for Social Development for the period 2009-2011. (Adopted without vote, 45th plenary meeting, 22 July 2010)

## SOCIAL DEVELOPMENT (Agenda item 14b) (continued)

**E/RES/2010/14** (E/2010/INF/2/Add.1) Future implementation of the Madrid International Plan of Action on Ageing, 2002.

Encourages Member States to continue their efforts to mainstream ageing into their policy agendas; recommends that Member States strengthen their networks of national focal points on ageing; decides that the procedure for the second review and appraisal of the Madrid Plan of Action will follow the set procedure of the 1st review and appraisal exercise and shall include preparatory activities at the national and regional levels, including those conducted by the regional commissions, to conclude in 2012; decides to conduct the 2nd global review and appraisal of the Madrid Plan of Action in 2013 at the 51st session of the Commission for Social Development. (Adopted without vote, 45th plenary meeting, 22 July 2010)

## STATISTICS (Agenda item 13c)

### Reports

**E/2010/24** (E/CN.3/2010/34) (ESCOR, 2010, Suppl. no. 4) Statistical Commission : report on the 41st session (23 to 26 February 2009).
Issued: 2010.

### Discussion in plenary

**E/2010/SR.43** (21 July 2010).
At the 43rd meeting, draft decision in E/2010/24 entitled "Report of the Statistical Commission on its 41st session and provisional agenda and dates for the 42nd session of the Commission" was adopted without vote: decision 2010/235.

## SUSTAINABLE DEVELOPMENT (Agenda item 13a)

### Reports

**E/2010/29** (E/CN.17/2010/15) (ESCOR, 2010, Suppl. no. 9) Commission on Sustainable Development : report on the 18th session (15 May 2009 and 3-14 May 2010).
Issued: 2010.

**E/2010/33** (ESCOR, 2010, Suppl. no. 13) Committee for Development Policy : report on the 12th session (22-26 March 2010).
Issued: 2010.

### General documents

**E/2010/51** (A/65/73) Note [transmitting note by the Chairperson of the Committee on World Food Security on the reform of the Committee and on progress made towards implementation] / by the Secretary-General.

**E/2010/NGO/2** Statement / submitted by Social Development Association.
Transmits statement entitled "Our dying rivers".

**E/2010/NGO/29** Statement / submitted by Institute for Planetary Synthesis.
Transmits statement entitled "People and commons: global partnership missing links".

## SUSTAINABLE DEVELOPMENT (Agenda item 13a) (continued)

### Draft resolutions/decisions

**E/2010/L.24** Review of United Nations support for small island developing States : draft resolution / Maldives.
Additional sponsors: Comoros and Saint Lucia (E/2010/SR.43).

**E/2010/L.30** Report of the Committee for Development Policy on its 12th session : draft resolution / submitted by the Vice-President of the Council, Somduth Soborun (Mauritius), on the basis of informal consultations.

**E/2010/L.33** Review of United Nations support for small island developing States : draft resolution / submitted by the Vice-President of the Council, Somduth Soborun (Mauritius), on the basis of informal consultations.

### Discussion in plenary

**E/2010/SR.43** (21 July 2010).
At the 43rd meeting, draft decision in E/2010/29 entitled "Report of the Commission on Sustainable Development on its 18th session and provisional agenda for the 19th session of the Commission" was adopted without vote: decision 2010/234.

**E/2010/SR.45** (22 July 2010).
At the 45th meeting, draft resolution E/2010/L.30 was adopted without vote: resolution 2010/9.

**E/2010/SR.46** (23 July 2010).
At the 46th meeting, the Council took note of a note by the Chairperson of the Committee on World Food Security on the reform of the Committee and on progress made towards implementation (E/2010/51): decision 2010/255.

**E/2010/SR.47** (23 July 2010).
At the 47th meeting, action on draft resolutions was as follows: draft resolution E/2010/L.33, adopted without vote: resolution 2010/34; draft resolution E/2010/L.24, withdrawn.

### Resolutions

**E/RES/2010/9** (E/2010/INF/2/Add.1) Report of the Committee for Development Policy on its 12th session.
Decides to forward the chapter on international support measures for the least developed countries to the Preparatory Committee of the 4th UN Conference on the Least Developed Countries for further consideration in the preparations for that Conference; requests the Committee for Development Policy, at its 13th session, to examine and make recommendations on the themes chosen by the Economic and Social Council for the high-level segment of its substantive session of 2011; requests the Committee to continue to monitor the development progress of countries graduating from the list of least developed countries and to include its findings in its annual report to the Economic and Social Council. (Adopted without vote, 45th plenary meeting, 22 July 2010)

## SUSTAINABLE DEVELOPMENT (Agenda item 13a) (continued)

**E/RES/2010/34** (E/2010/INF/2/Add.1) Review of United Nations support for small island developing States.
Decides to make available the independent views and perspectives of the Committee for Development Policy, together with a summary of the debate held during this substantive session, as a contribution to the 2-day high-level review to be conducted during the 65th session of the General Assembly, of progress made in addressing the vulnerabilities of small island developing States; requests the Secretary-General to submit a report to the Economic and Social Council. (Adopted without vote, 47th plenary meeting, 23 July 2010)

## TAXATION (Agenda item 13h)
### Reports

**E/2010/45** (E/C.18/2010/7) (ESCOR, 2010, Suppl. no. 25) Committee of Experts on International Cooperation in Tax Matters : report on the 6th session (18-22 October 2010).
Issued: 2011.

### General documents

**E/2010/L.28** Committee of Experts on International Cooperation in Tax Matters : programme budget implications of draft resolution E/2010/L.10 : statement / submitted by the Secretary-General in accordance with rule 31 of the rules of procedure of the Economic and Social Council.

### Draft resolutions/decisions

**E/2010/L.10** Committee of Experts on International Cooperation in Tax Matters : draft resolution / Yemen [on behalf of the Group of 77 and China].
The draft resolution was withdrawn (E/2010/SR.46).

**E/2010/L.36** Provisional agenda and dates for the 6th session of the Committee of Experts on International Cooperation in Tax Matters : draft decision / submitted by the Vice-President of the Council, Somduth Soborun (Mauritius), on the basis of informal consultations.

**E/2010/L.39** Committee of Experts on International Cooperation in Tax Matters : draft resolution / submitted by the Vice-President of the Council, Somduth Soborun (Mauritius), on the basis of informal consultations on draft resolution E/2010/L.10.

### Discussion in plenary

**E/2010/SR.43** (21 July 2010).

**E/2010/SR.46** (23 July 2010).
At the 46th meeting, action on draft resolution and draft decision was as follows: draft decision E/2010/L.36, adopted without vote: decision 2010/257; draft resolution E/2010/L.39, adopted without vote: resolution 2010/33; draft resolution E/2010/L.10, withdrawn.

## TAXATION (Agenda item 13h) (continued)
### Resolutions

**E/RES/2010/33** (E/2010/INF/2/Add.1) Committee of Experts on International Cooperation in Tax Matters.
Requests the Secretary-General to submit to the Council by Mar. 2011 a report examining the strengthening of institutional arrangements to promote international cooperation in tax matters, including the Committee of Experts on International Cooperation in Tax Matters; requests the President of the Economic and Social Council to convene a discussion within the Council by spring 2011 on international cooperation in tax matters; reiterates its appeal to Member States and relevant organizations to consider contributing generously to the trust fund for international cooperation in tax matters established by the Secretary-General; takes note with appreciation of the proposed Code of Conduct on Cooperation in Combating International Tax Evasion adopted by the Committee. (Adopted without vote, 46th plenary meeting, 23 July 2010)

## TOBACCO–HEALTH (Agenda item 7g)
### Reports

**E/2010/55** Ad Hoc Inter-Agency Task Force on Tobacco Control : report of the Secretary-General.
Issued: 4 May 2010.

**E/2010/55/Corr.1** Ad Hoc Inter-Agency Task Force on Tobacco Control : report of the Secretary-General : corrigendum.
Issued: 7 June 2010. - Corrects text.

### Draft resolutions/decisions

**E/2010/L.14** Tobacco use and maternal and child health : draft resolution / Yemen [on behalf of the Group of 77 and China].
The draft resolution was withdrawn by its sponsors in the light of the adoption of draft resolution E/2010/L.26 (E/2010/SR.45).

**E/2010/L.26** Tobacco use and maternal and child health : draft resolution / submitted by the Vice-President of the Council, Somduth Soborun (Mauritius), on the basis of informal consultations.

### Discussion in plenary

**E/2010/SR.37** (16 July 2010).

**E/2010/SR.38** (16 July 2010).

**E/2010/SR.45** (22 July 2010).
At the 45th meeting, draft resolution E/2010/L.26 was adopted without vote: resolution 2010/8; the Council also decided to withdraw draft resolution E/2010/L.14, in view of the adoption of draft resolution E/2010/L.26, the earlier draft resolution on the subject.

## TOBACCO–HEALTH (Agenda item 7g) (continued)

### Resolutions

**E/RES/2010/8** (E/2010/INF/2/Add.1) Tobacco use and maternal and child health.

Urges Member States to consider the importance of tobacco control in improving maternal and child health as part of their public health policies and in their development cooperation programmes; requests the Secretary-General to convene a meeting of the Ad Hoc Inter-Agency Task Force on Tobacco Control; also requests the Secretary-General to submit a report on the work of the Ad Hoc Inter-Agency Task Force on Tobacco Control to the Economic and Social Council at its substantive session of 2012. (Adopted without vote, 45th plenary meeting, 22 July 2010)

## UN–BUDGET (2012-2013) (Agenda item 7b)

### Discussion in plenary

**E/2010/SR.37** (16 July 2010).

## UN. COMMISSION ON POPULATION AND DEVELOPMENT–MEMBERS (Agenda item 1)

### Discussion in plenary

**E/2010/SR.42** (20 July 2010).

At the 42nd meeting, the Council elected Portugal for a 4-year term beginning at the 1st meeting of the Commission's 45th session, in 2011, and expiring at the close of the Commission's 48th session, in 2015, to fill a vacancy arising from the resignation of the United States, and the United States for a term beginning on the date of election and expiring at the close of the Commission's 47th session, in 2014, to fill a vacancy arising from the resignation of Portugal: decision 2010/201 C.

## UN. COMMISSION ON SCIENCE AND TECHNOLOGY FOR DEVELOPMENT–MEMBERS (Agenda item 1)

### Discussion in plenary

**E/2010/SR.52** (15 Dec. 2010).

At the 52nd meeting, France was elected as a member of the Commission on Science and Technology for Development by acclamation for a 4-year term beginning on 1 Jan. 2011; the Council postponed the election of 1 member from the Group of Asian States, 2 members from the Group of Eastern European States and 3 members from the Group of Western European and other States for a 4-year term beginning on 1 Jan. 2011: decision 2010/201 G.

## UN. COMMITTEE FOR DEVELOPMENT POLICY–MEMBERS (Agenda item 1)

### General documents

**E/2010/9/Add.14** Appointment of a new member to the Committee for Development Policy : note / by the Secretary-General.

## UN. COMMITTEE FOR DEVELOPMENT POLICY–MEMBERS (Agenda item 1) (continued)

### Discussion in plenary

**E/2010/SR.42** (20 July 2010).

At the 42nd meeting, Victor Polterovich (Russian Federation) was appointed as a member of the Committee for Development Policy for a term of office beginning immediately and expiring on 31 Dec. 2012: decision 2010/201 C.

## UN. COMMITTEE OF EXPERTS ON INTERNATIONAL COOPERATION IN TAX MATTERS–MEMBERS (Agenda item 1)

### General documents

**E/2010/9/Add.20** Appointment of a new member to the Committee of Experts on International Cooperation in Tax Matters : note : addendum / by the Secretary-General.

Concerns resignation of Miguel Ferre Navarrete (Spain) and reports the Secretary-General's decision to appoint Julia Martínez Rico (Spain) to complete the term of office of Ferre Navarrete, which expires on 30 June 2013; transmits the candidate's curriculum vitae.

### Discussion in plenary

**E/2010/SR.49** (25 Oct. 2010).

At the 49th meeting, the Council took note of the appointment of Julia Martínez Rico (Spain) to complete the term of office of Miguel Navarrete who resigned as a member of the Committee of Experts on International Cooperation in Tax Matters: decision 2010/201 E.

## UN. COMMITTEE ON ECONOMIC, SOCIAL AND CULTURAL RIGHTS–MEMBERS (Agenda item 1)

### General documents

**E/2010/9/Add.21** Election to fill a vacancy in the Committee on Economic, Social and Cultural Rights : note / by the Secretary-General.

**UN. ECONOMIC AND SOCIAL COUNCIL (2010, SUBSTANTIVE SESS. : NEW YORK)–AGENDA (Agenda item 1)**

**General documents**

**E/2010/97** Requests from non-governmental organizations to be heard by the Economic and Social Council.

**E/2010/100** Annotated provisional agenda : Economic and Social Council, substantive session of 2010, New York, 28 June-23 July 2010.

**E/2010/103** Note verbale, 12 July 2010, from Congo. Reports the decision of the Government of the Congo to present its candidature for membership in the Executive Committee of the Programme of the UN High Commissioner for Refugees.

**E/2010/L.5** Proposed programme of work for the substantive session of 2010 : Economic and Social Council.

**E/2010/L.6** Status of documentation for the session : Economic and Social Council, substantive session of 2010, New York, 28 June-23 July 2010 : note / by the Secretariat.

**Discussion in plenary**

**E/2010/SR.11** (28 June 2010).
At the 11th meeting, the provisional agenda, as contained in document E/2010/100, was adopted; the proposed programme of work in E/2010/L.5, as orally revised, was adopted; at the same meeting, the Council, upon the recommendation of the Committee on Non-Governmental Organizations in E/2010/97, approved requests made by non-governmental organizations to be heard during the high-level segment of the 2010 substantive session: decision 2010/210.

**E/2010/SR.50** (10 Nov. 2010).
At the 50th meeting, the Council adopted the theme "Current global and national trends and challenges and their impact on education" for the thematic discussion of the high-level segment of the 2011 substantive session: decision 2010/262.

**UN. ECONOMIC AND SOCIAL COUNCIL (2010, SUBSTANTIVE SESS. : NEW YORK)–CLOSING**

**Discussion in plenary**

**E/2010/SR.47** (23 July 2010).
The President declared closed the 2010 substantive session.

**UN. ECONOMIC AND SOCIAL COUNCIL (2010, SUBSTANTIVE SESS. : NEW YORK)–DOCUMENTS**

**General documents**

**E/2010/CRP.1** Updated status of documentation, 14 July 2010 : Economic and Social Council, substantive session of 2010, New York, 28 June-23 July 2010.

**UN. ECONOMIC AND SOCIAL COUNCIL (2010, SUBSTANTIVE SESS. : NEW YORK)–OPENING**

**Discussion in plenary**

**E/2010/SR.11** (28 June 2010).

**UN. ECONOMIC AND SOCIAL COUNCIL (2010, SUBSTANTIVE SESS. : NEW YORK)–PARTICIPANTS**

**General documents**

**E/2010/INF/1** List of delegations : Special High-Level Meeting with the Bretton Woods institutions, the World Trade Organization and the United Nations Conference on Trade and Development, New York, 18-19 March 2010 = Liste des délégations = Lista de las delegaciones.

**E/2010/INF/3** List of delegations : Economic and Social Council, substantive session of 2010, New York, 28 June-23 July 2010.

**UN. ECONOMIC AND SOCIAL COUNCIL (2010, SUBSTANTIVE SESS. : NEW YORK)–RESOLUTIONS AND DECISIONS**

**General documents**

**E/2010/99** (ESCOR, 2010, Suppl. no. 1) Resolutions and decisions of the Economic and Social Council : organizational session for 2010, New York, 19 January, 9 and 12 February 2010; resumed organizational session for 2010, New York, 28 April and 21 May 2010; substantive session of 2010, New York, 28 June-23 July 2010; resumed substantive session of 2010, New York, 9 September, 25 October, 10 November and 14-15 December 2010.

**E/2010/INF/2/Add.1** (To be issued in ESCOR, 2010, Suppl. no. 1.) Resolutions and decisions adopted by the Economic and Social Council at its substantive session of 2010 (New York, 28 June-23 July 2010).

**E/2010/INF/2/Add.2** (To be issued in ESCOR, 2010, Suppl. no. 1.) Resolutions and decisions adopted by the Economic and Social Council at its resumed substantive session of 2010 (New York, 9 September, 25 October, 10 November and 14 and 15 December 2010).

## UN. INTERGOVERNMENTAL WORKING GROUP OF EXPERTS ON INTERNATIONAL STANDARDS OF ACCOUNTING AND REPORTING–MEMBERS (Agenda item 1)

### Discussion in plenary

**E/2010/SR.52** (15 Dec. 2010).

At the 52nd meeting, Croatia was elected as a member of the Intergovernmental Working Group of Experts on International Standards of Accounting and Reporting by acclamation for a term beginning on the date of the election and expiring on 31 Dec. 2012; the Council postponed the election of 3 members from the Group of Latin American and Caribbean States and 4 members from the Group of Western European and other States, for a term beginning on the date of election and expiring on 31 Dec. 2011, and 4 members from the Group of Asian States and 1 member from the Group of Latin American and Caribbean Sates for a term beginning on the date of election and expiring on 31 Dec. 2012: decision 2010/201 G.

## UN. PEACEBUILDING COMMISSION. ORGANIZATIONAL COMMITTEE–MEMBERS (Agenda item 1)

### Draft resolutions/decisions

**E/2010/L.42** Membership of the Economic and Social Council in the Organizational Committee of the Peacebuilding Commission : draft resolution / submitted by the President of the Council.

### Discussion in plenary

**E/2010/SR.51** (14 Dec. 2010).

At the 51st meeting, draft resolution E/2010/L.42 was adopted without vote: resolution 2010/36.

**E/2010/SR.52** (15 Dec. 2010).

At the 52nd meeting, the Council elected Egypt, Guatemala, Republic of Korea, Rwanda, Spain, Ukraine and Zambia as members of the Organizational Committee of the Peacebuilding Commission for a 2-year term beginning on 1 Jan. 2011: decision 2010/201 G.

## UN. PEACEBUILDING COMMISSION. ORGANIZATIONAL COMMITTEE–MEMBERS (Agenda item 1) (continued)

### Resolutions

**E/RES/2010/36** (E/2010/INF/2/Add.2) Membership of the Economic and Social Council in the Organizational Committee of the Peacebuilding Commission.

Decides that the distribution of the 7 seats allocated to the Economic and Social Council on the Organizational Committee of the Peacebuilding Commission shall be as follows: 1 seat for each of the 5 regional groups, namely, African States, Asian States, Eastern European States, Latin American and Caribbean States and Western European and other States; in the election of members of the Economic and Social Council to the Organizational Committee whose term of office shall start on 1 Jan. 2011, the 2 remaining seats shall be allocated to the regional group of African States; also decides that the established practice of the Economic and Social Council regarding members elected to its subsidiary bodies who are not able to complete their term of office shall apply to members elected to the Organizational Committee by the Council. (Adopted without vote, 51st plenary meeting, 14 Dec. 2010)

## UN. PERMANENT FORUM ON INDIGENOUS ISSUES (Agenda item 14h)

### Reports

**E/2010/43** (E/C.19/2010/15) (ESCOR, 2010, Suppl. no. 23) Permanent Forum on Indigenous Issues : report on the 9th session (19-30 April 2010).
Issued: 2010.

### Discussion in plenary

**E/2010/SR.44** (22 July 2010).

**E/2010/SR.45** (22 July 2010).

At the 45th meeting, action on draft decisions in E/2010/43 was as follows: draft decision I entitled "International expert group meeting on the theme 'Indigenous peoples and forests'", adopted without vote: decision 2010/248; draft decision II entitled "Venue and dates of the 10th session of the Permanent Forum", adopted without vote: decision 2010/249; draft decision III entitled "Provisional agenda for the 10th session of the Permanent Forum", adopted without vote: decision 2010/250.

**E/2010/SR.46** (23 July 2010).

At the 46th meeting, the Council took note of the report of the Permanent Forum on Indigenous Issues on its 9th session (E/2010/43): decision 2010/258.

## UN. PERMANENT FORUM ON INDIGENOUS ISSUES–MEMBERS (Agenda item 1)

### General documents

**E/2010/9/Add.22** Election of a member to the Permanent Forum on Indigenous Issues : note / by the Secretary-General.

## UN. PERMANENT FORUM ON INDIGENOUS ISSUES–MEMBERS (Agenda item 1) (continued)

### Discussion in plenary

**E/2010/SR.52**  (15 Dec. 2010).
At the 52nd meeting, Bertie Xavier (Guyana) was elected as a member of the Permanent Forum on Indigenous Issues: decision 2010/201 G.

## UN. SUBCOMMITTEE OF EXPERTS ON THE TRANSPORT OF DANGEROUS GOODS–MEMBERS (Agenda item 1)

### General documents

**E/2010/9/Add.19**  Committee of Experts on the Transport of Dangerous Goods and on the Globally Harmonized System of Classification and Labelling of Chemicals : Subcommittee of Experts on the Transport of Dangerous Goods : note / by the Secretary-General.

### Discussion in plenary

**E/2010/SR.49**  (25 Oct. 2010).
At the 49th meeting, the Council decided to endorse the decision of the Secretary-General (E/2010/9/Add.19) to approve an application from the Republic of Korea for full membership in the Subcommittee of Experts on the Transport of Dangerous Goods: decision 2010/201 E.

## UN CONFERENCES–FOLLOW-UP (Agenda item 6)

### Reports

**E/2010/90**  (A/65/84)  Role of the Economic and Social Council in the integrated and coordinated implementation of the outcomes of and follow-up to major United Nations conferences and summits, in the light of relevant General Assembly resolutions, including resolution 61/16 : report of the Secretary-General.
Issued: 3 June 2010.

### General documents

**E/2010/91**  (A/64/803)  Letter, 25 May 2010, from Spain. Transmits Madrid Declaration entitled "Towards a new stage in the biregional partnership: innovation and technology for sustainable development and social inclusion", adopted by the Heads of State and Government meeting at the 6th summit of the European Union and the Latin American and Caribbean States, which was held in Madrid on 18 May 2010.

### Draft resolutions/decisions

**E/2010/L.11**  Role of the Council in the integrated and coordinated implementation of the outcomes of and follow-up to major United Nations conferences and summits, in the light of relevant General Assembly resolutions, including resolution 61/16 : draft decision / submitted by Vice-President of the Council, Morten Wetland (Norway), on the basis of informal consultations.

### Discussion in plenary

**E/2010/SR.22**  (6 July 2010).

**E/2010/SR.23**  (7 July 2010).

## UN CONFERENCES–FOLLOW-UP (Agenda item 6) (continued)

**E/2010/SR.26**  (8 July 2010).

**E/2010/SR.46**  (23 July 2010).
At the 46th meeting, draft decision E/2010/L.11, as orally revised, was adopted without vote: decision 2010/252.

## UN POLICY RECOMMENDATIONS–FOLLOW-UP (Agenda item 3a)

### Reports

**E/2010/4**  (E/CN.6/2010/2)  Review of the implementation of the Beijing Declaration and Platform for Action, the outcomes of the 23rd special session of the General Assembly and its contribution to shaping a gender perspective towards the full realization of the Millennium Development Goals : report of the Secretary-General.
Issued: 7 Dec. 2009.

### General documents

**E/2010/3**  (A/64/578)  Letter, 3 Dec. 2009, from Rwanda addressed to the Secretary-General. Transmits statement of outcome and way forward adopted at the Intergovernmental Meeting of the programme country pilots on Delivering as One, held in Kigali, 19-21 October 2009.

### Draft resolutions/decisions

**E/2010/L.32**  Progress in the implementation of General Assembly resolution 62/208 on the triennial comprehensive policy review of operational activities for development of the United Nations system : draft resolution / submitted by the Vice-President of the Council, Alexandru Cujba (Republic of Moldova) on the basis of informal consultations.

### Discussion in plenary

**E/2010/SR.27**  (9 July 2010).

**E/2010/SR.28**  (9 July 2010).

**E/2010/SR.29**  (12 July 2010).

**E/2010/SR.30**  (12 July 2010).

**E/2010/SR.31**  (13 July 2010).

**E/2010/SR.46**  (23 July 2010).
At the 46th meeting, draft resolution E/2010/L.32 was adopted without vote: resolution 2010/22.

## UN POLICY RECOMMENDATIONS–FOLLOW-UP (Agenda item 3a) (continued)

### Resolutions

**E/RES/2010/22** (E/2010/INF/2/Add.1) Progress in the implementation of General Assembly resolution 62/208 on the triennial comprehensive policy review of operational activities for development of the United Nations system.

Requests the Secretary-General to include in his report to the Council at its substantive session of 2011 information on further progress on an inter-agency collaborative framework on South-South cooperation and triangular cooperation, and on progress in the preparation of the operational guidelines to support the implementation of the Nairobi outcome document of the High-level UN Conference on South-South Cooperation to be prepared as mandated by the High-level Committee on South-South Cooperation at its 16th session; encourages the UN Development Group to continue working to improve the quality of the UN Development Assistance Framework and its regular monitoring; reiterates its request to the UN funds and programmes and specialized agencies to explore sources of financing to support the implementation of the Plan of Action for the Harmonization of Business Practices in the UN System. (Adopted without vote, 46th plenary meeting, 23 July 2010)

## UN-HABITAT. GOVERNING COUNCIL–MEMBERS (Agenda item 1)

### Discussion in plenary

**E/2010/SR.42** (20 July 2010).

At the 42nd meeting, the Council elected Chile and Grenada as members of the Governing Council of the UN Human Settlements Programme for a 4-year term beginning on 1 Jan. 2011; the Council postponed the election of 3 members from the Group of Western European and other States for a 4-year term beginning on 1 Jan. 2011; the Council further postponed the election of 4 members from the Group of Western European and other States for a term beginning on the date of election, 2 for a term expiring on 31 Dec. 2011 and 2 for a term expiring on 31 Dec. 2012: decision 2010/201 C.

## UN-WOMEN. EXECUTIVE BOARD–MEMBERS (Agenda item 1)

### Draft resolutions/decisions

**E/2010/L.40** Procedures for the election of the members of the Executive Board of the United Nations Entity for Gender Equality and the Empowerment of Women : draft resolution / submitted by the President of the Council, Hamidon Ali (Malaysia), on the basis of informal consultations.

### Discussion in plenary

**E/2010/SR.48** (9 Sept. 2010).

At the 48th meeting, the Council adopted the oral draft decision on the procedures for the election of the members of the Executive Board of the UN Entity for Gender Equality and the Empowerment of Women (UN Women), prepared on the basis of informal consultations: decision 2010/261.

## UN-WOMEN. EXECUTIVE BOARD–MEMBERS (Agenda item 1) (continued)

**E/2010/SR.49** (25 Oct. 2010).

At the 49th meeting, draft resolution E/2010/L.40 was adopted without vote: resolution 2010/35.

**E/2010/SR.50** (10 Nov. 2010).

At the 50th meeting, the following 41 members were elected members of the Executive Board of the UN Women: Angola, Argentina, Bangladesh, Brazil, Cape Verde, China, Congo, Côte d'Ivoire, Democratic Republic of the Congo, Denmark, Dominican Republic, El Salvador, Estonia, Ethiopia, France, Grenada, Hungary, India, Indonesia, Italy, Japan, Kazakhstan, Lesotho, Libyan Arab Jamahiriya, Luxembourg, Malaysia, Mexico, Nigeria, Norway, Pakistan, Peru, Republic of Korea, Russian Federation, Saudi Arabia, Spain, Sweden, Timor-Leste, Ukraine, United Kingdom, United Republic of Tanzania and United States; the Council also decided the following: 17 members were elected for a 2 year term of office beginning on the date of election and expiring on 31 Dec. 2012: Argentina, Bangladesh, Brazil, Côte d'Ivoire, Democratic Republic of the Congo, El Salvador, Estonia, France, India, Italy, Lesotho, Libyan Arab Jamahiriya, Malaysia, Pakistan, Russian Federation, Timor-Leste and United Republic of Tanzania; 18 members were elected for a 3 year term of office beginning on the date of election and expiring on 31 Dec. 2013: Angola, Cape Verde, China, Congo, Denmark, Dominican Republic, Ethiopia, Grenada, Hungary, Indonesia, Japan, Kazakhstan, Luxembourg, Nigeria, Peru, Republic of Korea, Sweden and Ukraine and 4 members were elected for a 3 year term of office beginning on the date of election and expiring on 31 Dec. 2013: Norway, Spain, United Kingdom and United States: decision 2010/201 F.

### Resolutions

**E/RES/2010/35** (E/2010/INF/2/Add.2) Procedures for the election of the members of the Executive Board of the United Nations Entity for Gender Equality and the Empowerment of Women.

Decides that the term of membership for the 35 members of the Executive Board elected from the 5 regional groups shall be staggered; also decides that the 6 contributing countries to serve as members of the Executive Board shall be elected for a 3-year term; further decides that the term of office of the 41 members of the Executive Board elected during the 1st election will begin on the date of the election and run until 31 Dec. of the year in which their term ends; decides that in subsequent elections members will be elected for a term of office of 3 years, beginning on 1 Jan. of the year following their election and running until 31 Dec. of the year in which their term ends. (Adopted without vote, 49th plenary meeting, 25 Oct. 2010)

## UNDP/UNFPA (Agenda item 3b)

### Reports

**E/2009/35** (ESCOR, 2009, Suppl. no. 15) Executive Board of the United Nations Development Programme/United Nations Population Fund : report of the Executive Board on its work during 2009.
Issued: 2009.

## UNDP/UNFPA (Agenda item 3b) (continued)

**E/2010/5**  Report to the Economic and Social Council : report of the Administrator of the United Nations Development Programme and the Executive Director of the United Nations Population Fund.
Issued: 25 Nov. 2009.

**E/2010/35**  (ESCOR, 2010, Suppl. no. 15)  Executive Board of the United Nations Development Programme/United Nations Population Fund : report of the Executive Board on its work during 2010.
Issued: 2010.

### Draft resolutions/decisions

**E/2010/L.17**  Renaming of the title of the Executive Board of the United Nations Development Programme and the United Nations Population Fund to include the United Nations Office for Project Services : draft resolution / submitted by the Vice-President of the Council, Alexandru Cujba (Republic of Moldova), on the basis of informal consultations.

### Discussion in plenary

**E/2010/SR.27**  (9 July 2010).

**E/2010/SR.28**  (9 July 2010).

**E/2010/SR.29**  (12 July 2010).

**E/2010/SR.30**  (12 July 2010).

**E/2010/SR.31**  (13 July 2010).

**E/2010/SR.46**  (23 July 2010).
At the 46th meeting, draft resolution E/2010/L.17 was adopted without vote: resolution 2010/23; the Council took note of the following documents: Report to the Economic and Social Council of the Administrator of the UN Development Programme and the Executive Director of the UN Population Fund (E/2010/5) and Report of the Executive Board of the UN Development Programme/United Nations Population Fund on its work in 2009 (E/2009/35): decision 2010/251.

### Resolutions

**E/RES/2010/23**  (E/2010/INF/2/Add.1)  Renaming of the title of the Executive Board of the United Nations Development Programme and the United Nations Population Fund to include the United Nations Office for Project Services.
Decides that the name of the Executive Board of the UN Development Programme and the UN Population Fund shall be changed to the Executive Board of the UN Development Programme, the UN Population Fund and the UN Office for Project Services; also decides that the functions of the Executive Board as set forth in General Assembly resolution 48/162 shall apply mutatis mutandis to the UN Office for Project Services. (Adopted without vote, 46th plenary meeting, 23 July 2010)

## UNICEF (Agenda item 3b)

### Reports

**E/2010/6**  (E/ICEF/2010/3)  Annual report to the Economic and Social Council.
Issued: 16 Nov. 2009.

**E/2010/34(PartI)**  (E/ICEF/2010/7(PartI))  (To be issued as ESCOR, 2010, Suppl. no. 14 (E/2010/34/Rev.1-E/ICEF/2010/7/Rev.1).)  Report of the Executive Board of the United Nations Children's Fund on the work of its 1st regular session of 2010 (12-14 January 2010).
Issued: 9 Feb. 2010.

**E/2010/34(PartI)/Add.1**  (E/ICEF/2010/7(PartI)/Add.1)  Report of the Executive Board of the United Nations Children's Fund on the work of its 2010 1st regular session (15 and 18 January 2010) : addendum.
Issued: 22 Feb. 2010.

**E/2010/34(PartII)**  (E/ICEF/2010/7(PartII))  (To be issued as ESCOR, 2010, Suppl. no. 14 (E/2010/34/Rev.1-E/ICEF/2010/7/Rev.1).)  Report of the Executive Board of the United Nations Children's Fund on the work of its 2010 annual session (1-4 June 2010).
Issued: 8 July 2010.

**E/2010/34(PartII)/Corr.1**  (E/ICEF/2010/7(PartII)/Corr.1)  Report of the Executive Board of the United Nations Children's Fund on the work of its 2010 annual session (1-4 June 2010) : corrigendum.
Issued: 12 Oct. 2010. - Corrects text.

**E/2010/34/Rev.1**  (E/ICEF/2010/7/Rev.1)  (ESCOR, 2010, Suppl. no. 14)  Executive Board of the United Nations Children's Fund : report on the 1st and 2nd regular sessions and annual session of 2010.
Issued: 2010.

**E/2010/L.7**  Extract from the report of the Executive Board of the United Nations Children's Fund on its 2010 annual session (1-4 June 2010) : decisions adopted by the Executive Board at its annual session of 2010.
Issued: 8 June 2010.

### Discussion in plenary

**E/2010/SR.27**  (9 July 2010).

**E/2010/SR.28**  (9 July 2010).

**E/2010/SR.29**  (12 July 2010).

**E/2010/SR.30**  (12 July 2010).

**E/2010/SR.31**  (13 July 2010).

**E/2010/SR.46**  (23 July 2010).
At the 46th meeting, the Council took note of the following documents: Annual report of the Executive Board of UNICEF (E/2010/6); Report of the Executive Board of the UNICEF on the work of its 1st regular session of 2010 (E/2010/34 (Part I)); Addendum to the report of the Executive Board of UNICEF on the work of its 1st regular session of 2010 (E/2010/34 (Part I/Add.1) and Extract from the report of the Executive Board of the UNICEF on its 2010 annual session: decisions adopted by the Executive Board at its annual session of 2010 (E/2010/L.7): decision 2010/251.

## WOMEN IN DEVELOPMENT (Agenda item 13k)

### Discussion in plenary

**E/2010/SR.11**  (28 June 2010).

**E/2010/SR.19(B)**  (2 July 2010).

## WOMEN'S ADVANCEMENT (Agenda item 14a)

### Reports

**E/2010/27**  (E/CN.6/2010/11)  (ESCOR, 2010, Suppl. no. 7) Commission on the Status of Women : report on the 54th session (13 March and 14 October 2009 and 1-12 March 2010).
Issued: 2010.

**E/2010/27/Corr.1**  (E/CN.6/2010/11/Corr.1)  (ESCOR, 2010, Suppl. no. 7) Commission on the Status of Women : report on the 54th session (13 March and 14 October 2009 and 1-12 March 2010) : corrigendum.
Issued: 31 Jan. 2011. - Corrects text.

### General documents

**E/2010/74**  Social and human rights questions : advancement of women : note / by the Secretariat.

### Draft resolutions/decisions

**E/2010/L.21**  Strengthening the institutional arrangements for support of gender equality and the empowerment of women : draft resolution / submitted by the President of the Economic and Social Council, Hamidon Ali (Malaysia).

### Discussion in plenary

**E/2010/SR.11**  (28 June 2010).

**E/2010/SR.19(B)**  (2 July 2010).

**E/2010/SR.42**  (20 July 2010).
At the 42nd meeting, action on draft resolution and draft decisions in E/2010/27 was as follows: draft resolution entitled "Situation of and assistance to Palestinian women", adopted (24-3-15): resolution 2010/6; draft decision entitled "Declaration on the occasion of the 15th anniversary of the 4th World Conference on Women", adopted without vote: decision 2010/232; draft decision entitled "Report of the Commission on the Status of Women on its 54th session and provisional agenda for its 55th session", adopted without vote: decision 2010/233; at the same meeting, draft resolution E/2010/L.21, as orally revised, was adopted without vote: resolution 2010/7.

### Resolutions

**E/RES/2010/6**  (E/2010/INF/2/Add.1)  Situation of and assistance to Palestinian women.
Urges the international community to continue to give special attention to the promotion and protection of the human rights of Palestinian women and girls. (Adopted 24-3-15, 42nd plenary meeting, 20 July 2010)

## WOMEN'S ADVANCEMENT (Agenda item 14a) (continued)

**E/RES/2010/7**  (E/2010/INF/2/Add.1)  Strengthening the institutional arrangements for support of gender equality and the empowerment of women.
Decides to dissolve the International Research and Training Institute for the Advancement of Women as of the date of the adoption of the present resolution. (Adopted without vote, 42nd plenary meeting, 20 July 2010)

## WORLD FOOD PROGRAMME (Agenda item 3b)

### Reports

**E/2010/14**  Annual report of the World Food Programme for 2009 : note / by the Secretary-General.
Issued: 4 Mar. 2010. - Transmits annual report of the World Food Programme (WFP) for 2009, as adopted at the 1st regular session of 2010 (8-11 February 2010) by the Board of the WFP in its decision 2010/EB.1/2, which is also attached.

**E/2010/36**  (ESCOR, 2010, Suppl. no. 16) Executive Board of the World Food Programme : report on the 1st and 2nd regular sessions and annual session of 2009.
Issued: 2010.

### Discussion in plenary

**E/2010/SR.27**  (9 July 2010).

**E/2010/SR.28**  (9 July 2010).

**E/2010/SR.29**  (12 July 2010).

**E/2010/SR.31**  (13 July 2010).

**E/2010/SR.46**  (23 July 2010).
At the 46th meeting, the Council took note of the following documents: Note by the Secretary-General transmitting the annual report of the World Food Programme for 2009 (E/2010/14); Report of the Executive Board of the World Food Programme on the 1st and 2nd regular sessions and annual session of 2009 (E/2010/36): decision 2010/251.

# INDEX TO SPEECHES

## EXPLANATORY NOTE

Certain speakers are permitted to address the
*Economic and Social* Council in their personal capacity.
In such cases, a triple asterisk (***) appears in place of
the corporate name/country affiliation in each section
of the Index to speeches.

## Angola

GENDER EQUALITY (Agenda item 2c)
Chicoty, George – E/2010/SR.11

## Argentina

DECOLONIZATION (Agenda item 9)
Díaz Bartolomé, Gerardo – E/2010/SR.46
EMPOWERMENT OF WOMEN (Agenda item 2d)
Argüello, Jorge – E/2010/SR.18(B)
GENDER EQUALITY (Agenda item 2c)
Rutilo, Gustavo – E/2010/SR.11
HUMANITARIAN ASSISTANCE (Agenda item 5)
Porretti, Eduardo – E/2010/SR.36
NON-GOVERNMENTAL ORGANIZATIONS (Agenda item 12)
Melon, María Luz – E/2010/SR.39

## Association Femmes Soleil d'Haiti

BRETTON WOODS INSTITUTIONS
Edmond, Jean Paul – E/2010/SR.6

## Australia

BRETTON WOODS INSTITUTIONS
Davies, Fleur Margaret – E/2010/SR.5; E/2010/SR.6
DEVELOPMENT FINANCE–CONFERENCE (2002 : MONTERREY, MEXICO)–FOLLOW-UP (Agenda item 6a)
Lin, Katy – E/2010/SR.47
EMPOWERMENT OF WOMEN (Agenda item 2d)
McMullan, Bob – E/2010/SR.17(B)
GENDER EQUALITY (Agenda item 2c)
McMullan, Bob – E/2010/SR.17(B); E/2010/SR.18(A)
HUMANITARIAN ASSISTANCE (Agenda item 5)
Yarlett, Kathryn – E/2010/SR.34
NON-GOVERNMENTAL ORGANIZATIONS (Agenda item 12)
Goledzinowski, Andrew – E/2010/SR.39
PALESTINIANS–TERRITORIES OCCUPIED BY ISRAEL–LIVING CONDITIONS (Agenda item 11)
Windsor, David Anthony – E/2010/SR.46
UN POLICY RECOMMENDATIONS–FOLLOW-UP (Agenda item 3a)
Cohen, Nathalie – E/2010/SR.29; E/2010/SR.31
UNDP/UNFPA (Agenda item 3b)
Cohen, Nathalie – E/2010/SR.31
UNICEF (Agenda item 3b)
Cohen, Nathalie – E/2010/SR.31
WOMEN'S ADVANCEMENT (Agenda item 14a)
Windsor, David Anthony – E/2010/SR.42
WORLD FOOD PROGRAMME (Agenda item 3b)
Cohen, Nathalie – E/2010/SR.31

## Austria

EMPOWERMENT OF WOMEN (Agenda item 2d)
Freudenschuss-Reichl, Irene – E/2010/SR.17(B)
GENDER EQUALITY (Agenda item 2c)
Freudenschuss-Reichl, Irene – E/2010/SR.17(B)

## Azerbaijan

GENDER EQUALITY (Agenda item 2c)
Garayev, Asif – E/2010/SR.12

## Bahamas

EMPOWERMENT OF WOMEN (Agenda item 2d)
Bethel, Paulette A. – E/2010/SR.18(B)
HUMANITARIAN ASSISTANCE (Agenda item 5)
Bethel, Paulette A. – E/2010/SR.36
POVERTY MITIGATION (Agenda item 4)
Bethel, Paulette A. – E/2010/SR.26
RESOLUTIONS–UN. GENERAL ASSEMBLY–IMPLEMENTATION (Agenda item 8)
Bethel, Paulette A. – E/2010/SR.26
TAXATION (Agenda item 13h)
Bethel, Paulette A. – E/2010/SR.43
UN CONFERENCES–FOLLOW-UP (Agenda item 6)
Bethel, Paulette A. – E/2010/SR.26

## Bangladesh

BRETTON WOODS INSTITUTIONS
Rahman, Nojibur – E/2010/SR.4
DEVELOPMENT FINANCE–CONFERENCE (2002 : MONTERREY, MEXICO)–FOLLOW-UP (Agenda item 6a)
Rahman, A.K.M. Mashiur – E/2010/SR.26
EMPOWERMENT OF WOMEN (Agenda item 2d)
Rahman, Nojibur – E/2010/SR.19(B)
GENDER EQUALITY (Agenda item 2c)
Rahman, Nojibur – E/2010/SR.15(A); E/2010/SR.19(B)
HUMANITARIAN ASSISTANCE (Agenda item 5)
Momen, Abulkalam Abdul – E/2010/SR.36
Rahman, A.K.M. Mashiur – E/2010/SR.35
LEAST DEVELOPED COUNTRIES–INTERNATIONAL DECADE (2001-2010) (Agenda item 6b)
Rahman, Nojibur – E/2010/SR.46
UN. PERMANENT FORUM ON INDIGENOUS ISSUES (Agenda item 14h)
Momen, Abulkalam Abdul – E/2010/SR.44
UN POLICY RECOMMENDATIONS–FOLLOW-UP (Agenda item 3a)
Momen, Abulkalam Abdul – E/2010/SR.31
Rahman, Nojibur – E/2010/SR.29
UNDP/UNFPA (Agenda item 3b)
Momen, Abulkalam Abdul – E/2010/SR.31
Rahman, Nojibur – E/2010/SR.29
UNICEF (Agenda item 3b)
Momen, Abulkalam Abdul – E/2010/SR.31
WOMEN IN DEVELOPMENT (Agenda item 13k)
Rahman, Nojibur – E/2010/SR.19(B)
WOMEN'S ADVANCEMENT (Agenda item 14a)
Rahman, Nojibur – E/2010/SR.19(B)
WORLD FOOD PROGRAMME (Agenda item 3b)
Momen, Abulkalam Abdul – E/2010/SR.31
Rahman, Nojibur – E/2010/SR.29

## Belarus

CRIME PREVENTION (Agenda item 14c)
Velichko, Irina – E/2010/SR.44
DEVELOPMENT FINANCE–CONFERENCE (2002 : MONTERREY, MEXICO)–FOLLOW-UP (Agenda item 6a)
Zdorov, Denis – E/2010/SR.26
EMPOWERMENT OF WOMEN (Agenda item 2d)
Dapkiunas, Andrei – E/2010/SR.18(B)

## Belarus (continued)

INFORMATICS–INTERNATIONAL COOPERATION
(Agenda item 7c)
Sergeev, Sergei – E/2010/SR.38
NARCOTIC DRUGS (Agenda item 14d)
Velichko, Irina – E/2010/SR.44
OPERATIONAL ACTIVITIES–UN (Agenda item 3)
Sergeev, Sergei – E/2010/SR.30
REFUGEES (Agenda item 14e)
Velichko, Irina – E/2010/SR.44
REGIONAL COOPERATION (Agenda item 10)
Zdorov, Denis – E/2010/SR.41
SCIENCE AND TECHNOLOGY–DEVELOPMENT
(Agenda item 13b)
Sergeev, Sergei – E/2010/SR.38
SUSTAINABLE DEVELOPMENT (Agenda item 13a)
Sergeev, Sergei – E/2010/SR.43
WOMEN'S ADVANCEMENT (Agenda item 14a)
Velichko, Irina – E/2010/SR.42

## Belgium

BRETTON WOODS INSTITUTIONS
Bassompierre, Christophe de – E/2010/SR.6
Leroy, Marcus – E/2010/SR.5
DEVELOPMENT FINANCE–CONFERENCE (2002 :
MONTERREY, MEXICO)–FOLLOW-UP (Agenda item
6a)
Bassompierre, Christophe de – E/2010/SR.26
INFORMATICS–INTERNATIONAL COOPERATION
(Agenda item 7c)
Bassompierre, Christophe de – E/2010/SR.52

## Benin

BRETTON WOODS INSTITUTIONS
Zinsou, Jean-Francis Régis – E/2010/SR.6
ECONOMIC ASSISTANCE–HAITI (Agenda item 7d)
Zinsou, Jean-Francis Régis – E/2010/SR.32

## Bolivia (Plurinational State of)

EMPOWERMENT OF WOMEN (Agenda item 2d)
Daza, Varinia – E/2010/SR.17(B)
GENDER EQUALITY (Agenda item 2c)
Daza, Varinia – E/2010/SR.17(B)

## Brazil

BRETTON WOODS INSTITUTIONS
Dunlop, Regina Maria Cordeiro – E/2010/SR.4
Patriota, Guilherme de Aguiar – E/2010/SR.5;
E/2010/SR.6
CRIME PREVENTION (Agenda item 14c)
Andrade, Pedro Aurélio Florencio Cabral de –
E/2010/SR.44
DEVELOPMENT FINANCE–CONFERENCE (2002 :
MONTERREY, MEXICO)–FOLLOW-UP (Agenda item
6a)
Almeida, João Lucas Quental Novaes de –
E/2010/SR.46
ECONOMIC ASSISTANCE–HAITI (Agenda item 7d)
Dunlop, Regina Maria Cordeiro – E/2010/SR.32
EMPOWERMENT OF WOMEN (Agenda item 2d)
Freire, Nilcéa – E/2010/SR.17(B)

## Brazil (continued)

GENDER EQUALITY (Agenda item 2c)
Freire, Nilcéa – E/2010/SR.11; E/2010/SR.17(B)
HUMAN SETTLEMENTS (Agenda item 13d)
Farias, Fábio Moreira Carbonell – E/2010/SR.43
HUMANITARIAN ASSISTANCE (Agenda item 5)
Dunlop, Regina Maria Cordeiro – E/2010/SR.33
INFORMATICS–INTERNATIONAL COOPERATION
(Agenda item 7c)
Farias, Fábio Moreira Carbonell – E/2010/SR.38
INTERNATIONAL FINANCIAL INSTITUTIONS (Agenda
item 2a)
Dunlop, Regina Maria Cordeiro – E/2010/SR.19(A)
LEAST DEVELOPED COUNTRIES–INTERNATIONAL
DECADE (2001-2010) (Agenda item 6b)
Farias, Fábio Moreira Carbonell – E/2010/SR.37
OPERATIONAL ACTIVITIES–UN (Agenda item 3)
Dunlop, Regina Maria Cordeiro – E/2010/SR.30
POVERTY MITIGATION (Agenda item 4)
Almeida, João Lucas Quental Novaes de –
E/2010/SR.23
REGIONAL COOPERATION–LATIN AMERICA AND
THE CARIBBEAN (Agenda item 10)
Brichta, Daniella Poppius – E/2010/SR.20
RESOLUTIONS–UN. GENERAL ASSEMBLY–
IMPLEMENTATION (Agenda item 8)
Almeida, João Lucas Quental Novaes de –
E/2010/SR.23
SCIENCE AND TECHNOLOGY–DEVELOPMENT
(Agenda item 13b)
Farias, Fábio Moreira Carbonell – E/2010/SR.38
UN CONFERENCES–FOLLOW-UP (Agenda item 6)
Almeida, João Lucas Quental Novaes de –
E/2010/SR.23
UN POLICY RECOMMENDATIONS–FOLLOW-UP
(Agenda item 3a)
Leite, Bruno – E/2010/SR.29

## Burundi

GENDER EQUALITY (Agenda item 2c)
Nahayo, Adolphe – E/2010/SR.12

## Cameroon

ECONOMIC ASSISTANCE–HAITI (Agenda item 7d)
Tommo Monthe, Michel – E/2010/SR.44
REFUGEES (Agenda item 14e)
Tommo Monthe, Michel – E/2010/SR.45
REGIONAL COOPERATION–AFRICA (Agenda item 10)
Tommo Monthe, Michel – E/2010/SR.20

## Canada

BRETTON WOODS INSTITUTIONS
McNee, John – E/2010/SR.4
ECONOMIC ASSISTANCE–HAITI (Agenda item 7d)
McNee, John – E/2010/SR.32
Morrill, Keith – E/2010/SR.44
HUMAN SETTLEMENTS (Agenda item 13d)
Morrill, Keith – E/2010/SR.43
HUMANITARIAN ASSISTANCE (Agenda item 5)
Bonser, Michael – E/2010/SR.35
McNee, John – E/2010/SR.33

## Canada (continued)

INFORMATICS–INTERNATIONAL COOPERATION
(Agenda item 7c)
Morrill, Keith – E/2010/SR.38
NON-GOVERNMENTAL ORGANIZATIONS (Agenda
item 12)
Morrill, Keith – E/2010/SR.39
REGIONAL COOPERATION (Agenda item 10)
Morrill, Keith – E/2010/SR.42
SCIENCE AND TECHNOLOGY–DEVELOPMENT
(Agenda item 13b)
Morrill, Keith – E/2010/SR.38
UN. ECONOMIC AND SOCIAL COUNCIL (2010,
SUBSTANTIVE SESS. : NEW YORK)–AGENDA
(Agenda item 1)
Morrill, Keith – E/2010/SR.47

## Cape Verde

GENDER EQUALITY (Agenda item 2c)
Lima, Antonio Pedro Monteiro – E/2010/SR.17(A)

## Caribbean Community

BRETTON WOODS INSTITUTIONS
St. Aimee, Donatus Keith (Saint Lucia) –
E/2010/SR.4; E/2010/SR.7

## Chamber of Commerce of the United States of America

BRETTON WOODS INSTITUTIONS
Jordan, Stephen – E/2010/SR.6

## Chile

COORDINATION AND PROGRAMMES (Agenda item 7)
Tagle, Jorge – E/2010/SR.40
ECONOMIC ASSISTANCE–HAITI (Agenda item 7d)
Errázuriz, Octavio – E/2010/SR.32
EMPOWERMENT OF WOMEN (Agenda item 2d)
Errázuriz, Octavio – E/2010/SR.19(B)
GENDER EQUALITY (Agenda item 2c)
Bachelet, Michelle – E/2010/SR.11
Errázuriz, Octavio – E/2010/SR.17(A);
E/2010/SR.18(A); E/2010/SR.19(B)
GENDER MAINSTREAMING–UN SYSTEM (Agenda
item 7e)
Errázuriz, Octavio – E/2010/SR.47
HUMANITARIAN ASSISTANCE (Agenda item 5)
Errázuriz, Octavio – E/2010/SR.47
Gálvez, Eduardo – E/2010/SR.33
POST-CONFLICT RECONSTRUCTION–AFRICA
(Agenda item 7f)
Tagle, Jorge – E/2010/SR.40
WOMEN IN DEVELOPMENT (Agenda item 13k)
Errázuriz, Octavio – E/2010/SR.19(B)
WOMEN'S ADVANCEMENT (Agenda item 14a)
Errázuriz, Octavio – E/2010/SR.19(B)
Peña, Belén Muñoz de la – E/2010/SR.42

## China

BRETTON WOODS INSTITUTIONS
Li, Baodong – E/2010/SR.4

## China (continued)

DEVELOPMENT COOPERATION FORUM (Agenda
item 2b)
Yi, Xiaozhun – E/2010/SR.13
EMPOWERMENT OF WOMEN (Agenda item 2d)
Li, Baodong – E/2010/SR.18(B)
ENVIRONMENT (Agenda item 3e)
Wang, Qun – E/2010/SR.43
GENDER EQUALITY (Agenda item 2c)
Zhang, Dan – E/2010/SR.18(A)
HUMANITARIAN ASSISTANCE (Agenda item 5)
Wang, Hongbo – E/2010/SR.33
INFORMATICS–INTERNATIONAL COOPERATION
(Agenda item 7c)
Chen, Yin – E/2010/SR.38
LEAST DEVELOPED COUNTRIES–INTERNATIONAL
DECADE (2001-2010) (Agenda item 6b)
Wang, Min – E/2010/SR.37
NON-GOVERNMENTAL ORGANIZATIONS (Agenda
item 12)
Xu, Jing – E/2010/SR.39
OPERATIONAL ACTIVITIES–UN (Agenda item 3)
Wang, Min – E/2010/SR.30
POVERTY MITIGATION (Agenda item 4)
Wang, Min – E/2010/SR.23
RESOLUTIONS–UN. GENERAL ASSEMBLY–
IMPLEMENTATION (Agenda item 8)
Wang, Min – E/2010/SR.23
SCIENCE AND TECHNOLOGY–DEVELOPMENT
(Agenda item 13b)
Chen, Yin – E/2010/SR.38
UN CONFERENCES–FOLLOW-UP (Agenda item 6)
Wang, Min – E/2010/SR.23

## Colombia

BRETTON WOODS INSTITUTIONS
Guerra, María Paula – E/2010/SR.5
EMPOWERMENT OF WOMEN (Agenda item 2d)
Blum, Claudia – E/2010/SR.19(B)
GENDER EQUALITY (Agenda item 2c)
Blum, Claudia – E/2010/SR.19(B)
HUMANITARIAN ASSISTANCE (Agenda item 5)
Suárez Garzón, Carlos Alberto – E/2010/SR.34;
E/2010/SR.36
WOMEN IN DEVELOPMENT (Agenda item 13k)
Blum, Claudia – E/2010/SR.19(B)
WOMEN'S ADVANCEMENT (Agenda item 14a)
Blum, Claudia – E/2010/SR.19(B)

## Congo

GENDER EQUALITY (Agenda item 2c)
Itoua, Martin – E/2010/SR.18(A)
Leckomba Loumeto-Pombo, Jeanne Françoise –
E/2010/SR.12; E/2010/SR.18(A)
Ngapi, Cornelie Adou – E/2010/SR.18(A)
POVERTY MITIGATION (Agenda item 4)
Fila, Jean-Lezin – E/2010/SR.26
REFUGEES (Agenda item 14e)
Maboundou, Raphael Dieudonné – E/2010/SR.50
REGIONAL COOPERATION–AFRICA (Agenda item 10)
Bidounga, Ruffin – E/2010/SR.20

## European Union (continued)

DEVELOPMENT FINANCE–CONFERENCE (2002 : MONTERREY, MEXICO)–FOLLOW-UP (Agenda item 6a)
    Bassompierre, Christophe de (Belgium) – E/2010/SR.47
EMPOWERMENT OF WOMEN (Agenda item 2d)
    Grauls, Jan (Belgium) – E/2010/SR.17(B)
ENVIRONMENT (Agenda item 13e)
    Delieux, Delphine (Belgium) – E/2010/SR.43
GENDER EQUALITY (Agenda item 2c)
    Bassompierre, Christophe de (Belgium) – E/2010/SR.19(A)
    Grauls, Jan (Belgium) – E/2010/SR.17(B)
HUMAN SETTLEMENTS (Agenda item 13d)
    Delieux, Delphine (Belgium) – E/2010/SR.43
HUMANITARIAN ASSISTANCE (Agenda item 5)
    Grauls, Jan (Belgium) – E/2010/SR.33
    Lallemand Zeller, Loïc – E/2010/SR.35
    Stewart-David, Julia – E/2010/SR.34
INFORMATICS–INTERNATIONAL COOPERATION (Agenda item 7c)
    Bassompierre, Christophe de (Belgium) – E/2010/SR.38
INTERNATIONAL FINANCIAL INSTITUTIONS (Agenda item 2a)
    Spatolisano, Maria – E/2010/SR.19(A)
LEAST DEVELOPED COUNTRIES–INTERNATIONAL DECADE (2001-2010) (Agenda item 6b)
    Lambert, Thomas (Belgium) – E/2010/SR.37
NARCOTIC DRUGS (Agenda item 14d)
    Geest, Ellen de (Belgium) – E/2010/SR.44
NON-GOVERNMENTAL ORGANIZATIONS (Agenda item 12)
    Grauls, Jan (Belgium) – E/2010/SR.39
OPERATIONAL ACTIVITIES–UN (Agenda item 3)
    Grauls, Jan (Belgium) – E/2010/SR.30
POVERTY MITIGATION (Agenda item 4)
    Bassompierre, Christophe de (Belgium) – E/2010/SR.23
RESOLUTIONS–UN. GENERAL ASSEMBLY–IMPLEMENTATION (Agenda item 8)
    Bassompierre, Christophe de (Belgium) – E/2010/SR.23
SCIENCE AND TECHNOLOGY–DEVELOPMENT (Agenda item 13b)
    Bassompierre, Christophe de (Belgium) – E/2010/SR.38
SOCIAL DEVELOPMENT (Agenda item 14b)
    Geest, Ellen de (Belgium) – E/2010/SR.44
SUSTAINABLE DEVELOPMENT (Agenda item 13a)
    Delieux, Delphine (Belgium) – E/2010/SR.43
TAXATION (Agenda item 13h)
    Bassompierre, Christophe de (Belgium) – E/2010/SR.43
UN CONFERENCES–FOLLOW-UP (Agenda item 6)
    Bassompierre, Christophe de (Belgium) – E/2010/SR.23
UN POLICY RECOMMENDATIONS–FOLLOW-UP (Agenda item 3a)
    Charlier, Pierre (Belgium) – E/2010/SR.29; E/2010/SR.46
UNDP/UNFPA (Agenda item 3b)
    Charlier, Pierre (Belgium) – E/2010/SR.29

## European Union (continued)

UNICEF (Agenda item 3b)
    Charlier, Pierre (Belgium) – E/2010/SR.29
WOMEN'S ADVANCEMENT (Agenda item 14a)
    Nihon, Nicolas (Belgium) – E/2010/SR.42
WORLD FOOD PROGRAMME (Agenda item 3b)
    Charlier, Pierre (Belgium) – E/2010/SR.29

## FAO

EMPOWERMENT OF WOMEN (Agenda item 2d)
    Ratsifandrihamanana, Lila Hanitra – E/2010/SR.19(B)
GENDER EQUALITY (Agenda item 2c)
    Ratsifandrihamanana, Lila Hanitra – E/2010/SR.19(B)
WOMEN IN DEVELOPMENT (Agenda item 13k)
    Ratsifandrihamanana, Lila Hanitra – E/2010/SR.19(B)

## FAO. Committee on World Food Security. Chair

SUSTAINABLE DEVELOPMENT (Agenda item 13a)
    De Luna, Noel – E/2010/SR.43

## FAO. Emergency Operations and Rehabilitation Division. Director

HUMANITARIAN ASSISTANCE (Agenda item 5)
    Thomas, Laurent – E/2010/SR.35; E/2010/SR.35

## Feinstein International Center

HUMANITARIAN ASSISTANCE (Agenda item 5)
    Walker, Peter – E/2010/SR.35

## Finland

DEVELOPMENT COOPERATION FORUM (Agenda item 2b)
    Vayrynen, Paavo – E/2010/SR.13
GENDER EQUALITY (Agenda item 2c)
    Koukku-Ronde, Ritva – E/2010/SR.15(A); E/2010/SR.17(A)

## France

BRETTON WOODS INSTITUTIONS
    Cormon-Veyssière, Florence – E/2010/SR.7
    Follain, Moncef – E/2010/SR.5; E/2010/SR.6
GENDER EQUALITY (Agenda item 2c)
    Heyfries, Fabrice – E/2010/SR.15(A)
    Sportis, Cécile – E/2010/SR.12; E/2010/SR.15(A); E/2010/SR.18(A)
    Vianès, Michèle – E/2010/SR.15(A)

## Gambia

EMPOWERMENT OF WOMEN (Agenda item 2d)
    Waffa-Ogoo, Susan – E/2010/SR.18(B)

## Geena Davis Institute on Gender in Media

GENDER EQUALITY (Agenda item 2c)
    Davis, Geena – E/2010/SR.11

## Germany

BRETTON WOODS INSTITUTIONS
    Wittig, Peter – E/2010/SR.5

## Germany (continued)

EMPOWERMENT OF WOMEN (Agenda item 2d)
Wittig, Peter – E/2010/SR.18(B)
GENDER EQUALITY (Agenda item 2c)
Wittig, Peter – E/2010/SR.12

## Ghana

EMPOWERMENT OF WOMEN (Agenda item 2d)
Christian, Leslie – E/2010/SR.18(B)
HUMANITARIAN ASSISTANCE (Agenda item 5)
Christian, Leslie – E/2010/SR.33
Tachie-Menson, Henry – E/2010/SR.34

## Global Facility for Disaster Reduction and Recovery

HUMANITARIAN ASSISTANCE (Agenda item 5)
Jha, Saroj Kumar – E/2010/SR.35

## Group of 77

BRETTON WOODS INSTITUTIONS
Alyemany, Khaled (Yemen) – E/2010/SR.4;
E/2010/SR.5
DECOLONIZATION (Agenda item 9)
Al-Aud, Awsan Abdullah (Yemen) – E/2010/SR.41
DEVELOPMENT FINANCE–CONFERENCE (2002 :
MONTERREY, MEXICO)–FOLLOW-UP (Agenda item
6a)
Al Shami, Waheed Abdulwahab Ahmed (Yemen) –
E/2010/SR.46
Al-Aud, Awsan Abdullah (Yemen) – E/2010/SR.47
EMPOWERMENT OF WOMEN (Agenda item 2d)
Al Shami, Waheed Abdulwahab Ahmed (Yemen) –
E/2010/SR.47
Alsaidi, Abdullah M. (Yemen) – E/2010/SR.17(B)
GENDER EQUALITY (Agenda item 2c)
Al Shami, Waheed Abdulwahab Ahmed (Yemen) –
E/2010/SR.47
Alsaidi, Abdullah M. (Yemen) – E/2010/SR.17(B)
HUMANITARIAN ASSISTANCE (Agenda item 5)
Al Shami, Waheed Abdulwahab Ahmed (Yemen) –
E/2010/SR.33
INFORMATICS–INTERNATIONAL COOPERATION
(Agenda item 7c)
Al-Aud, Awsan Abdullah (Yemen) – E/2010/SR.38
LEAST DEVELOPED COUNTRIES–INTERNATIONAL
DECADE (2001-2010) (Agenda item 6b)
Al-Aud, Awsan Abdullah (Yemen) – E/2010/SR.37;
E/2010/SR.41
OPERATIONAL ACTIVITIES–UN (Agenda item 3)
Alsaidi, Abdullah M. (Yemen) – E/2010/SR.30
PALESTINIANS–TERRITORIES OCCUPIED BY
ISRAEL–LIVING CONDITIONS (Agenda item 11)
Al-Aud, Awsan Abdullah (Yemen) – E/2010/SR.41
POVERTY MITIGATION (Agenda item 4)
Alsaidi, Abdullah M. (Yemen) – E/2010/SR.23
REGIONAL COOPERATION (Agenda item 10)
Al-Aud, Awsan Abdullah (Yemen) – E/2010/SR.41
RESOLUTIONS–UN. GENERAL ASSEMBLY–
IMPLEMENTATION (Agenda item 8)
Alsaidi, Abdullah M. (Yemen) – E/2010/SR.23
SCIENCE AND TECHNOLOGY–DEVELOPMENT
(Agenda item 13b)
Al-Aud, Awsan Abdullah (Yemen) – E/2010/SR.38

## Group of 77 (continued)

TOBACCO–HEALTH (Agenda item 7g)
Al-Aud, Awsan Abdullah (Yemen) – E/2010/SR.38
UN CONFERENCES–FOLLOW-UP (Agenda item 6)
Alsaidi, Abdullah M. (Yemen) – E/2010/SR.23

## Group of Landlocked Developing Countries

BRETTON WOODS INSTITUTIONS
Dos Santos, José Antonio (Paraguay) –
E/2010/SR.7

## Group of Least Developed Countries

BRETTON WOODS INSTITUTIONS
Acharya, Gyan Chandra (Nepal) – E/2010/SR.4
Acharya, Madhu Raman (Nepal) – E/2010/SR.5
Aguirre, Patricio (Nepal) – E/2010/SR.6
EMPOWERMENT OF WOMEN (Agenda item 2d)
Acharya, Gyan Chandra (Nepal) – E/2010/SR.17(B)
GENDER EQUALITY (Agenda item 2c)
Acharya, Gyan Chandra (Nepal) – E/2010/SR.17(B)
LEAST DEVELOPED COUNTRIES–INTERNATIONAL
DECADE (2001-2010) (Agenda item 6b)
Acharya, Gyan Chandra (Nepal) – E/2010/SR.37;
E/2010/SR.46

## Guatemala

BRETTON WOODS INSTITUTIONS
Rosenthal, Gert – E/2010/SR.4; E/2010/SR.6;
E/2010/SR.7
GENDER EQUALITY (Agenda item 2c)
Argueta de Barillas, Marisol – E/2010/SR.17(A)
Montenegro, Mirna – E/2010/SR.12
Rodríguez Pineda, Ana Cristina – E/2010/SR.12
Rosenthal, Gert – E/2010/SR.11; E/2010/SR.12;
E/2010/SR.15(A); E/2010/SR.17(A);
E/2010/SR.19(B)
Slowing-Umaña, Karin – E/2010/SR.12
GENDER MAINSTREAMING–UN SYSTEM (Agenda
item 7e)
Rosenthal, Gert – E/2010/SR.19(B)
HUMANITARIAN ASSISTANCE (Agenda item 5)
Del Águila-Castillo, María José – E/2010/SR.36
REGIONAL COOPERATION–LATIN AMERICA AND
THE CARIBBEAN (Agenda item 10)
Rosenthal, Gert – E/2010/SR.20
SUSTAINABLE DEVELOPMENT (Agenda item 13a)
Leiva Roesch, Jimena – E/2010/SR.43
UN. PERMANENT FORUM ON INDIGENOUS ISSUES
(Agenda item 14h)
Taracena Secaira, Connie – E/2010/SR.44
WOMEN'S ADVANCEMENT (Agenda item 14a)
Taracena Secaira, Connie – E/2010/SR.42

## Haiti

ECONOMIC ASSISTANCE–HAITI (Agenda item 7d)
Exantus, William – E/2010/SR.46
Voltaire, Leslie – E/2010/SR.32

## HelpAge International

EMPOWERMENT OF WOMEN (Agenda item 2d)
Lear, Judy – E/2010/SR.19(B)

## HelpAge International (continued)

GENDER EQUALITY (Agenda item 2c)
Lear, Judy – E/2010/SR.19(B)

## Holy See

EMPOWERMENT OF WOMEN (Agenda item 2d)
Migliore, Celestino – E/2010/SR.18(B)
HUMANITARIAN ASSISTANCE (Agenda item 5)
Bharanikulangara, Kuriakose – E/2010/SR.36

## Honduras

EMPOWERMENT OF WOMEN (Agenda item 2d)
Flores, Mary Elizabeth – E/2010/SR.18(B)

## IBRD

BRETTON WOODS INSTITUTIONS
Braga, Carlos Alberto Primo – E/2010/SR.4;
E/2010/SR.5; E/2010/SR.6
Brandt, Anna Margaretha – E/2010/SR.4
Cliffe, Sarah – E/2010/SR.6
Dib, Sid Ahmed – E/2010/SR.5
Kleist, Ruediger Wilhelm von – E/2010/SR.5
Kvasov, Alexey – E/2010/SR.4; E/2010/SR.6
Moorehead, Susanna – E/2010/SR.4
Treffers, Rudolf Jan – E/2010/SR.6

## IBRD. Poverty Reduction and Economic Management

BRETTON WOODS INSTITUTIONS
Lewis, Jeffrey D. – E/2010/SR.5
INTERNATIONAL FINANCIAL INSTITUTIONS (Agenda item 2a)
Santos Filho, Otavio Canuto dos – E/2010/SR.19(A)

## ILO

BRETTON WOODS INSTITUTIONS
Stewart, Jane – E/2010/SR.5
DEVELOPMENT FINANCE–CONFERENCE (2002 : MONTERREY, MEXICO)–FOLLOW-UP (Agenda item 6a)
Diop, Assane – E/2010/SR.23
ECONOMIC ASSISTANCE–HAITI (Agenda item 7d)
Lazarte, Alfredo – E/2010/SR.32
EMPOWERMENT OF WOMEN (Agenda item 2d)
Gastaldo, Elena – E/2010/SR.19(B)
GENDER EQUALITY (Agenda item 2c)
Gastaldo, Elena – E/2010/SR.19(B)

## IMF

BRETTON WOODS INSTITUTIONS
Barendregt, Ester – E/2010/SR.5; E/2010/SR.7
Geadah, Sami – E/2010/SR.7
Luo, Yang – E/2010/SR.7

## IMF. Strategy, Policy and Review Department. Director

INTERNATIONAL FINANCIAL INSTITUTIONS (Agenda item 2a)
Moghadam, Reza – E/2010/SR.19(A)

## India

BRETTON WOODS INSTITUTIONS
Puri, Hardeep Singh – E/2010/SR.6
EMPOWERMENT OF WOMEN (Agenda item 2d)
Kaur, Preneet – E/2010/SR.19(B)
GENDER EQUALITY (Agenda item 2c)
Kaur, Preneet – E/2010/SR.19(B)
HUMANITARIAN ASSISTANCE (Agenda item 5)
Jaiswal, Randhir Kumar – E/2010/SR.36
LEAST DEVELOPED COUNTRIES–INTERNATIONAL DECADE (2001-2010) (Agenda item 6b)
Jaiswal, Randhir Kumar – E/2010/SR.37
POVERTY MITIGATION (Agenda item 4)
Gómez Durán, Rosa Delia – E/2010/SR.26
Jaiswal, Randhir Kumar – E/2010/SR.26
RESOLUTIONS–UN. GENERAL ASSEMBLY–IMPLEMENTATION (Agenda item 8)
Gómez Durán, Rosa Delia – E/2010/SR.26
Jaiswal, Randhir Kumar – E/2010/SR.26
UN. PERMANENT FORUM ON INDIGENOUS ISSUES (Agenda item 14h)
Jaiswal, Randhir Kumar – E/2010/SR.44
UN CONFERENCES–FOLLOW-UP (Agenda item 6)
Gómez Durán, Rosa Delia – E/2010/SR.26
Jaiswal, Randhir Kumar – E/2010/SR.26
UN POLICY RECOMMENDATIONS–FOLLOW-UP (Agenda item 3a)
Jaiswal, Randhir Kumar – E/2010/SR.31
UNDP/UNFPA (Agenda item 3b)
Jaiswal, Randhir Kumar – E/2010/SR.31
UNICEF (Agenda item 3b)
Jaiswal, Randhir Kumar – E/2010/SR.31
WOMEN IN DEVELOPMENT (Agenda item 13k)
Kaur, Preneet – E/2010/SR.19(B)
WOMEN'S ADVANCEMENT (Agenda item 14a)
Kaur, Preneet – E/2010/SR.19(B)
WORLD FOOD PROGRAMME (Agenda item 3b)
Jaiswal, Randhir Kumar – E/2010/SR.31

## Indonesia

BRETTON WOODS INSTITUTIONS
Kleib, Hasan – E/2010/SR.4
Nasir, Arrmanatha – E/2010/SR.7
Wahab, Dewi Savitri – E/2010/SR.5; E/2010/SR.6
CRIME PREVENTION (Agenda item 14c)
Tutuhatunewa, Spica Alphanya – E/2010/SR.44
GENDER EQUALITY (Agenda item 2c)
Kleib, Hasan – E/2010/SR.17(A)
HUMANITARIAN ASSISTANCE (Agenda item 5)
Petranto, Ade – E/2010/SR.36
INTERNATIONAL FINANCIAL INSTITUTIONS (Agenda item 2a)
Herawan, Cecep – E/2010/SR.19(A)
NARCOTIC DRUGS (Agenda item 14d)
Tutuhatunewa, Spica Alphanya – E/2010/SR.44
OPERATIONAL ACTIVITIES–UN (Agenda item 3)
Sardjana, Agus – E/2010/SR.30
PALESTINIANS–TERRITORIES OCCUPIED BY ISRAEL–LIVING CONDITIONS (Agenda item 11)
Khan, Yusra – E/2010/SR.41
POVERTY MITIGATION (Agenda item 4)
Petranto, Ade – E/2010/SR.23

## Indonesia (continued)

REGIONAL COOPERATION (Agenda item 10)
  Herawan, Cecep – E/2010/SR.20
RESOLUTIONS–UN. GENERAL ASSEMBLY–
IMPLEMENTATION (Agenda item 8)
  Petranto, Ade – E/2010/SR.23
SUSTAINABLE DEVELOPMENT (Agenda item 13a)
  Rahdiansyah, Danny – E/2010/SR.43
UN CONFERENCES–FOLLOW-UP (Agenda item 6)
  Petranto, Ade – E/2010/SR.23

## Inter-Parliamentary Union

EMPOWERMENT OF WOMEN (Agenda item 2d)
  Mporogomyi, Kilontsi – E/2010/SR.19(B)
WOMEN'S ADVANCEMENT (Agenda item 14a)
  Mporogomyi, Kilontsi – E/2010/SR.19(B)

## International Alliance of Women

EMPOWERMENT OF WOMEN (Agenda item 2d)
  Sarlis, Irini – E/2010/SR.19(B)
GENDER EQUALITY (Agenda item 2c)
  Sarlis, Irini – E/2010/SR.19(B)

## International Association of Economic and Social Councils and Similar Institutions

EMPOWERMENT OF WOMEN (Agenda item 2d)
  Marzano, Antonio – E/2010/SR.19(B)
GENDER EQUALITY (Agenda item 2c)
  Marzano, Antonio – E/2010/SR.19(B)
POVERTY MITIGATION (Agenda item 4)
  Marzano, Antonio – E/2010/SR.21

## International Chamber of Commerce

BRETTON WOODS INSTITUTIONS
  Kantrow, Louise – E/2010/SR.4
  Onambèlè, Joseph – E/2010/SR.7

## International Committee for Arab-Israeli Reconciliation

EMPOWERMENT OF WOMEN (Agenda item 2d)
  Karmakar, Sudhangshu – E/2010/SR.19(B)
GENDER EQUALITY (Agenda item 2c)
  Karmakar, Sudhangshu – E/2010/SR.19(B)

## International Committee of the Red Cross

HUMANITARIAN ASSISTANCE (Agenda item 5)
  Stillhart, Dominik – E/2010/SR.34

## International Federation of Red Cross and Red Crescent Societies

EMPOWERMENT OF WOMEN (Agenda item 2d)
  Jilani, Marwan – E/2010/SR.19(B)
POVERTY MITIGATION (Agenda item 4)
  Oosterhof, Pytrik Dieuwke – E/2010/SR.26
UN CONFERENCES–FOLLOW-UP (Agenda item 6)
  Oosterhof, Pytrik Dieuwke – E/2010/SR.26
WOMEN'S ADVANCEMENT (Agenda item 14a)
  Jilani, Marwan – E/2010/SR.19(B)

## International Institute for Human Rights, Environment and Development (Kathmandu)

BRETTON WOODS INSTITUTIONS
  Siwakoti, Gopal Krishna – E/2010/SR.6

## International Labour Office

UN POLICY RECOMMENDATIONS–FOLLOW-UP
(Agenda item 3a)
  Amorim, Anita – E/2010/SR.31
UNDP/UNFPA (Agenda item 3b)
  Amorim, Anita – E/2010/SR.31
UNICEF (Agenda item 3b)
  Amorim, Anita – E/2010/SR.31
WORLD FOOD PROGRAMME (Agenda item 3b)
  Amorim, Anita – E/2010/SR.31

## International Monetary and Financial Committee

BRETTON WOODS INSTITUTIONS
  Dimian, Hany (Egypt) – E/2010/SR.4

## International Narcotics Control Board. President

NARCOTIC DRUGS (Agenda item 14d)
  Ghodse, Hamid A. – E/2010/SR.44

## International Olympic Committee

GENDER EQUALITY (Agenda item 2c)
  DeFrantz, Anita L. – E/2010/SR.19(B)

## International Organization for Migration

GENDER EQUALITY (Agenda item 2c)
  Muedin, Amy – E/2010/SR.19(B)
GENDER MAINSTREAMING–UN SYSTEM (Agenda
item 7e)
  Muedin, Amy – E/2010/SR.19(B)
HUMANITARIAN ASSISTANCE (Agenda item 5)
  Muedin, Amy – E/2010/SR.36

## International Red Cross

HUMANITARIAN ASSISTANCE (Agenda item 5)
  Mosquini, Elyse – E/2010/SR.36

## International Right to Life Federation

EMPOWERMENT OF WOMEN (Agenda item 2d)
  Head, Jeanne – E/2010/SR.17(B)
GENDER EQUALITY (Agenda item 2c)
  Head, Jeanne – E/2010/SR.17(B)

## International Trade Centre UNCTAD/WTO. Executive Director

INTERNATIONAL FINANCIAL INSTITUTIONS (Agenda
item 2a)
  Francis, Patricia – E/2010/SR.19(A)

## Iran (Islamic Republic of)

BRETTON WOODS INSTITUTIONS
  Hassani Nejad Pirkouhi, Mohammad – E/2010/SR.6
EMPOWERMENT OF WOMEN (Agenda item 2d)
  Farahi, Hossin – E/2010/SR.17(B)
GENDER EQUALITY (Agenda item 2c)
  Farahi, Hossin – E/2010/SR.17(B)

## Iran (Islamic Republic of) (continued)

INFORMATICS–INTERNATIONAL COOPERATION
(Agenda item 7c)
Rajabi, Ahmad – E/2010/SR.38
NARCOTIC DRUGS (Agenda item 14d)
Rajabi, Ahmad – E/2010/SR.44
PALESTINIANS–TERRITORIES OCCUPIED BY
ISRAEL–LIVING CONDITIONS (Agenda item 11)
Rajabi, Ahmad – E/2010/SR.41
SCIENCE AND TECHNOLOGY–DEVELOPMENT
(Agenda item 13b)
Rajabi, Ahmad – E/2010/SR.38

## Iraq

EMPOWERMENT OF WOMEN (Agenda item 2d)
Al Bayati, Hamid – E/2010/SR.19(B)
ENVIRONMENT (Agenda item 13e)
Al Bayati, Hamid – E/2010/SR.43
GENDER EQUALITY (Agenda item 2c)
Al Bayati, Hamid – E/2010/SR.19(B)
HUMAN RIGHTS (Agenda item 14g)
Al-Obaidi, Yahya Ibraheem Fadhil – E/2010/SR.44
HUMANITARIAN ASSISTANCE (Agenda item 5)
Al Bayati, Hamid – E/2010/SR.36
Al-Seedi, Razzaq Khleef Mansoor – E/2010/SR.34
INFORMATICS–INTERNATIONAL COOPERATION
(Agenda item 7c)
Al Bayati, Hamid – E/2010/SR.38
REGIONAL COOPERATION (Agenda item 10)
Al-Seedi, Razzaq Khleef Mansoor – E/2010/SR.20
SCIENCE AND TECHNOLOGY–DEVELOPMENT
(Agenda item 13b)
Al Bayati, Hamid – E/2010/SR.38
SUSTAINABLE DEVELOPMENT (Agenda item 13a)
Al Bayati, Hamid – E/2010/SR.43
WOMEN IN DEVELOPMENT (Agenda item 13k)
Al Bayati, Hamid – E/2010/SR.19(B)
WOMEN'S ADVANCEMENT (Agenda item 14a)
Al Bayati, Hamid – E/2010/SR.19(B)
Mohammed, Ahmed Hameed – E/2010/SR.42

## Israel

EMPOWERMENT OF WOMEN (Agenda item 2d)
Renford, Mazal – E/2010/SR.17(B)
GENDER EQUALITY (Agenda item 2c)
Renford, Mazal – E/2010/SR.12; E/2010/SR.15(A);
E/2010/SR.17(B); E/2010/SR.18(A)
NON-GOVERNMENTAL ORGANIZATIONS (Agenda
item 12)
Carmon, Daniel – E/2010/SR.39
PALESTINIANS–TERRITORIES OCCUPIED BY
ISRAEL–LIVING CONDITIONS (Agenda item 11)
Davidovich, Shulamit Yona – E/2010/SR.41;
E/2010/SR.46
POVERTY MITIGATION (Agenda item 4)
Fluss, Ilan Simon – E/2010/SR.26
REGIONAL COOPERATION (Agenda item 10)
Renford, Mazal – E/2010/SR.20
RESOLUTIONS–UN. GENERAL ASSEMBLY–
IMPLEMENTATION (Agenda item 8)
Fluss, Ilan Simon – E/2010/SR.26
UN CONFERENCES–FOLLOW-UP (Agenda item 6)
Fluss, Ilan Simon – E/2010/SR.26

## Israel (continued)

UN POLICY RECOMMENDATIONS–FOLLOW-UP
(Agenda item 3a)
Fluss, Ilan Simon – E/2010/SR.29; E/2010/SR.31
UNDP/UNFPA (Agenda item 3b)
Fluss, Ilan Simon – E/2010/SR.31
UNICEF (Agenda item 3b)
Fluss, Ilan Simon – E/2010/SR.31
WOMEN'S ADVANCEMENT (Agenda item 14a)
Davidovich, Shulamit Yona – E/2010/SR.42
WORLD FOOD PROGRAMME (Agenda item 3b)
Fluss, Ilan Simon – E/2010/SR.31

## Italy

EMPOWERMENT OF WOMEN (Agenda item 2d)
Carfagna, Mara – E/2010/SR.17(B)
GENDER EQUALITY (Agenda item 2c)
Carfagna, Mara – E/2010/SR.17(B)

## Ius Primi Viri International Association

SOCIAL DEVELOPMENT (Agenda item 14b)
Filiotis, Georgia – E/2010/SR.44

## Japan

BRETTON WOODS INSTITUTIONS
Murakami, Kenju – E/2010/SR.5
Sumi, Shigeki – E/2010/SR.4; E/2010/SR.6
EMPOWERMENT OF WOMEN (Agenda item 2d)
Okuda, Norihiro – E/2010/SR.19(B)
GENDER EQUALITY (Agenda item 2c)
Okuda, Norihiro – E/2010/SR.18(A);
E/2010/SR.19(B)
HUMANITARIAN ASSISTANCE (Agenda item 5)
Sumi, Shigeki – E/2010/SR.33
NON-GOVERNMENTAL ORGANIZATIONS (Agenda
item 12)
Fujimoto, Shoko – E/2010/SR.39
UN POLICY RECOMMENDATIONS–FOLLOW-UP
(Agenda item 3a)
Yamashita, Nozomu – E/2010/SR.31
UNDP/UNFPA (Agenda item 3b)
Yamashita, Nozomu – E/2010/SR.31
UNICEF (Agenda item 3b)
Yamashita, Nozomu – E/2010/SR.31
WOMEN IN DEVELOPMENT (Agenda item 13k)
Okuda, Norihiro – E/2010/SR.19(B)
WOMEN'S ADVANCEMENT (Agenda item 14a)
Okuda, Norihiro – E/2010/SR.19(B)
WORLD FOOD PROGRAMME (Agenda item 3b)
Yamashita, Nozomu – E/2010/SR.31

## Jubilee Campaign

BRETTON WOODS INSTITUTIONS
Hanfstaengl, Eva – E/2010/SR.5

## Kenya

EMPOWERMENT OF WOMEN (Agenda item 2d)
Manyala Keya, Atanas – E/2010/SR.17(B)
GENDER EQUALITY (Agenda item 2c)
Manyala Keya, Atanas – E/2010/SR.17(B)
HUMANITARIAN ASSISTANCE (Agenda item 5)
Shaban, Naomi N. – E/2010/SR.33; E/2010/SR.35

## Kenya (continued)

INTERNATIONAL FINANCIAL INSTITUTIONS (Agenda item 2a)
Sambili, Edward – E/2010/SR.19(A)

## Latvia

EMPOWERMENT OF WOMEN (Agenda item 2d)
Silkalna, Solveiga – E/2010/SR.17(B)
GENDER EQUALITY (Agenda item 2c)
Silkalna, Solveiga – E/2010/SR.17(B)

## Liberia

GENDER EQUALITY (Agenda item 2c)
Chenoweth, Florence – E/2010/SR.11

## Libyan Arab Jamahiriya

BRETTON WOODS INSTITUTIONS
Alahraf, Mohamed A. A. – E/2010/SR.4

## Liechtenstein

EMPOWERMENT OF WOMEN (Agenda item 2d)
Wenaweser, Christian – E/2010/SR.18(B)
HUMANITARIAN ASSISTANCE (Agenda item 5)
Dornig, Swen – E/2010/SR.36

## Lithuania

EMPOWERMENT OF WOMEN (Agenda item 2d)
Cekuolis, Dalius – E/2010/SR.18(B)

## Malawi

UN POLICY RECOMMENDATIONS–FOLLOW-UP (Agenda item 3a)
Ning'ang'a, Eric – E/2010/SR.29
UNDP/UNFPA (Agenda item 3b)
Ning'ang'a, Eric – E/2010/SR.29
UNICEF (Agenda item 3b)
Ning'ang'a, Eric – E/2010/SR.29
WORLD FOOD PROGRAMME (Agenda item 3b)
Ning'ang'a, Eric – E/2010/SR.29

## Malaysia

BRETTON WOODS INSTITUTIONS
Zainal Abidin, Raja Nushirwan – E/2010/SR.4;
E/2010/SR.5

## Maldives

SUSTAINABLE DEVELOPMENT (Agenda item 13a)
Hussain, Thilmeeza – E/2010/SR.43

## Malta

HUMANITARIAN ASSISTANCE (Agenda item 5)
Looz Karageorgiades, Bertrand de – E/2010/SR.36

## Mexico

BRETTON WOODS INSTITUTIONS
González Segura, Noel – E/2010/SR.6; E/2010/SR.7
Heller, Claude – E/2010/SR.5
Rovirosa, Socorro – E/2010/SR.4

## Mexico (continued)

DEVELOPMENT FINANCE–CONFERENCE (2002 : MONTERREY, MEXICO)–FOLLOW-UP (Agenda item 6a)
González Segura, Noel – E/2010/SR.26;
E/2010/SR.46
EMPOWERMENT OF WOMEN (Agenda item 2d)
Heller, Claude – E/2010/SR.18(B)
GENDER EQUALITY (Agenda item 2c)
Carreño, Aida – E/2010/SR.12
García Gaytán, Maria del Rocio – E/2010/SR.11
HUMANITARIAN ASSISTANCE (Agenda item 5)
Heller, Claude – E/2010/SR.36

## Mongolia

BRETTON WOODS INSTITUTIONS
Enkhtsetseg, Ochir – E/2010/SR.6
Nyam-Osor, Tuya – E/2010/SR.5
GENDER EQUALITY (Agenda item 2c)
Enkhnasan, Nasan-Ulzii – E/2010/SR.18(A)
Tugsjargal, Gandi – E/2010/SR.18(A)
Urantsooj, Gombosuren – E/2010/SR.18(A)

## Morocco

BRETTON WOODS INSTITUTIONS
Iziraren, Tarik – E/2010/SR.5
EMPOWERMENT OF WOMEN (Agenda item 2d)
Skalli, Nouzha – E/2010/SR.17(B)
GENDER EQUALITY (Agenda item 2c)
Skalli, Nouzha – E/2010/SR.11; E/2010/SR.15(A);
E/2010/SR.17(B)
HUMANITARIAN ASSISTANCE (Agenda item 5)
Loulichki, Mohammed – E/2010/SR.36
LEAST DEVELOPED COUNTRIES–INTERNATIONAL DECADE (2001-2010) (Agenda item 6b)
Loulichki, Mohammed – E/2010/SR.37
TOBACCO–HEALTH (Agenda item 7g)
Belakhel, Latifa – E/2010/SR.37

## Mozambique

BRETTON WOODS INSTITUTIONS
Macheve, António – E/2010/SR.7
EMPOWERMENT OF WOMEN (Agenda item 2d)
Abreu, Alcinda Antonio de – E/2010/SR.17(B)
GENDER EQUALITY (Agenda item 2c)
Abreu, Alcinda Antonio de – E/2010/SR.17(B)

## Namibia

EMPOWERMENT OF WOMEN (Agenda item 2d)
Sioka, Doreen – E/2010/SR.17(B)
GENDER EQUALITY (Agenda item 2c)
Chirawu, Tapera O. – E/2010/SR.15(A)
Sioka, Doreen – E/2010/SR.15(A); E/2010/SR.17(B)

## National Right to Life Educational Trust Fund (United States)

REGIONAL COOPERATION (Agenda item 10)
Head, Jeanne – E/2010/SR.20

## Netherlands

GENDER EQUALITY (Agenda item 2c)
Dijksterhuis, Robert – E/2010/SR.12
Klerk, Piet de – E/2010/SR.17(A)
Schaper, Herman – E/2010/SR.12; E/2010/SR.15(A)
PALESTINIANS–TERRITORIES OCCUPIED BY
ISRAEL–LIVING CONDITIONS (Agenda item 11)
Van der Velden, Mark – E/2010/SR.46

## New Rules for Global Finance Coalition

BRETTON WOODS INSTITUTIONS
Griesgraber, Jo Marie – E/2010/SR.7

## NGO Committee on Financing for Development

BRETTON WOODS INSTITUTIONS
Dance, Kevin – E/2010/SR.4

## NGO Coordination Committee for Iraq

HUMANITARIAN ASSISTANCE (Agenda item 5)
Mawazini, Fyras – E/2010/SR.34

## Nicaragua

INTERNATIONAL FINANCIAL INSTITUTIONS (Agenda
item 2a)
Oquist, Paul – E/2010/SR.19(A)

## Nigeria

EMPOWERMENT OF WOMEN (Agenda item 2d)
Nwadinobi, Ezinne – E/2010/SR.19(B)
WOMEN IN DEVELOPMENT (Agenda item 13k)
Nwadinobi, Ezinne – E/2010/SR.19(B)
WOMEN'S ADVANCEMENT (Agenda item 14a)
Nwadinobi, Ezinne – E/2010/SR.19(B)

## Norway

BRETTON WOODS INSTITUTIONS
Fiskaa, Ingrid – E/2010/SR.4
GENDER EQUALITY (Agenda item 2c)
Fiskaa, Ingrid – E/2010/SR.17(A)
Moberg, Mette – E/2010/SR.17(A)
Oppegaard, Svein – E/2010/SR.17(A)
Sundnes, Trine Lise – E/2010/SR.17(A)
HUMANITARIAN ASSISTANCE (Agenda item 5)
Eckey, Susan – E/2010/SR.33; E/2010/SR.34
NON-GOVERNMENTAL ORGANIZATIONS (Agenda
item 12)
Tollefsen, Petter – E/2010/SR.39
UN POLICY RECOMMENDATIONS–FOLLOW-UP
(Agenda item 3a)
Ajamay, Astrid Helle – E/2010/SR.29; E/2010/SR.31
UNDP/UNFPA (Agenda item 3b)
Ajamay, Astrid Helle – E/2010/SR.29; E/2010/SR.31
UNICEF (Agenda item 3b)
Ajamay, Astrid Helle – E/2010/SR.29; E/2010/SR.31
WORLD FOOD PROGRAMME (Agenda item 3b)
Ajamay, Astrid Helle – E/2010/SR.29; E/2010/SR.31

## Organisation of the Islamic Conference

EMPOWERMENT OF WOMEN (Agenda item 2d)
Kalyoncu, Mehmet – E/2010/SR.19(B)

## Organisation of the Islamic Conference (continued)

GENDER EQUALITY (Agenda item 2c)
Kalyoncu, Mehmet – E/2010/SR.19(B)
HUMANITARIAN ASSISTANCE (Agenda item 5)
Gokcen, Ufuk – E/2010/SR.36
WOMEN IN DEVELOPMENT (Agenda item 13k)
Kalyoncu, Mehmet – E/2010/SR.19(B)
WOMEN'S ADVANCEMENT (Agenda item 14a)
Kalyoncu, Mehmet – E/2010/SR.19(B)

## Pakistan

EMPOWERMENT OF WOMEN (Agenda item 2d)
Khosa, Sardar Muhammad Latif Khan –
E/2010/SR.17(B)
GENDER EQUALITY (Agenda item 2c)
Khosa, Sardar Muhammad Latif Khan –
E/2010/SR.17(B)
HUMANITARIAN ASSISTANCE (Agenda item 5)
Sial, Amjad Hussain B. – E/2010/SR.33
INTERNATIONAL FINANCIAL INSTITUTIONS (Agenda
item 2a)
Khosa, Sardar Muhammad Latif Khan –
E/2010/SR.19(A)

## Palestine

PALESTINIANS–TERRITORIES OCCUPIED BY
ISRAEL–LIVING CONDITIONS (Agenda item 11)
Barghouti, Somaia – E/2010/SR.46
Hijazi, Ammar M.B. – E/2010/SR.41
WOMEN'S ADVANCEMENT (Agenda item 14a)
Zeidan, Yousef – E/2010/SR.42

## Papua New Guinea

GENDER EQUALITY (Agenda item 2c)
Aisi, Robert Guba – E/2010/SR.18(A)

## Peru

BRETTON WOODS INSTITUTIONS
Chávez, Luis Enrique – E/2010/SR.7
DEVELOPMENT FINANCE–CONFERENCE (2002 :
MONTERREY, MEXICO)–FOLLOW-UP (Agenda item
6a)
Gutiérrez, Gonzalo – E/2010/SR.26
ECONOMIC ASSISTANCE–HAITI (Agenda item 7d)
Gutiérrez, Gonzalo – E/2010/SR.32
EMPOWERMENT OF WOMEN (Agenda item 2d)
Gutiérrez, Gonzalo – E/2010/SR.18(B)
INTERNATIONAL FINANCIAL INSTITUTIONS (Agenda
item 2a)
Gutiérrez, Gonzalo – E/2010/SR.19(A)
NON-GOVERNMENTAL ORGANIZATIONS (Agenda
item 12)
Rodríguez, Roberto – E/2010/SR.39
POVERTY MITIGATION (Agenda item 4)
Gutiérrez, Gonzalo – E/2010/SR.23
REGIONAL COOPERATION–LATIN AMERICA AND
THE CARIBBEAN (Agenda item 10)
Morales, Fabiola – E/2010/SR.20
RESOLUTIONS–UN. GENERAL ASSEMBLY–
IMPLEMENTATION (Agenda item 8)
Gutiérrez, Gonzalo – E/2010/SR.23

## Peru (continued)

UN CONFERENCES–FOLLOW-UP (Agenda item 6)
Gutiérrez, Gonzalo – E/2010/SR.23
WOMEN'S ADVANCEMENT (Agenda item 14a)
Rodríguez, Roberto – E/2010/SR.42

## Philippines

EMPOWERMENT OF WOMEN (Agenda item 2d)
Cabactulan, Libran N. – E/2010/SR.19(B)
WOMEN IN DEVELOPMENT (Agenda item 13k)
Cabactulan, Libran N. – E/2010/SR.19(B)
WOMEN'S ADVANCEMENT (Agenda item 14a)
Cabactulan, Libran N. – E/2010/SR.19(B)

## Poland

EMPOWERMENT OF WOMEN (Agenda item 2d)
Fedak, Jolanta – E/2010/SR.17(B)
GENDER EQUALITY (Agenda item 2c)
Fedak, Jolanta – E/2010/SR.17(B)

## Portugal

GENDER EQUALITY (Agenda item 2c)
Cravinho, Joao Gomes – E/2010/SR.17(A);
E/2010/SR.18(A)
Pais, Elza – E/2010/SR.17(A)

## Rambhau Mhalgi Prabodhini (Organization : India)

GENDER EQUALITY (Agenda item 2c)
Sahasrabuddhe, Vinay – E/2010/SR.12;
E/2010/SR.15(A)

## Republic of Korea

BRETTON WOODS INSTITUTIONS
Shin, Boonam – E/2010/SR.5
CRIME PREVENTION (Agenda item 14c)
Hwang, Hyuni – E/2010/SR.44
EMPOWERMENT OF WOMEN (Agenda item 2d)
Shin, Kak-soo – E/2010/SR.18(B)
GENDER EQUALITY (Agenda item 2c)
Kim, Bonghyun – E/2010/SR.17(A)
Paik, Hee-Young – E/2010/SR.17(A)
HUMANITARIAN ASSISTANCE (Agenda item 5)
Kim, Soo Gwon – E/2010/SR.33
Lee, So-rie – E/2010/SR.35
INFORMATICS–INTERNATIONAL COOPERATION
(Agenda item 7c)
Kim, Chang-mo – E/2010/SR.38
LEAST DEVELOPED COUNTRIES–INTERNATIONAL
DECADE (2001-2010) (Agenda item 6b)
Kim, Chang-mo – E/2010/SR.37
REFUGEES (Agenda item 14e)
Hwang, Hyuni – E/2010/SR.44
SCIENCE AND TECHNOLOGY–DEVELOPMENT
(Agenda item 13b)
Kim, Chang-mo – E/2010/SR.38
UN POLICY RECOMMENDATIONS–FOLLOW-UP
(Agenda item 3a)
Lee, So-rie – E/2010/SR.29
UNDP/UNFPA (Agenda item 3b)
Lee, So-rie – E/2010/SR.29
WOMEN'S ADVANCEMENT (Agenda item 14a)
Hwang, Hyuni – E/2010/SR.42

## Republic of Moldova

GENDER EQUALITY (Agenda item 2c)
Bodiu, Victor – E/2010/SR.12
Bodrug-Lungu, Valentina – E/2010/SR.12
Pistrinciuk, Vadim – E/2010/SR.12

## Rio Group

BRETTON WOODS INSTITUTIONS
Aguirre, Patricio (Chile) – E/2010/SR.6
Gálvez, Eduardo (Chile) – E/2010/SR.4;
E/2010/SR.5; E/2010/SR.7

## Romania

GENDER EQUALITY (Agenda item 2c)
Miculescu, Simona Mirela – E/2010/SR.12

## Russian Federation

BRETTON WOODS INSTITUTIONS
Korneev, Mikhail – E/2010/SR.5
Vasiliev, Sergey Yu. – E/2010/SR.7
COORDINATION–REPORTS (Agenda item 7a)
Birichevskiy, Dimitry – E/2010/SR.37
DECOLONIZATION (Agenda item 9)
Alimov, Alexander S. – E/2010/SR.46
DEVELOPMENT FINANCE–CONFERENCE (2002 :
MONTERREY, MEXICO)–FOLLOW-UP (Agenda item
6a)
Birichevskiy, Dimitry – E/2010/SR.26
EMPOWERMENT OF WOMEN (Agenda item 2d)
Yakovenko, Alexander V. – E/2010/SR.17(B)
ENVIRONMENT (Agenda item 13e)
Kononuchenko, Sergei – E/2010/SR.43
GENDER EQUALITY (Agenda item 2c)
Yakovenko, Alexander V. – E/2010/SR.17(B)
GENETIC PRIVACY–DISCRIMINATION (Agenda item
14i)
Birichevskiy, Dimitry – E/2010/SR.37
HUMAN RIGHTS (Agenda item 14g)
Lukiyantsev, Grigory Y. – E/2010/SR.44
HUMANITARIAN ASSISTANCE (Agenda item 5)
Nebenzia, Vasilii – E/2010/SR.33
INFORMATICS–INTERNATIONAL COOPERATION
(Agenda item 7c)
Sirotkina, Marina A. – E/2010/SR.38
INTERNATIONAL FINANCIAL INSTITUTIONS (Agenda
item 2a)
Yakovenko, Alexander V. – E/2010/SR.19(A)
NON-GOVERNMENTAL ORGANIZATIONS (Agenda
item 12)
Lukiyantsev, Grigory Y. – E/2010/SR.39
OPERATIONAL ACTIVITIES–UN (Agenda item 3)
Piminov, Denis V. – E/2010/SR.30
POVERTY MITIGATION (Agenda item 4)
Nebenzia, Vasilii – E/2010/SR.23
REGIONAL COOPERATION–ASIA AND THE PACIFIC
(Agenda item 10)
Yakovenko, Alexander V. – E/2010/SR.20
REGIONAL COOPERATION–EUROPE (Agenda item
10)
Yakovenko, Alexander V. – E/2010/SR.20
RESOLUTIONS–UN. GENERAL ASSEMBLY–
IMPLEMENTATION (Agenda item 8)
Nebenzia, Vasilii – E/2010/SR.23

## Russian Federation (continued)

SCIENCE AND TECHNOLOGY–DEVELOPMENT
(Agenda item 13b)
    Sirotkina, Marina A. – E/2010/SR.38
SOCIAL DEVELOPMENT (Agenda item 14b)
    Rakovskiy, Nikolay S. – E/2010/SR.44
SUSTAINABLE DEVELOPMENT (Agenda item 13a)
    Kononuchenko, Sergei – E/2010/SR.43
TAXATION (Agenda item 13h)
    Kononuchenko, Sergei – E/2010/SR.43
TOBACCO–HEALTH (Agenda item 7g)
    Birichevskiy, Dimitry – E/2010/SR.37
UN CONFERENCES–FOLLOW-UP (Agenda item 6)
    Nebenzia, Vasilii – E/2010/SR.23
UN POLICY RECOMMENDATIONS–FOLLOW-UP
(Agenda item 3a)
    Savostianov, Mikhail Y. – E/2010/SR.29
WOMEN'S ADVANCEMENT (Agenda item 14a)
    Rakovskiy, Nikolay S. – E/2010/SR.42

## Rwanda

EMPOWERMENT OF WOMEN (Agenda item 2d)
    Sayinzoga, Kampeta – E/2010/SR.17(B)
GENDER EQUALITY (Agenda item 2c)
    Sayinzoga, Kampeta – E/2010/SR.17(B)

## Saint Lucia

INTERNATIONAL FINANCIAL INSTITUTIONS (Agenda
item 2a)
    St. Aimee, Donatus Keith – E/2010/SR.19(A)
NON-GOVERNMENTAL ORGANIZATIONS (Agenda
item 12)
    St. Aimee, Donatus Keith – E/2010/SR.39
PALESTINIANS–TERRITORIES OCCUPIED BY
ISRAEL–LIVING CONDITIONS (Agenda item 11)
    St. Aimee, Donatus Keith – E/2010/SR.46

## Saudi Arabia

EMPOWERMENT OF WOMEN (Agenda item 2d)
    Al Nafisee, Khalid Abdalrazaq – E/2010/SR.18(B)
NON-GOVERNMENTAL ORGANIZATIONS (Agenda
item 12)
    Al Nafisee, Khalid Abdalrazaq – E/2010/SR.39

## Senegal

GENDER EQUALITY (Agenda item 2c)
    Diop, Maymouna – E/2010/SR.11

## SIDSNet

SUSTAINABLE DEVELOPMENT (Agenda item 13a)
    St. Aimee, Donatus Keith (Saint Lucia) –
    E/2010/SR.43

## Slovakia

EMPOWERMENT OF WOMEN (Agenda item 2d)
    Algayerová, Olga – E/2010/SR.17(B)
GENDER EQUALITY (Agenda item 2c)
    Algayerová, Olga – E/2010/SR.17(B)

## Solomon Islands

LEAST DEVELOPED COUNTRIES–INTERNATIONAL
DECADE (2001-2010) (Agenda item 6b)
    Beck, Collin D. – E/2010/SR.37

## South Africa

EMPOWERMENT OF WOMEN (Agenda item 2d)
    Sangqu, Baso – E/2010/SR.18(B)
GENDER EQUALITY (Agenda item 2c)
    Dzivhani, Mbangiseni – E/2010/SR.15(A)
HUMANITARIAN ASSISTANCE (Agenda item 5)
    Nofukuka, Xolulela Lawrence – E/2010/SR.36

## Spain

BRETTON WOODS INSTITUTIONS
    Martín Carretero, José Moisés – E/2010/SR.7
GENDER EQUALITY (Agenda item 2c)
    Yánez-Barnuevo, Juan Antonio – E/2010/SR.15(A)

## Sweden

GENDER EQUALITY (Agenda item 2c)
    Grunditz, Marten – E/2010/SR.17(A)
HUMANITARIAN ASSISTANCE (Agenda item 5)
    Byman, Per – E/2010/SR.35

## Switzerland

BRETTON WOODS INSTITUTIONS
    Bachmann, Matthias – E/2010/SR.6
EMPOWERMENT OF WOMEN (Agenda item 2d)
    Chave, Olivier – E/2010/SR.17(B)
GENDER EQUALITY (Agenda item 2c)
    Chave, Olivier – E/2010/SR.17(B)
HUMANITARIAN ASSISTANCE (Agenda item 5)
    Frisch, Toni – E/2010/SR.33
OPERATIONAL ACTIVITIES–UN (Agenda item 3)
    Poretti, Mattia – E/2010/SR.30
POVERTY MITIGATION (Agenda item 4)
    Chave, Olivier – E/2010/SR.26
RESOLUTIONS–UN. GENERAL ASSEMBLY–
IMPLEMENTATION (Agenda item 8)
    Chave, Olivier – E/2010/SR.26
UN CONFERENCES–FOLLOW-UP (Agenda item 6)
    Chave, Olivier – E/2010/SR.26

## Syrian Arab Republic

PALESTINIANS–TERRITORIES OCCUPIED BY
ISRAEL–LIVING CONDITIONS (Agenda item 11)
    Ja'afari, Bashar – E/2010/SR.41

## Timor-Leste

GENDER EQUALITY (Agenda item 2c)
    Borges, Sofia – E/2010/SR.18(A)

## Turkey

BRETTON WOODS INSTITUTIONS
    Dilekli, Evren – E/2010/SR.5; E/2010/SR.6
EMPOWERMENT OF WOMEN (Agenda item 2d)
    Apakan, Ertugrul – E/2010/SR.18(B)
LEAST DEVELOPED COUNTRIES–INTERNATIONAL
DECADE (2001-2010) (Agenda item 6b)
    Corman, Fazli – E/2010/SR.37

## Ukraine

CRIME PREVENTION (Agenda item 14c)
Kavun, Olha – E/2010/SR.44
DEVELOPMENT FINANCE–CONFERENCE (2002 :
MONTERREY, MEXICO)–FOLLOW-UP (Agenda item
6a)
Sergeyev, Yuriy – E/2010/SR.26
EMPOWERMENT OF WOMEN (Agenda item 2d)
Sergeyev, Yuriy – E/2010/SR.18(B)
HUMAN RIGHTS (Agenda item 14g)
Kavun, Olha – E/2010/SR.44
HUMANITARIAN ASSISTANCE (Agenda item 5)
Sergeyev, Yuriy – E/2010/SR.36
NARCOTIC DRUGS (Agenda item 14d)
Kavun, Olha – E/2010/SR.44
POVERTY MITIGATION (Agenda item 4)
Kavun, Olha – E/2010/SR.26
REGIONAL COOPERATION (Agenda item 10)
Tsymbaliuk, Yevhenii – E/2010/SR.41
RESOLUTIONS–UN. GENERAL ASSEMBLY–
IMPLEMENTATION (Agenda item 8)
Kavun, Olha – E/2010/SR.26
SOCIAL DEVELOPMENT (Agenda item 14b)
Kavun, Olha – E/2010/SR.44
SUSTAINABLE DEVELOPMENT (Agenda item 13a)
Pavlichenko, Oleksandr – E/2010/SR.43
UN CONFERENCES–FOLLOW-UP (Agenda item 6)
Kavun, Olha – E/2010/SR.26
UNDP/UNFPA (Agenda item 3b)
Prorok, Hanna V. – E/2010/SR.30
UNICEF (Agenda item 3b)
Prorok, Hanna V. – E/2010/SR.30
WOMEN'S ADVANCEMENT (Agenda item 14a)
Kavun, Olha – E/2010/SR.42

## UN. Assistant Secretary-General for Economic Development

INFORMATICS–INTERNATIONAL COOPERATION
(Agenda item 7c)
Jomo K.S. (Jomo Kwame Sundaram) –
E/2010/SR.38
SCIENCE AND TECHNOLOGY–DEVELOPMENT
(Agenda item 13b)
Jomo K.S. (Jomo Kwame Sundaram) –
E/2010/SR.38

## UN. Assistant Secretary-General for Policy Coordination and Inter-Agency Affairs

COORDINATION–REPORTS (Agenda item 7a)
Stelzer, Thomas – E/2010/SR.23; E/2010/SR.26
POVERTY MITIGATION (Agenda item 4)
Stelzer, Thomas – E/2010/SR.21

## UN. Committee for Development Policy

GENDER EQUALITY (Agenda item 2c)
Stewart, Frances – E/2010/SR.11
SUSTAINABLE DEVELOPMENT (Agenda item 13a)
Najam, Adil – E/2010/SR.43

## UN. Department of Economic and Social Affairs. Development Policy Analysis Division. Director

BRETTON WOODS INSTITUTIONS
Vos, Robert – E/2010/SR.5; E/2010/SR.7

## UN. Deputy High Commissioner for Refugees

HUMANITARIAN ASSISTANCE (Agenda item 5)
Aleinikoff, Thomas Alexander – E/2010/SR.34

## UN. Deputy Secretary-General

COORDINATION AND PROGRAMMES (Agenda item 7)
Migiro, Asha-Rose Mtengeti – E/2010/SR.40
POST-CONFLICT RECONSTRUCTION–AFRICA
(Agenda item 7f)
Migiro, Asha-Rose Mtengeti – E/2010/SR.40

## UN. ECA. Under-Secretary-General and Executive Secretary

REGIONAL COOPERATION–AFRICA (Agenda item 10)
Janneh, Abdoulie – E/2010/SR.20

## UN. ECE. Under-Secretary-General and Executive Secretary

REGIONAL COOPERATION–EUROPE (Agenda item
10)
Kubis, Ján – E/2010/SR.20

## UN. ECLAC. Under-Secretary-General and Executive Secretary

REGIONAL COOPERATION–LATIN AMERICA AND
THE CARIBBEAN (Agenda item 10)
Prado, Antonio – E/2010/SR.20

## UN. Economic and Social Council (2010 : New York). Deputy Secretary

ECONOMIC ASSISTANCE–HAITI (Agenda item 7d)
Pliner, Vivian C. – E/2010/SR.46
REGIONAL COOPERATION–WESTERN ASIA (Agenda
item 10)
Pliner, Vivian C. – E/2010/SR.42

## UN. Economic and Social Council (2010 : New York). President

BRETTON WOODS INSTITUTIONS
Ali, Hamidon (Malaysia) – E/2010/SR.4;
E/2010/SR.7
COORDINATION AND PROGRAMMES (Agenda item 7)
Ali, Hamidon (Malaysia) – E/2010/SR.40
CRIME PREVENTION (Agenda item 14c)
Ali, Hamidon (Malaysia) – E/2010/SR.45
DEVELOPMENT COOPERATION FORUM (Agenda
item 2b)
Ali, Hamidon (Malaysia) – E/2010/SR.11;
E/2010/SR.13; E/2010/SR.14; E/2010/SR.47
Mérorès, Léo (Haiti) – E/2010/SR.16
ECONOMIC ASSISTANCE–HAITI (Agenda item 7d)
Ali, Hamidon (Malaysia) – E/2010/SR.47
EMPOWERMENT OF WOMEN (Agenda item 2d)
Ali, Hamidon (Malaysia) – E/2010/SR.47
GENDER EQUALITY (Agenda item 2c)
Ali, Hamidon (Malaysia) – E/2010/SR.19(A);
E/2010/SR.47
HUMAN RIGHTS (Agenda item 14g)
Ali, Hamidon (Malaysia) – E/2010/SR.45
HUMANITARIAN ASSISTANCE (Agenda item 5)
Ali, Hamidon (Malaysia) – E/2010/SR.47

## UN. Economic and Social Council (2010 : New York). President (continued)

NARCOTIC DRUGS (Agenda item 14d)
Ali, Hamidon (Malaysia) – E/2010/SR.45
OPERATIONAL ACTIVITIES–UN (Agenda item 3)
Ali, Hamidon (Malaysia) – E/2010/SR.47
POST-CONFLICT RECONSTRUCTION–AFRICA
(Agenda item 7f)
Ali, Hamidon (Malaysia) – E/2010/SR.40
REFUGEES (Agenda item 14e)
Ali, Hamidon (Malaysia) – E/2010/SR.45
SOCIAL DEVELOPMENT (Agenda item 14b)
Ali, Hamidon (Malaysia) – E/2010/SR.11;
E/2010/SR.45
SUSTAINABLE DEVELOPMENT (Agenda item 13a)
Ali, Hamidon (Malaysia) – E/2010/SR.45
TOBACCO–HEALTH (Agenda item 7g)
Ali, Hamidon (Malaysia) – E/2010/SR.45
UN. COMMITTEE OF EXPERTS ON INTERNATIONAL
COOPERATION IN TAX MATTERS–MEMBERS
(Agenda item 1)
Ali, Hamidon (Malaysia) – E/2010/SR.49
UN. PERMANENT FORUM ON INDIGENOUS ISSUES
(Agenda item 14h)
Ali, Hamidon (Malaysia) – E/2010/SR.45
UN. SUBCOMMITTEE OF EXPERTS ON THE
TRANSPORT OF DANGEROUS GOODS–MEMBERS
(Agenda item 1)
Ali, Hamidon (Malaysia) – E/2010/SR.49
UN-WOMEN. EXECUTIVE BOARD–MEMBERS
(Agenda item 1)
Ali, Hamidon (Malaysia) – E/2010/SR.48;
E/2010/SR.49; E/2010/SR.50
WOMEN IN DEVELOPMENT (Agenda item 13k)
Ali, Hamidon (Malaysia) – E/2010/SR.11
WOMEN'S ADVANCEMENT (Agenda item 14a)
Ali, Hamidon (Malaysia) – E/2010/SR.11

## UN. Economic and Social Council (2010 : New York). Secretary

ECONOMIC, SOCIAL AND CULTURAL RIGHTS–
TREATY (1966) (Agenda item 14g)
De Laurentis, Jennifer – E/2010/SR.51
HUMANITARIAN ASSISTANCE (Agenda item 5)
Khane, Moncef – E/2010/SR.36
NON-GOVERNMENTAL ORGANIZATIONS (Agenda
item 12)
Gustafik, Otto – E/2010/SR.39
UN-WOMEN. EXECUTIVE BOARD–MEMBERS
(Agenda item 1)
De Laurentis, Jennifer – E/2010/SR.50

## UN. Economic and Social Council (2010 : New York). Vice-President

CRIME PREVENTION (Agenda item 14c)
Soborun, Somduth (Mauritius) – E/2010/SR.45
EMPOWERMENT OF WOMEN (Agenda item 2d)
Soborun, Somduth (Mauritius) – E/2010/SR.17(B)
GENDER EQUALITY (Agenda item 2c)
Soborun, Somduth (Mauritius) – E/2010/SR.17(B)
HUMAN RIGHTS (Agenda item 14g)
Soborun, Somduth (Mauritius) – E/2010/SR.45

## UN. Economic and Social Council (2010 : New York). Vice-President (continued)

HUMANITARIAN ASSISTANCE (Agenda item 5)
Errázuriz, Octavio (Chile) – E/2010/SR.33
INFORMATICS–INTERNATIONAL COOPERATION
(Agenda item 7c)
Soborun, Somduth (Mauritius) – E/2010/SR.38
INTERNATIONAL NARCOTICS CONTROL BOARD–
MEMBERS (Agenda item 1)
Soborun, Somduth (Mauritius) – E/2010/SR.42
NARCOTIC DRUGS (Agenda item 14d)
Soborun, Somduth (Mauritius) – E/2010/SR.45
OPERATIONAL ACTIVITIES–UN (Agenda item 3)
Cujba, Alexandru (Republic of Moldova) –
E/2010/SR.27
POVERTY MITIGATION (Agenda item 4)
Wetland, Morten (Norway) – E/2010/SR.21
REFUGEES (Agenda item 14e)
Soborun, Somduth (Mauritius) – E/2010/SR.45
REGIONAL COOPERATION–LATIN AMERICA AND
THE CARIBBEAN (Agenda item 10)
Soborun, Somduth (Mauritius) – E/2010/SR.42
SCIENCE AND TECHNOLOGY–DEVELOPMENT
(Agenda item 13b)
Soborun, Somduth (Mauritius) – E/2010/SR.38
SOCIAL DEVELOPMENT (Agenda item 14b)
Soborun, Somduth (Mauritius) – E/2010/SR.45
SUSTAINABLE DEVELOPMENT (Agenda item 13a)
Soborun, Somduth (Mauritius) – E/2010/SR.45
TOBACCO–HEALTH (Agenda item 7g)
Soborun, Somduth (Mauritius) – E/2010/SR.45
UN. COMMISSION ON POPULATION AND
DEVELOPMENT–MEMBERS (Agenda item 1)
Soborun, Somduth (Mauritius) – E/2010/SR.42
UN. COMMITTEE FOR DEVELOPMENT POLICY–
MEMBERS (Agenda item 1)
Soborun, Somduth (Mauritius) – E/2010/SR.42
UN. PERMANENT FORUM ON INDIGENOUS ISSUES
(Agenda item 14h)
Soborun, Somduth (Mauritius) – E/2010/SR.45
UN POLICY RECOMMENDATIONS–FOLLOW-UP
(Agenda item 3a)
Cujba, Alexandru (Republic of Moldova) –
E/2010/SR.27; E/2010/SR.31
UN-HABITAT. GOVERNING COUNCIL–MEMBERS
(Agenda item 1)
Soborun, Somduth (Mauritius) – E/2010/SR.42
UNDP/UNFPA (Agenda item 3b)
Cujba, Alexandru (Republic of Moldova) –
E/2010/SR.31
UNICEF (Agenda item 3b)
Cujba, Alexandru (Republic of Moldova) –
E/2010/SR.31
WORLD FOOD PROGRAMME (Agenda item 3b)
Cujba, Alexandru (Republic of Moldova) –
E/2010/SR.31

## UN. ESCAP. Under-Secretary-General and Executive Secretary

REGIONAL COOPERATION–ASIA AND THE PACIFIC
(Agenda item 10)
Heyzer, Noeleen – E/2010/SR.20

**UN. ESCWA. Centre for Women. Chief**

REGIONAL COOPERATION–WESTERN ASIA (Agenda item 10)
    Omer, Afaf – E/2010/SR.20

**UN. High Representative of the Secretary-General for the Least Developed Countries, Landlocked Developing Countries and Small Island Developing States**

LEAST DEVELOPED COUNTRIES–INTERNATIONAL DECADE (2001-2010) (Agenda item 6b)
    Diarra, Cheick Sidi – E/2010/SR.37

**UN. Information Technology Services Division. Director**

INFORMATICS–INTERNATIONAL COOPERATION (Agenda item 7c)
    Blinder, Eduardo – E/2010/SR.38

**UN. Office of the High Commissioner for Human Rights. New York Office. Assistant Secretary-General**

HUMAN RIGHTS (Agenda item 14g)
    Simonovic, Ivan – E/2010/SR.44

**UN. Office of the United Nations Humanitarian Coordinator for Pakistan**

HUMANITARIAN ASSISTANCE (Agenda item 5)
    Mogwanja, Martin – E/2010/SR.34

**UN. Peacebuilding Commission. Chairman**

COORDINATION AND PROGRAMMES (Agenda item 7)
    Wittig, Peter – E/2010/SR.40
POST-CONFLICT RECONSTRUCTION–AFRICA (Agenda item 7f)
    Wittig, Peter – E/2010/SR.40

**UN. Regional Commissions New York Office. Director**

PALESTINIANS–TERRITORIES OCCUPIED BY ISRAEL–LIVING CONDITIONS (Agenda item 11)
    Nour, Amr – E/2010/SR.41
REGIONAL COOPERATION (Agenda item 10)
    Nour, Amr – E/2010/SR.41

**UN. Secretary-General**

SOCIAL DEVELOPMENT (Agenda item 14b)
    Ban, Ki-moon, 1944- – E/2010/SR.11
WOMEN IN DEVELOPMENT (Agenda item 13k)
    Ban, Ki-moon, 1944- – E/2010/SR.11
WOMEN'S ADVANCEMENT (Agenda item 14a)
    Ban, Ki-moon, 1944- – E/2010/SR.11

**UN. Special Adviser to the Secretary-General on Gender Issues and Advancement of Women**

WOMEN'S ADVANCEMENT (Agenda item 14a)
    Mayanja, Rachel N. – E/2010/SR.42

**UN. Special Committee of 24. Chairman**

DECOLONIZATION (Agenda item 9)
    St. Aimee, Donatus Keith (Saint Lucia) – E/2010/SR.41

**UN. Under-Secretary-General for Economic and Social Affairs**

DEVELOPMENT COOPERATION FORUM (Agenda item 2b)
    Sha, Zukang – E/2010/SR.13; E/2010/SR.47
DEVELOPMENT FINANCE–CONFERENCE (2002 : MONTERREY, MEXICO)–FOLLOW-UP (Agenda item 6a)
    Sha, Zukang – E/2010/SR.26
EMPOWERMENT OF WOMEN (Agenda item 2d)
    Sha, Zukang – E/2010/SR.15(B); E/2010/SR.47
GENDER EQUALITY (Agenda item 2c)
    Sha, Zukang – E/2010/SR.15(A); E/2010/SR.15(B); E/2010/SR.47
INTERNATIONAL FINANCIAL INSTITUTIONS (Agenda item 2a)
    Sha, Zukang – E/2010/SR.19(A)
OPERATIONAL ACTIVITIES–UN (Agenda item 3)
    Sha, Zukang – E/2010/SR.27; E/2010/SR.47
UN POLICY RECOMMENDATIONS–FOLLOW-UP (Agenda item 3a)
    Sha, Zukang – E/2010/SR.27

**UN. Under-Secretary-General for Humanitarian Affairs and Emergency Relief Coordinator**

HUMANITARIAN ASSISTANCE (Agenda item 5)
    Holmes, John – E/2010/SR.33; E/2010/SR.34; E/2010/SR.35; E/2010/SR.36

**UN. Under-Secretary-General for Safety and Security**

HUMANITARIAN ASSISTANCE (Agenda item 5)
    Starr, Gregory B. – E/2010/SR.34

**UN Office on Drugs and Crime**

CRIME PREVENTION (Agenda item 14c)
    Monasebian, Simone – E/2010/SR.44
HUMAN RIGHTS (Agenda item 14g)
    Monasebian, Simone – E/2010/SR.44
NARCOTIC DRUGS (Agenda item 14d)
    Monasebian, Simone – E/2010/SR.46

**UN-HABITAT**

HUMAN SETTLEMENTS (Agenda item 13d)
    Djacta, Yamina – E/2010/SR.43

**UNCTAD**

BRETTON WOODS INSTITUTIONS
    Gore, Charles – E/2010/SR.6

**UNCTAD. Division on Globalization and Development Strategies. Macroeconomic and Development Policies Branch**

BRETTON WOODS INSTITUTIONS
    Kotte, Detlef J. – E/2010/SR.7

**UNCTAD. Division on Technology and Logistics. Science, Technology and ICT Branch**

INFORMATICS–INTERNATIONAL COOPERATION (Agenda item 7c)
Hamdi, Mongi – E/2010/SR.38
SCIENCE AND TECHNOLOGY–DEVELOPMENT (Agenda item 13b)
Hamdi, Mongi – E/2010/SR.38

**UNCTAD. Secretary-General**

INTERNATIONAL FINANCIAL INSTITUTIONS (Agenda item 2a)
Panitchpakdi, Supachai – E/2010/SR.19(A)

**UNCTAD. Trade and Development Board. President**

BRETTON WOODS INSTITUTIONS
Feyder, Jean – E/2010/SR.4; E/2010/SR.6

**UNDP**

GENDER EQUALITY (Agenda item 2c)
Immonen, Kaarina – E/2010/SR.12

**UNDP. Administrator**

UN POLICY RECOMMENDATIONS–FOLLOW-UP (Agenda item 3a)
Clark, Helen – E/2010/SR.29
UNDP/UNFPA (Agenda item 3b)
Clark, Helen – E/2010/SR.29
UNICEF (Agenda item 3b)
Clark, Helen – E/2010/SR.29

**UNEP**

ENVIRONMENT (Agenda item 13e)
Castaño, Juanita – E/2010/SR.43

**Unesco**

GENETIC PRIVACY–DISCRIMINATION (Agenda item 14i)
Alfsen-Norodom, Christine – E/2010/SR.37
HUMANITARIAN ASSISTANCE (Agenda item 5)
Falatar, Boris – E/2010/SR.36
INFORMATICS–INTERNATIONAL COOPERATION (Agenda item 7c)
Alfsen-Norodom, Christine – E/2010/SR.38
SCIENCE AND TECHNOLOGY–DEVELOPMENT (Agenda item 13b)
Alfsen-Norodom, Christine – E/2010/SR.38

**UNFPA. Executive Director**

UN POLICY RECOMMENDATIONS–FOLLOW-UP (Agenda item 3a)
Obaid, Thoraya – E/2010/SR.29
UNDP/UNFPA (Agenda item 3b)
Obaid, Thoraya – E/2010/SR.29

**UNFPA. Humanitarian Response Branch. Chief**

HUMANITARIAN ASSISTANCE (Agenda item 5)
Mahmood, Jemilah – E/2010/SR.35

**UNHCR**

HUMANITARIAN ASSISTANCE (Agenda item 5)
Janz, Udo – E/2010/SR.36

**UNHCR. New York Liaison Office. Director**

REFUGEES (Agenda item 14e)
Janz, Udo – E/2010/SR.44

**UNICEF**

HUMANITARIAN ASSISTANCE (Agenda item 5)
Iyer, Akhil – E/2010/SR.36
UN POLICY RECOMMENDATIONS–FOLLOW-UP (Agenda item 3a)
Lake, Tony – E/2010/SR.29
UNICEF (Agenda item 3b)
Lake, Tony – E/2010/SR.29

**United Kingdom**

BRETTON WOODS INSTITUTIONS
Dodd, Eleanor – E/2010/SR.5
GENDER EQUALITY (Agenda item 2c)
Mitchell, Andrew – E/2010/SR.11
NON-GOVERNMENTAL ORGANIZATIONS (Agenda item 12)
Parham, Philip John – E/2010/SR.39

**United Republic of Tanzania**

GENDER EQUALITY (Agenda item 2c)
Likwelile, Servacius – E/2010/SR.15(A)
UN. ECONOMIC AND SOCIAL COUNCIL (2010, SUBSTANTIVE SESS. : NEW YORK)–AGENDA (Agenda item 1)
Mero, Modest Jonathan – E/2010/SR.47

**United States**

BRETTON WOODS INSTITUTIONS
Barton, Frederick D. – E/2010/SR.5
Sammis, John F. – E/2010/SR.4
DECOLONIZATION (Agenda item 9)
Sammis, John F. – E/2010/SR.46
EMPOWERMENT OF WOMEN (Agenda item 2d)
Barton, Frederick D. – E/2010/SR.19(B)
GENDER EQUALITY (Agenda item 2c)
Barton, Frederick D. – E/2010/SR.11; E/2010/SR.12; E/2010/SR.19(B)
Fulgham, Alonzo – E/2010/SR.15(A)
Verveer, Melanne – E/2010/SR.15(A)
HUMAN SETTLEMENTS (Agenda item 13d)
Farrell, Sita – E/2010/SR.43
HUMANITARIAN ASSISTANCE (Agenda item 5)
Mercado, Douglas E. – E/2010/SR.34; E/2010/SR.36
INFORMATICS–INTERNATIONAL COOPERATION (Agenda item 7c)
Nemroff, Courtney – E/2010/SR.38
NON-GOVERNMENTAL ORGANIZATIONS (Agenda item 12)
DiCarlo, Rosemary A. – E/2010/SR.39
SCIENCE AND TECHNOLOGY–DEVELOPMENT (Agenda item 13b)
Nemroff, Courtney – E/2010/SR.38

## United States (continued)

UN POLICY RECOMMENDATIONS–FOLLOW-UP
(Agenda item 3a)
    Barton, Frederick D. – E/2010/SR.29
WOMEN IN DEVELOPMENT (Agenda item 13k)
    Barton, Frederick D. – E/2010/SR.19(B)
WOMEN'S ADVANCEMENT (Agenda item 14a)
    Barton, Frederick D. – E/2010/SR.19(B)
    Phipps, Laurie Shestack – E/2010/SR.42

## Uruguay

BRETTON WOODS INSTITUTIONS
    Cancela, José Luis – E/2010/SR.5
    Novoa, Natalia – E/2010/SR.7
EMPOWERMENT OF WOMEN (Agenda item 2d)
    Cancela, José Luis – E/2010/SR.18(B)
HUMANITARIAN ASSISTANCE (Agenda item 5)
    Cancela, José Luis – E/2010/SR.33
NON-GOVERNMENTAL ORGANIZATIONS (Agenda
item 12)
    Alvarez, Gustavo – E/2010/SR.39

## Venezuela (Bolivarian Republic of)

BRETTON WOODS INSTITUTIONS
    Ovalles-Santos, Víctor Lautaro – E/2010/SR.5;
    E/2010/SR.6; E/2010/SR.7
    Valero Briceño, Jorge – E/2010/SR.4
DECOLONIZATION (Agenda item 9)
    Anzola Padrón, Mariaelena Margarita –
    E/2010/SR.41
GENDER EQUALITY (Agenda item 2c)
    Escalona Ojeda, Julio Rafael – E/2010/SR.19(B)
NON-GOVERNMENTAL ORGANIZATIONS (Agenda
item 12)
    Romero, Moira Méndez – E/2010/SR.39
PALESTINIANS–TERRITORIES OCCUPIED BY
ISRAEL–LIVING CONDITIONS (Agenda item 11)
    Valero Briceño, Jorge – E/2010/SR.41
WOMEN'S ADVANCEMENT (Agenda item 14a)
    Escalona Ojeda, Julio Rafael – E/2010/SR.19(B)

## WHO

HUMANITARIAN ASSISTANCE (Agenda item 5)
    Milovanovic, Ivana – E/2010/SR.36
TOBACCO–HEALTH (Agenda item 7g)
    Bettcher, Douglas – E/2010/SR.37

## WHO. Health Action in Crises. Assistant Director-General

HUMANITARIAN ASSISTANCE (Agenda item 5)
    Laroche, Eric – E/2010/SR.35

## Wisconsin Women's Business Initiative Corporation

BRETTON WOODS INSTITUTIONS
    Baumann, Wendy Katherine – E/2010/SR.5

## WMO

GENDER EQUALITY (Agenda item 2c)
    Batjargal, Zamba – E/2010/SR.18(A)

## World Food Programme

HUMANITARIAN ASSISTANCE (Agenda item 5)
    Silva, Ramiro Armando de Oliveira Lopes da –
    E/2010/SR.34
UN POLICY RECOMMENDATIONS–FOLLOW-UP
(Agenda item 3a)
    Silva, Ramiro Armando de Oliveira Lopes da –
    E/2010/SR.29
WORLD FOOD PROGRAMME (Agenda item 3b)
    Silva, Ramiro Armando de Oliveira Lopes da –
    E/2010/SR.29

## World Society for the Protection of Animals

WOMEN IN DEVELOPMENT (Agenda item 13k)
    Sakoh, Mayumi – E/2010/SR.19(B)

## World Trade Organization

BRETTON WOODS INSTITUTIONS
    Priyadarshi, Shishir – E/2010/SR.4; E/2010/SR.5;
    E/2010/SR.6
INTERNATIONAL FINANCIAL INSTITUTIONS (Agenda
item 2a)
    Boonekamp, Clemens – E/2010/SR.19(A)

## Yemen

DEVELOPMENT FINANCE–CONFERENCE (2002 :
MONTERREY, MEXICO)–FOLLOW-UP (Agenda item
6a)
    Al-Aud, Awsan Abdullah – E/2010/SR.26
GENDER EQUALITY (Agenda item 2c)
    Al Shami, Waheed Abdulwahab Ahmed –
    E/2010/SR.19(A)

## Zambia

EMPOWERMENT OF WOMEN (Agenda item 2d)
    Kalamwina, Christine – E/2010/SR.19(B)
GENDER EQUALITY (Agenda item 2c)
    Kalamwina, Christine – E/2010/SR.19(B)
HUMANITARIAN ASSISTANCE (Agenda item 5)
    Kalamwina, Christine – E/2010/SR.36
WOMEN IN DEVELOPMENT (Agenda item 13k)
    Kalamwina, Christine – E/2010/SR.19(B)
WOMEN'S ADVANCEMENT (Agenda item 14a)
    Kalamwina, Christine – E/2010/SR.19(B)

**Abdelaziz, Maged Abdelfattah (Egypt)**

NON-GOVERNMENTAL ORGANIZATIONS (Agenda
item 12)
E/2010/SR.39

**Abreu, Alcinda Antonio de (Mozambique)**

EMPOWERMENT OF WOMEN (Agenda item 2d)
E/2010/SR.17(B)
GENDER EQUALITY (Agenda item 2c)
E/2010/SR.17(B)

**Acharya, Gyan Chandra (Nepal) (Group of Least
Developed Countries)**

BRETTON WOODS INSTITUTIONS
E/2010/SR.4
EMPOWERMENT OF WOMEN (Agenda item 2d)
E/2010/SR.17(B)
GENDER EQUALITY (Agenda item 2c)
E/2010/SR.17(B)
LEAST DEVELOPED COUNTRIES–INTERNATIONAL
DECADE (2001-2010) (Agenda item 6b)
E/2010/SR.37; E/2010/SR.46

**Acharya, Madhu Raman (Nepal) (Group of Least
Developed Countries)**

BRETTON WOODS INSTITUTIONS
E/2010/SR.5

**Aguirre, Patricio (Chile) (Rio Group)**

BRETTON WOODS INSTITUTIONS
E/2010/SR.6

**Aguirre, Patricio (Nepal) (Group of Least
Developed Countries)**

BRETTON WOODS INSTITUTIONS
E/2010/SR.6

**Aisi, Robert Guba (Papua New Guinea)**

GENDER EQUALITY (Agenda item 2c)
E/2010/SR.18(A)

**Ajamay, Astrid Helle (Norway)**

UN POLICY RECOMMENDATIONS–FOLLOW-UP
(Agenda item 3a)
E/2010/SR.29; E/2010/SR.31
UNDP/UNFPA (Agenda item 3b)
E/2010/SR.29; E/2010/SR.31
UNICEF (Agenda item 3b)
E/2010/SR.29; E/2010/SR.31
WORLD FOOD PROGRAMME (Agenda item 3b)
E/2010/SR.29; E/2010/SR.31

**Al Bayati, Hamid (Iraq)**

EMPOWERMENT OF WOMEN (Agenda item 2d)
E/2010/SR.19(B)
ENVIRONMENT (Agenda item 13e)
E/2010/SR.43
GENDER EQUALITY (Agenda item 2c)
E/2010/SR.19(B)
HUMANITARIAN ASSISTANCE (Agenda item 5)
E/2010/SR.36

**Al Bayati, Hamid (Iraq) (continued)**

INFORMATICS–INTERNATIONAL COOPERATION
(Agenda item 7c)
E/2010/SR.38
SCIENCE AND TECHNOLOGY–DEVELOPMENT
(Agenda item 13b)
E/2010/SR.38
SUSTAINABLE DEVELOPMENT (Agenda item 13a)
E/2010/SR.43
WOMEN IN DEVELOPMENT (Agenda item 13k)
E/2010/SR.19(B)
WOMEN'S ADVANCEMENT (Agenda item 14a)
E/2010/SR.19(B)

**Al Nafisee, Khalid Abdalrazaq (Saudi Arabia)**

EMPOWERMENT OF WOMEN (Agenda item 2d)
E/2010/SR.18(B)
NON-GOVERNMENTAL ORGANIZATIONS (Agenda
item 12)
E/2010/SR.39

**Al Shami, Waheed Abdulwahab Ahmed (Yemen)**

GENDER EQUALITY (Agenda item 2c)
E/2010/SR.19(A)

**Al Shami, Waheed Abdulwahab Ahmed (Yemen)
(Group of 77)**

DEVELOPMENT FINANCE–CONFERENCE (2002 :
MONTERREY, MEXICO)–FOLLOW-UP (Agenda item
6a)
E/2010/SR.46
EMPOWERMENT OF WOMEN (Agenda item 2d)
E/2010/SR.47
GENDER EQUALITY (Agenda item 2c)
E/2010/SR.47
HUMANITARIAN ASSISTANCE (Agenda item 5)
E/2010/SR.33

**Al-Aud, Awsan Abdullah (Yemen)**

DEVELOPMENT FINANCE–CONFERENCE (2002 :
MONTERREY, MEXICO)–FOLLOW-UP (Agenda item
6a)
E/2010/SR.26

**Al-Aud, Awsan Abdullah (Yemen) (Group of 77)**

DECOLONIZATION (Agenda item 9)
E/2010/SR.41
DEVELOPMENT FINANCE–CONFERENCE (2002 :
MONTERREY, MEXICO)–FOLLOW-UP (Agenda item
6a)
E/2010/SR.47
INFORMATICS–INTERNATIONAL COOPERATION
(Agenda item 7c)
E/2010/SR.38
LEAST DEVELOPED COUNTRIES–INTERNATIONAL
DECADE (2001-2010) (Agenda item 6b)
E/2010/SR.37; E/2010/SR.41
PALESTINIANS–TERRITORIES OCCUPIED BY
ISRAEL–LIVING CONDITIONS (Agenda item 11)
E/2010/SR.41
REGIONAL COOPERATION (Agenda item 10)
E/2010/SR.41

**Al-Aud, Awsan Abdullah (Yemen) (Group of 77) (continued)**

SCIENCE AND TECHNOLOGY–DEVELOPMENT (Agenda item 13b)
E/2010/SR.38
TOBACCO–HEALTH (Agenda item 7g)
E/2010/SR.38

**Al-Obaidi, Yahya Ibraheem Fadhil (Iraq)**

HUMAN RIGHTS (Agenda item 14g)
E/2010/SR.44

**Al-Seedi, Razzaq Khleef Mansoor (Iraq)**

HUMANITARIAN ASSISTANCE (Agenda item 5)
E/2010/SR.34
REGIONAL COOPERATION (Agenda item 10)
E/2010/SR.20

**Alahraf, Mohamed A. A. (Libyan Arab Jamahiriya)**

BRETTON WOODS INSTITUTIONS
E/2010/SR.4

**Aleinikoff, Thomas Alexander (UN. Deputy High Commissioner for Refugees)**

HUMANITARIAN ASSISTANCE (Agenda item 5)
E/2010/SR.34

**Alfsen-Norodom, Christine (Unesco)**

GENETIC PRIVACY–DISCRIMINATION (Agenda item 14i)
E/2010/SR.37
INFORMATICS–INTERNATIONAL COOPERATION (Agenda item 7c)
E/2010/SR.38
SCIENCE AND TECHNOLOGY–DEVELOPMENT (Agenda item 13b)
E/2010/SR.38

**Algayerová, Olga (Slovakia)**

EMPOWERMENT OF WOMEN (Agenda item 2d)
E/2010/SR.17(B)
GENDER EQUALITY (Agenda item 2c)
E/2010/SR.17(B)

**Ali, Hamidon (Malaysia) (UN. Economic and Social Council (2010 : New York). President)**

BRETTON WOODS INSTITUTIONS
E/2010/SR.4; E/2010/SR.7
COORDINATION AND PROGRAMMES (Agenda item 7)
E/2010/SR.40
CRIME PREVENTION (Agenda item 14c)
E/2010/SR.45
DEVELOPMENT COOPERATION FORUM (Agenda item 2b)
E/2010/SR.11; E/2010/SR.13; E/2010/SR.14; E/2010/SR.47
ECONOMIC ASSISTANCE–HAITI (Agenda item 7d)
E/2010/SR.47
EMPOWERMENT OF WOMEN (Agenda item 2d)
E/2010/SR.47

**Ali, Hamidon (Malaysia) (UN. Economic and Social Council (2010 : New York). President) (continued)**

GENDER EQUALITY (Agenda item 2c)
E/2010/SR.19(A); E/2010/SR.47
HUMAN RIGHTS (Agenda item 14g)
E/2010/SR.45
HUMANITARIAN ASSISTANCE (Agenda item 5)
E/2010/SR.47
NARCOTIC DRUGS (Agenda item 14d)
E/2010/SR.45
OPERATIONAL ACTIVITIES–UN (Agenda item 3)
E/2010/SR.47
POST-CONFLICT RECONSTRUCTION–AFRICA (Agenda item 7f)
E/2010/SR.40
REFUGEES (Agenda item 14e)
E/2010/SR.45
SOCIAL DEVELOPMENT (Agenda item 14b)
E/2010/SR.11; E/2010/SR.45
SUSTAINABLE DEVELOPMENT (Agenda item 13a)
E/2010/SR.45
TOBACCO–HEALTH (Agenda item 7g)
E/2010/SR.45
UN. COMMITTEE OF EXPERTS ON INTERNATIONAL COOPERATION IN TAX MATTERS–MEMBERS (Agenda item 1)
E/2010/SR.49
UN. PERMANENT FORUM ON INDIGENOUS ISSUES (Agenda item 14h)
E/2010/SR.45
UN. SUBCOMMITTEE OF EXPERTS ON THE TRANSPORT OF DANGEROUS GOODS–MEMBERS (Agenda item 1)
E/2010/SR.49
UN-WOMEN. EXECUTIVE BOARD–MEMBERS (Agenda item 1)
E/2010/SR.48; E/2010/SR.49; E/2010/SR.50
WOMEN IN DEVELOPMENT (Agenda item 13k)
E/2010/SR.11
WOMEN'S ADVANCEMENT (Agenda item 14a)
E/2010/SR.11

**Alimov, Alexander S. (Russian Federation)**

DECOLONIZATION (Agenda item 9)
E/2010/SR.46

**Almeida, João Lucas Quental Novaes de (Brazil)**

DEVELOPMENT FINANCE–CONFERENCE (2002 : MONTERREY, MEXICO)–FOLLOW-UP (Agenda item 6a)
E/2010/SR.46
POVERTY MITIGATION (Agenda item 4)
E/2010/SR.23
RESOLUTIONS–UN. GENERAL ASSEMBLY–IMPLEMENTATION (Agenda item 8)
E/2010/SR.23
UN CONFERENCES–FOLLOW-UP (Agenda item 6)
E/2010/SR.23

**Alsaidi, Abdullah M. (Yemen) (Group of 77)**

EMPOWERMENT OF WOMEN (Agenda item 2d)
E/2010/SR.17(B)

**Alsaidi, Abdullah M. (Yemen) (Group of 77) (continued)**

GENDER EQUALITY (Agenda item 2c)
E/2010/SR.17(B)
OPERATIONAL ACTIVITIES–UN (Agenda item 3)
E/2010/SR.30
POVERTY MITIGATION (Agenda item 4)
E/2010/SR.23
RESOLUTIONS–UN. GENERAL ASSEMBLY–
IMPLEMENTATION (Agenda item 8)
E/2010/SR.23
UN CONFERENCES–FOLLOW-UP (Agenda item 6)
E/2010/SR.23

**Alvarez, Gustavo (Uruguay)**

NON-GOVERNMENTAL ORGANIZATIONS (Agenda item 12)
E/2010/SR.39

**Alyemany, Khaled (Yemen) (Group of 77)**

BRETTON WOODS INSTITUTIONS
E/2010/SR.4; E/2010/SR.5

**Amorim, Anita (International Labour Office)**

UN POLICY RECOMMENDATIONS–FOLLOW-UP
(Agenda item 3a)
E/2010/SR.31
UNDP/UNFPA (Agenda item 3b)
E/2010/SR.31
UNICEF (Agenda item 3b)
E/2010/SR.31
WORLD FOOD PROGRAMME (Agenda item 3b)
E/2010/SR.31

**Andrade, Pedro Aurélio Florencio Cabral de (Brazil)**

CRIME PREVENTION (Agenda item 14c)
E/2010/SR.44

**Anzola Padrón, Mariaelena Margarita (Venezuela (Bolivarian Republic of))**

DECOLONIZATION (Agenda item 9)
E/2010/SR.41

**Apakan, Ertugrul (Turkey)**

EMPOWERMENT OF WOMEN (Agenda item 2d)
E/2010/SR.18(B)

**Argüello, Jorge (Argentina)**

EMPOWERMENT OF WOMEN (Agenda item 2d)
E/2010/SR.18(B)

**Argueta de Barillas, Marisol (Guatemala)**

GENDER EQUALITY (Agenda item 2c)
E/2010/SR.17(A)

**Bachelet, Michelle (Chile)**

GENDER EQUALITY (Agenda item 2c)
E/2010/SR.11

**Bachmann, Matthias (Switzerland)**

BRETTON WOODS INSTITUTIONS
E/2010/SR.6

**Bame, Aman Hassen (Ethiopia)**

EMPOWERMENT OF WOMEN (Agenda item 2d)
E/2010/SR.18(B)
HUMANITARIAN ASSISTANCE (Agenda item 5)
E/2010/SR.33

**Ban, Ki-moon, 1944- (UN. Secretary-General)**

SOCIAL DEVELOPMENT (Agenda item 14b)
E/2010/SR.11
WOMEN IN DEVELOPMENT (Agenda item 13k)
E/2010/SR.11
WOMEN'S ADVANCEMENT (Agenda item 14a)
E/2010/SR.11

**Barendregt, Ester (IMF)**

BRETTON WOODS INSTITUTIONS
E/2010/SR.5; E/2010/SR.7

**Barghouti, Somaia (Palestine)**

PALESTINIANS–TERRITORIES OCCUPIED BY
ISRAEL–LIVING CONDITIONS (Agenda item 11)
E/2010/SR.46

**Barton, Frederick D. (United States)**

BRETTON WOODS INSTITUTIONS
E/2010/SR.5
EMPOWERMENT OF WOMEN (Agenda item 2d)
E/2010/SR.19(B)
GENDER EQUALITY (Agenda item 2c)
E/2010/SR.11; E/2010/SR.12; E/2010/SR.19(B)
UN POLICY RECOMMENDATIONS–FOLLOW-UP
(Agenda item 3a)
E/2010/SR.29
WOMEN IN DEVELOPMENT (Agenda item 13k)
E/2010/SR.19(B)
WOMEN'S ADVANCEMENT (Agenda item 14a)
E/2010/SR.19(B)

**Bassompierre, Christophe de (Belgium)**

BRETTON WOODS INSTITUTIONS
E/2010/SR.6
DEVELOPMENT FINANCE–CONFERENCE (2002 :
MONTERREY, MEXICO)–FOLLOW-UP (Agenda item
6a)
E/2010/SR.26
INFORMATICS–INTERNATIONAL COOPERATION
(Agenda item 7c)
E/2010/SR.52

**Bassompierre, Christophe de (Belgium) (European Union)**

DEVELOPMENT FINANCE–CONFERENCE (2002 :
MONTERREY, MEXICO)–FOLLOW-UP (Agenda item
6a)
E/2010/SR.47
GENDER EQUALITY (Agenda item 2c)
E/2010/SR.19(A)

**Bassompierre, Christophe de (Belgium)**
**(European Union) (continued)**

INFORMATICS–INTERNATIONAL COOPERATION
(Agenda item 7c)
E/2010/SR.38
POVERTY MITIGATION (Agenda item 4)
E/2010/SR.23
RESOLUTIONS–UN. GENERAL ASSEMBLY–
IMPLEMENTATION (Agenda item 8)
E/2010/SR.23
SCIENCE AND TECHNOLOGY–DEVELOPMENT
(Agenda item 13b)
E/2010/SR.38
TAXATION (Agenda item 13h)
E/2010/SR.43
UN CONFERENCES–FOLLOW-UP (Agenda item 6)
E/2010/SR.23

**Batjargal, Zamba (WMO)**

GENDER EQUALITY (Agenda item 2c)
E/2010/SR.18(A)

**Baumann, Wendy Katherine (Wisconsin Women's**
**Business Initiative Corporation)**

BRETTON WOODS INSTITUTIONS
E/2010/SR.5

**Beck, Collin D. (Solomon Islands)**

LEAST DEVELOPED COUNTRIES–INTERNATIONAL
DECADE (2001-2010) (Agenda item 6b)
E/2010/SR.37

**Belakhel, Latifa (Morocco)**

TOBACCO–HEALTH (Agenda item 7g)
E/2010/SR.37

**Benítez Versón, Rodolfo Eliseo (Cuba)**

DECOLONIZATION (Agenda item 9)
E/2010/SR.41
EMPOWERMENT OF WOMEN (Agenda item 2d)
E/2010/SR.18(B)
HUMANITARIAN ASSISTANCE (Agenda item 5)
E/2010/SR.33
PALESTINIANS–TERRITORIES OCCUPIED BY
ISRAEL–LIVING CONDITIONS (Agenda item 11)
E/2010/SR.41

**Bethel, Paulette A. (Bahamas)**

EMPOWERMENT OF WOMEN (Agenda item 2d)
E/2010/SR.18(B)
HUMANITARIAN ASSISTANCE (Agenda item 5)
E/2010/SR.36
POVERTY MITIGATION (Agenda item 4)
E/2010/SR.26
RESOLUTIONS–UN. GENERAL ASSEMBLY–
IMPLEMENTATION (Agenda item 8)
E/2010/SR.26
TAXATION (Agenda item 13h)
E/2010/SR.43
UN CONFERENCES–FOLLOW-UP (Agenda item 6)
E/2010/SR.26

**Bettcher, Douglas (WHO)**

TOBACCO–HEALTH (Agenda item 7g)
E/2010/SR.37

**Bharanikulangara, Kuriakose (Holy See)**

HUMANITARIAN ASSISTANCE (Agenda item 5)
E/2010/SR.36

**Bidounga, Ruffin (Congo)**

REGIONAL COOPERATION–AFRICA (Agenda item 10)
E/2010/SR.20

**Birichevskiy, Dimitry (Russian Federation)**

COORDINATION–REPORTS (Agenda item 7a)
E/2010/SR.37
DEVELOPMENT FINANCE–CONFERENCE (2002 :
MONTERREY, MEXICO)–FOLLOW-UP (Agenda item
6a)
E/2010/SR.26
GENETIC PRIVACY–DISCRIMINATION (Agenda item
14i)
E/2010/SR.37
TOBACCO–HEALTH (Agenda item 7g)
E/2010/SR.37

**Blinder, Eduardo (UN. Information Technology**
**Services Division. Director)**

INFORMATICS–INTERNATIONAL COOPERATION
(Agenda item 7c)
E/2010/SR.38

**Blum, Claudia (Colombia)**

EMPOWERMENT OF WOMEN (Agenda item 2d)
E/2010/SR.19(B)
GENDER EQUALITY (Agenda item 2c)
E/2010/SR.19(B)
WOMEN IN DEVELOPMENT (Agenda item 13k)
E/2010/SR.19(B)
WOMEN'S ADVANCEMENT (Agenda item 14a)
E/2010/SR.19(B)

**Bodiu, Victor (Republic of Moldova)**

GENDER EQUALITY (Agenda item 2c)
E/2010/SR.12

**Bodrug-Lungu, Valentina (Republic of Moldova)**

GENDER EQUALITY (Agenda item 2c)
E/2010/SR.12

**Bonser, Michael (Canada)**

HUMANITARIAN ASSISTANCE (Agenda item 5)
E/2010/SR.35

**Boonekamp, Clemens (World Trade Organization)**

INTERNATIONAL FINANCIAL INSTITUTIONS (Agenda
item 2a)
E/2010/SR.19(A)

**Borges, Sofia (Timor-Leste)**

GENDER EQUALITY (Agenda item 2c)
E/2010/SR.18(A)

**Braga, Carlos Alberto Primo (IBRD)**

BRETTON WOODS INSTITUTIONS
E/2010/SR.4; E/2010/SR.5; E/2010/SR.6

**Brandt, Anna Margaretha (IBRD)**

BRETTON WOODS INSTITUTIONS
E/2010/SR.4

**Brichta, Daniella Poppius (Brazil)**

REGIONAL COOPERATION–LATIN AMERICA AND
THE CARIBBEAN (Agenda item 10)
E/2010/SR.20

**Byman, Per (Sweden)**

HUMANITARIAN ASSISTANCE (Agenda item 5)
E/2010/SR.35

**Cabactulan, Libran N. (Philippines)**

EMPOWERMENT OF WOMEN (Agenda item 2d)
E/2010/SR.19(B)
WOMEN IN DEVELOPMENT (Agenda item 13k)
E/2010/SR.19(B)
WOMEN'S ADVANCEMENT (Agenda item 14a)
E/2010/SR.19(B)

**Cancela, José Luis (Uruguay)**

BRETTON WOODS INSTITUTIONS
E/2010/SR.5
EMPOWERMENT OF WOMEN (Agenda item 2d)
E/2010/SR.18(B)
HUMANITARIAN ASSISTANCE (Agenda item 5)
E/2010/SR.33

**Carfagna, Mara (Italy)**

EMPOWERMENT OF WOMEN (Agenda item 2d)
E/2010/SR.17(B)
GENDER EQUALITY (Agenda item 2c)
E/2010/SR.17(B)

**Carmon, Daniel (Israel)**

NON-GOVERNMENTAL ORGANIZATIONS (Agenda
item 12)
E/2010/SR.39

**Carreño, Aida (Mexico)**

GENDER EQUALITY (Agenda item 2c)
E/2010/SR.12

**Castaño, Juanita (UNEP)**

ENVIRONMENT (Agenda item 13e)
E/2010/SR.43

**Cekuolis, Dalius (Lithuania)**

EMPOWERMENT OF WOMEN (Agenda item 2d)
E/2010/SR.18(B)

**Charlier, Pierre (Belgium) (European Union)**

UN POLICY RECOMMENDATIONS–FOLLOW-UP
(Agenda item 3a)
E/2010/SR.29; E/2010/SR.46

**Charlier, Pierre (Belgium) (European Union)
(continued)**

UNDP/UNFPA (Agenda item 3b)
E/2010/SR.29
UNICEF (Agenda item 3b)
E/2010/SR.29
WORLD FOOD PROGRAMME (Agenda item 3b)
E/2010/SR.29

**Chave, Olivier (Switzerland)**

EMPOWERMENT OF WOMEN (Agenda item 2d)
E/2010/SR.17(B)
GENDER EQUALITY (Agenda item 2c)
E/2010/SR.17(B)
POVERTY MITIGATION (Agenda item 4)
E/2010/SR.26
RESOLUTIONS–UN. GENERAL ASSEMBLY–
IMPLEMENTATION (Agenda item 8)
E/2010/SR.26
UN CONFERENCES–FOLLOW-UP (Agenda item 6)
E/2010/SR.26

**Chávez, Luis Enrique (Peru)**

BRETTON WOODS INSTITUTIONS
E/2010/SR.7

**Chen, Yin (China)**

INFORMATICS–INTERNATIONAL COOPERATION
(Agenda item 7c)
E/2010/SR.38
SCIENCE AND TECHNOLOGY–DEVELOPMENT
(Agenda item 13b)
E/2010/SR.38

**Chenoweth, Florence (Liberia)**

GENDER EQUALITY (Agenda item 2c)
E/2010/SR.11

**Chicoty, George (Angola)**

GENDER EQUALITY (Agenda item 2c)
E/2010/SR.11

**Chirawu, Tapera O. (Namibia)**

GENDER EQUALITY (Agenda item 2c)
E/2010/SR.15(A)

**Christian, Leslie (Ghana)**

EMPOWERMENT OF WOMEN (Agenda item 2d)
E/2010/SR.18(B)
HUMANITARIAN ASSISTANCE (Agenda item 5)
E/2010/SR.33

**Clark, Helen (UNDP. Administrator)**

UN POLICY RECOMMENDATIONS–FOLLOW-UP
(Agenda item 3a)
E/2010/SR.29
UNDP/UNFPA (Agenda item 3b)
E/2010/SR.29
UNICEF (Agenda item 3b)
E/2010/SR.29

**Cliffe, Sarah (IBRD)**

BRETTON WOODS INSTITUTIONS
E/2010/SR.6

**Cohen, Nathalie (Australia)**

UN POLICY RECOMMENDATIONS–FOLLOW-UP
(Agenda item 3a)
E/2010/SR.29; E/2010/SR.31
UNDP/UNFPA (Agenda item 3b)
E/2010/SR.31
UNICEF (Agenda item 3b)
E/2010/SR.31
WORLD FOOD PROGRAMME (Agenda item 3b)
E/2010/SR.31

**Corman, Fazli (Turkey)**

LEAST DEVELOPED COUNTRIES–INTERNATIONAL
DECADE (2001-2010) (Agenda item 6b)
E/2010/SR.37

**Cormon-Veyssière, Florence (France)**

BRETTON WOODS INSTITUTIONS
E/2010/SR.7

**Cravinho, Joao Gomes (Portugal)**

GENDER EQUALITY (Agenda item 2c)
E/2010/SR.17(A); E/2010/SR.18(A)

**Cujba, Alexandru (Republic of Moldova) (UN. Economic and Social Council (2010 : New York). Vice-President)**

OPERATIONAL ACTIVITIES–UN (Agenda item 3)
E/2010/SR.27
UN POLICY RECOMMENDATIONS–FOLLOW-UP
(Agenda item 3a)
E/2010/SR.27; E/2010/SR.31
UNDP/UNFPA (Agenda item 3b)
E/2010/SR.31
UNICEF (Agenda item 3b)
E/2010/SR.31
WORLD FOOD PROGRAMME (Agenda item 3b)
E/2010/SR.31

**Cumberbatch Miguén, Jorge (Cuba)**

COORDINATION–REPORTS (Agenda item 7a)
E/2010/SR.26
POVERTY MITIGATION (Agenda item 4)
E/2010/SR.26
RESOLUTIONS–UN. GENERAL ASSEMBLY–
IMPLEMENTATION (Agenda item 8)
E/2010/SR.26
UN CONFERENCES–FOLLOW-UP (Agenda item 6)
E/2010/SR.26
UN POLICY RECOMMENDATIONS–FOLLOW-UP
(Agenda item 3a)
E/2010/SR.29; E/2010/SR.31
UNDP/UNFPA (Agenda item 3b)
E/2010/SR.29; E/2010/SR.31
UNICEF (Agenda item 3b)
E/2010/SR.31
WORLD FOOD PROGRAMME (Agenda item 3b)
E/2010/SR.31

**Dance, Kevin (NGO Committee on Financing for Development)**

BRETTON WOODS INSTITUTIONS
E/2010/SR.4

**Dapkiunas, Andrei (Belarus)**

EMPOWERMENT OF WOMEN (Agenda item 2d)
E/2010/SR.18(B)

**Davidovich, Shulamit Yona (Israel)**

PALESTINIANS–TERRITORIES OCCUPIED BY
ISRAEL–LIVING CONDITIONS (Agenda item 11)
E/2010/SR.41; E/2010/SR.46
WOMEN'S ADVANCEMENT (Agenda item 14a)
E/2010/SR.42

**Davies, Fleur Margaret (Australia)**

BRETTON WOODS INSTITUTIONS
E/2010/SR.5; E/2010/SR.6

**Davis, Geena (Geena Davis Institute on Gender in Media)**

GENDER EQUALITY (Agenda item 2c)
E/2010/SR.11

**Daza, Varinia (Bolivia (Plurinational State of))**

EMPOWERMENT OF WOMEN (Agenda item 2d)
E/2010/SR.17(B)
GENDER EQUALITY (Agenda item 2c)
E/2010/SR.17(B)

**De Laurentis, Jennifer (UN. Economic and Social Council (2010 : New York). Secretary)**

ECONOMIC, SOCIAL AND CULTURAL RIGHTS–
TREATY (1966) (Agenda item 14g)
E/2010/SR.51
UN-WOMEN. EXECUTIVE BOARD–MEMBERS
(Agenda item 1)
E/2010/SR.50

**De Luna, Noel (FAO. Committee on World Food Security. Chair)**

SUSTAINABLE DEVELOPMENT (Agenda item 13a)
E/2010/SR.43

**DeFrantz, Anita L. (International Olympic Committee)**

GENDER EQUALITY (Agenda item 2c)
E/2010/SR.19(B)

**Del Águila-Castillo, María José (Guatemala)**

HUMANITARIAN ASSISTANCE (Agenda item 5)
E/2010/SR.36

**Delieux, Delphine (Belgium) (European Union)**

ENVIRONMENT (Agenda item 13e)
E/2010/SR.43
HUMAN SETTLEMENTS (Agenda item 13d)
E/2010/SR.43
SUSTAINABLE DEVELOPMENT (Agenda item 13a)
E/2010/SR.43

**Diarra, Cheick Sidi (UN. High Representative of the Secretary-General for the Least Developed Countries, Landlocked Developing Countries and Small Island Developing States)**

LEAST DEVELOPED COUNTRIES–INTERNATIONAL DECADE (2001-2010) (Agenda item 6b)
E/2010/SR.37

**Díaz Bartolomé, Gerardo (Argentina)**

DECOLONIZATION (Agenda item 9)
E/2010/SR.46

**Dib, Sid Ahmed (IBRD)**

BRETTON WOODS INSTITUTIONS
E/2010/SR.5

**DiCarlo, Rosemary A. (United States)**

NON-GOVERNMENTAL ORGANIZATIONS (Agenda item 12)
E/2010/SR.39

**Dijksterhuis, Robert (Netherlands)**

GENDER EQUALITY (Agenda item 2c)
E/2010/SR.12

**Dilekli, Evren (Turkey)**

BRETTON WOODS INSTITUTIONS
E/2010/SR.5; E/2010/SR.6

**Dimian, Hany (Egypt) (International Monetary and Financial Committee)**

BRETTON WOODS INSTITUTIONS
E/2010/SR.4

**Diop, Assane (ILO)**

DEVELOPMENT FINANCE–CONFERENCE (2002 : MONTERREY, MEXICO)–FOLLOW-UP (Agenda item 6a)
E/2010/SR.23

**Diop, Maymouna (Senegal)**

GENDER EQUALITY (Agenda item 2c)
E/2010/SR.11

**Djacta, Yamina (UN-HABITAT)**

HUMAN SETTLEMENTS (Agenda item 13d)
E/2010/SR.43

**Dodd, Eleanor (United Kingdom)**

BRETTON WOODS INSTITUTIONS
E/2010/SR.5

**Dornig, Swen (Liechtenstein)**

HUMANITARIAN ASSISTANCE (Agenda item 5)
E/2010/SR.36

**Dos Santos, José Antonio (Paraguay) (Group of Landlocked Developing Countries)**

BRETTON WOODS INSTITUTIONS
E/2010/SR.7

**Dunlop, Regina Maria Cordeiro (Brazil)**

BRETTON WOODS INSTITUTIONS
E/2010/SR.4
ECONOMIC ASSISTANCE–HAITI (Agenda item 7d)
E/2010/SR.32
HUMANITARIAN ASSISTANCE (Agenda item 5)
E/2010/SR.33
INTERNATIONAL FINANCIAL INSTITUTIONS (Agenda item 2a)
E/2010/SR.19(A)
OPERATIONAL ACTIVITIES–UN (Agenda item 3)
E/2010/SR.30

**Dzivhani, Mbangiseni (South Africa)**

GENDER EQUALITY (Agenda item 2c)
E/2010/SR.15(A)

**Eckey, Susan (Norway)**

HUMANITARIAN ASSISTANCE (Agenda item 5)
E/2010/SR.33; E/2010/SR.34

**Edmond, Jean Paul (Association Femmes Soleil d'Haiti)**

BRETTON WOODS INSTITUTIONS
E/2010/SR.6

**Edrees, Mohamed Fathi (Egypt)**

BRETTON WOODS INSTITUTIONS
E/2010/SR.4

**Elshaar, Hussein (Egypt)**

UN POLICY RECOMMENDATIONS–FOLLOW-UP (Agenda item 3a)
E/2010/SR.29

**Enkhnasan, Nasan-Ulzii (Mongolia)**

GENDER EQUALITY (Agenda item 2c)
E/2010/SR.18(A)

**Enkhtsetseg, Ochir (Mongolia)**

BRETTON WOODS INSTITUTIONS
E/2010/SR.6

**Errázuriz, Octavio (Chile)**

ECONOMIC ASSISTANCE–HAITI (Agenda item 7d)
E/2010/SR.32
EMPOWERMENT OF WOMEN (Agenda item 2d)
E/2010/SR.19(B)
GENDER EQUALITY (Agenda item 2c)
E/2010/SR.17(A); E/2010/SR.18(A); E/2010/SR.19(B)
GENDER MAINSTREAMING–UN SYSTEM (Agenda item 7e)
E/2010/SR.47
HUMANITARIAN ASSISTANCE (Agenda item 5)
E/2010/SR.47
WOMEN IN DEVELOPMENT (Agenda item 13k)
E/2010/SR.19(B)
WOMEN'S ADVANCEMENT (Agenda item 14a)
E/2010/SR.19(B)

**Errázuriz, Octavio (Chile) (UN. Economic and Social Council (2010 : New York). Vice-President)**
HUMANITARIAN ASSISTANCE (Agenda item 5)
E/2010/SR.33

**Escalona Ojeda, Julio Rafael (Venezuela (Bolivarian Republic of))**
GENDER EQUALITY (Agenda item 2c)
E/2010/SR.19(B)
WOMEN'S ADVANCEMENT (Agenda item 14a)
E/2010/SR.19(B)

**Exantus, William (Haiti)**
ECONOMIC ASSISTANCE–HAITI (Agenda item 7d)
E/2010/SR.46

**Falatar, Boris (Unesco)**
HUMANITARIAN ASSISTANCE (Agenda item 5)
E/2010/SR.36

**Farahi, Hossin (Iran (Islamic Republic of))**
EMPOWERMENT OF WOMEN (Agenda item 2d)
E/2010/SR.17(B)
GENDER EQUALITY (Agenda item 2c)
E/2010/SR.17(B)

**Farias, Fábio Moreira Carbonell (Brazil)**
HUMAN SETTLEMENTS (Agenda item 13d)
E/2010/SR.43
INFORMATICS–INTERNATIONAL COOPERATION (Agenda item 7c)
E/2010/SR.38
LEAST DEVELOPED COUNTRIES–INTERNATIONAL DECADE (2001-2010) (Agenda item 6b)
E/2010/SR.37
SCIENCE AND TECHNOLOGY–DEVELOPMENT (Agenda item 13b)
E/2010/SR.38

**Farrell, Sita (United States)**
HUMAN SETTLEMENTS (Agenda item 13d)
E/2010/SR.43

**Fedak, Jolanta (Poland)**
EMPOWERMENT OF WOMEN (Agenda item 2d)
E/2010/SR.17(B)
GENDER EQUALITY (Agenda item 2c)
E/2010/SR.17(B)

**Feyder, Jean (UNCTAD. Trade and Development Board. President)**
BRETTON WOODS INSTITUTIONS
E/2010/SR.4; E/2010/SR.6

**Fila, Jean-Lezin (Congo)**
POVERTY MITIGATION (Agenda item 4)
E/2010/SR.26
RESOLUTIONS–UN. GENERAL ASSEMBLY–IMPLEMENTATION (Agenda item 8)
E/2010/SR.26

**Fila, Jean-Lezin (Congo) (continued)**
UN CONFERENCES–FOLLOW-UP (Agenda item 6)
E/2010/SR.26

**Filiotis, Georgia (Ius Primi Viri International Association)**
SOCIAL DEVELOPMENT (Agenda item 14b)
E/2010/SR.44

**Fiskaa, Ingrid (Norway)**
BRETTON WOODS INSTITUTIONS
E/2010/SR.4
GENDER EQUALITY (Agenda item 2c)
E/2010/SR.17(A)

**Flores, Mary Elizabeth (Honduras)**
EMPOWERMENT OF WOMEN (Agenda item 2d)
E/2010/SR.18(B)

**Fluss, Ilan Simon (Israel)**
POVERTY MITIGATION (Agenda item 4)
E/2010/SR.26
RESOLUTIONS–UN. GENERAL ASSEMBLY–IMPLEMENTATION (Agenda item 8)
E/2010/SR.26
UN CONFERENCES–FOLLOW-UP (Agenda item 6)
E/2010/SR.26
UN POLICY RECOMMENDATIONS–FOLLOW-UP (Agenda item 3a)
E/2010/SR.29; E/2010/SR.31
UNDP/UNFPA (Agenda item 3b)
E/2010/SR.31
UNICEF (Agenda item 3b)
E/2010/SR.31
WORLD FOOD PROGRAMME (Agenda item 3b)
E/2010/SR.31

**Follain, Moncef (France)**
BRETTON WOODS INSTITUTIONS
E/2010/SR.5; E/2010/SR.6

**Francis, Patricia (International Trade Centre UNCTAD/WTO. Executive Director)**
INTERNATIONAL FINANCIAL INSTITUTIONS (Agenda item 2a)
E/2010/SR.19(A)

**Freire, Nilcéa (Brazil)**
EMPOWERMENT OF WOMEN (Agenda item 2d)
E/2010/SR.17(B)
GENDER EQUALITY (Agenda item 2c)
E/2010/SR.11; E/2010/SR.17(B)

**Freudenschuss-Reichl, Irene (Austria)**
EMPOWERMENT OF WOMEN (Agenda item 2d)
E/2010/SR.17(B)
GENDER EQUALITY (Agenda item 2c)
E/2010/SR.17(B)

**Frisch, Toni (Switzerland)**

HUMANITARIAN ASSISTANCE (Agenda item 5)
E/2010/SR.33

**Fujimoto, Shoko (Japan)**

NON-GOVERNMENTAL ORGANIZATIONS (Agenda
item 12)
E/2010/SR.39

**Fulgham, Alonzo (United States)**

GENDER EQUALITY (Agenda item 2c)
E/2010/SR.15(A)

**Gallardo Hernández, Carmen María (El Salvador)**

BRETTON WOODS INSTITUTIONS
E/2010/SR.5

**Gálvez, Eduardo (Chile)**

HUMANITARIAN ASSISTANCE (Agenda item 5)
E/2010/SR.33

**Gálvez, Eduardo (Chile) (Rio Group)**

BRETTON WOODS INSTITUTIONS
E/2010/SR.4; E/2010/SR.5; E/2010/SR.7

**Garayev, Asif (Azerbaijan)**

GENDER EQUALITY (Agenda item 2c)
E/2010/SR.12

**García Gaytán, Maria del Rocio (Mexico)**

GENDER EQUALITY (Agenda item 2c)
E/2010/SR.11

**García González, Carlos Enrique (El Salvador)**

EMPOWERMENT OF WOMEN (Agenda item 2d)
E/2010/SR.18(B)

**Gastaldo, Elena (ILO)**

EMPOWERMENT OF WOMEN (Agenda item 2d)
E/2010/SR.19(B)
GENDER EQUALITY (Agenda item 2c)
E/2010/SR.19(B)

**Geadah, Sami (IMF)**

BRETTON WOODS INSTITUTIONS
E/2010/SR.7

**Geest, Ellen de (Belgium) (European Union)**

CRIME PREVENTION (Agenda item 14c)
E/2010/SR.44
NARCOTIC DRUGS (Agenda item 14d)
E/2010/SR.44
SOCIAL DEVELOPMENT (Agenda item 14b)
E/2010/SR.44

**Ghodse, Hamid A. (International Narcotics Control Board. President)**

NARCOTIC DRUGS (Agenda item 14d)
E/2010/SR.44

**Gokcen, Ufuk (Organisation of the Islamic Conference)**

HUMANITARIAN ASSISTANCE (Agenda item 5)
E/2010/SR.36

**Goledzinowski, Andrew (Australia)**

NON-GOVERNMENTAL ORGANIZATIONS (Agenda
item 12)
E/2010/SR.39

**Gómez Durán, Rosa Delia (India)**

POVERTY MITIGATION (Agenda item 4)
E/2010/SR.26
RESOLUTIONS–UN. GENERAL ASSEMBLY–
IMPLEMENTATION (Agenda item 8)
E/2010/SR.26
UN CONFERENCES–FOLLOW-UP (Agenda item 6)
E/2010/SR.26

**González Segura, Noel (Mexico)**

BRETTON WOODS INSTITUTIONS
E/2010/SR.6; E/2010/SR.7
DEVELOPMENT FINANCE–CONFERENCE (2002 :
MONTERREY, MEXICO)–FOLLOW-UP (Agenda item
6a)
E/2010/SR.26; E/2010/SR.46

**Gore, Charles (UNCTAD)**

BRETTON WOODS INSTITUTIONS
E/2010/SR.6

**Grauls, Jan (Belgium) (European Union)**

EMPOWERMENT OF WOMEN (Agenda item 2d)
E/2010/SR.17(B)
GENDER EQUALITY (Agenda item 2c)
E/2010/SR.17(B)
HUMANITARIAN ASSISTANCE (Agenda item 5)
E/2010/SR.33
NON-GOVERNMENTAL ORGANIZATIONS (Agenda
item 12)
E/2010/SR.39
OPERATIONAL ACTIVITIES–UN (Agenda item 3)
E/2010/SR.30

**Griesgraber, Jo Marie (New Rules for Global Finance Coalition)**

BRETTON WOODS INSTITUTIONS
E/2010/SR.7

**Grunditz, Marten (Sweden)**

GENDER EQUALITY (Agenda item 2c)
E/2010/SR.17(A)

**Guerra, María Paula (Colombia)**

BRETTON WOODS INSTITUTIONS
E/2010/SR.5

**Gustafik, Otto (UN. Economic and Social Council (2010 : New York). Secretary)**

NON-GOVERNMENTAL ORGANIZATIONS (Agenda item 12)
E/2010/SR.39

**Gutiérrez, Gonzalo (Peru)**

DEVELOPMENT FINANCE–CONFERENCE (2002 : MONTERREY, MEXICO)–FOLLOW-UP (Agenda item 6a)
E/2010/SR.26
ECONOMIC ASSISTANCE–HAITI (Agenda item 7d)
E/2010/SR.32
EMPOWERMENT OF WOMEN (Agenda item 2d)
E/2010/SR.18(B)
INTERNATIONAL FINANCIAL INSTITUTIONS (Agenda item 2a)
E/2010/SR.19(A)
POVERTY MITIGATION (Agenda item 4)
E/2010/SR.23
RESOLUTIONS–UN. GENERAL ASSEMBLY–IMPLEMENTATION (Agenda item 8)
E/2010/SR.23
UN CONFERENCES–FOLLOW-UP (Agenda item 6)
E/2010/SR.23

**Hamdi, Mongi (UNCTAD. Division on Technology and Logistics. Science, Technology and ICT Branch)**

INFORMATICS–INTERNATIONAL COOPERATION (Agenda item 7c)
E/2010/SR.38
SCIENCE AND TECHNOLOGY–DEVELOPMENT (Agenda item 13b)
E/2010/SR.38

**Hanfstaengl, Eva (Jubilee Campaign)**

BRETTON WOODS INSTITUTIONS
E/2010/SR.5

**Hassan, Yasser (Egypt)**

INFORMATICS–INTERNATIONAL COOPERATION (Agenda item 7c)
E/2010/SR.38
SCIENCE AND TECHNOLOGY–DEVELOPMENT (Agenda item 13b)
E/2010/SR.38

**Hassani Nejad Pirkouhi, Mohammad (Iran (Islamic Republic of))**

BRETTON WOODS INSTITUTIONS
E/2010/SR.6

**Head, Jeanne (International Right to Life Federation)**

EMPOWERMENT OF WOMEN (Agenda item 2d)
E/2010/SR.17(B)
GENDER EQUALITY (Agenda item 2c)
E/2010/SR.17(B)

**Head, Jeanne (National Right to Life Educational Trust Fund (United States))**

REGIONAL COOPERATION (Agenda item 10)
E/2010/SR.20

**Heller, Claude (Mexico)**

BRETTON WOODS INSTITUTIONS
E/2010/SR.5
EMPOWERMENT OF WOMEN (Agenda item 2d)
E/2010/SR.18(B)
HUMANITARIAN ASSISTANCE (Agenda item 5)
E/2010/SR.36

**Herawan, Cecep (Indonesia)**

INTERNATIONAL FINANCIAL INSTITUTIONS (Agenda item 2a)
E/2010/SR.19(A)
REGIONAL COOPERATION (Agenda item 10)
E/2010/SR.20

**Heyfries, Fabrice (France)**

GENDER EQUALITY (Agenda item 2c)
E/2010/SR.15(A)

**Heyzer, Noeleen (UN. ESCAP. Under-Secretary-General and Executive Secretary)**

REGIONAL COOPERATION–ASIA AND THE PACIFIC (Agenda item 10)
E/2010/SR.20

**Hijazi, Ammar M.B. (Palestine)**

PALESTINIANS–TERRITORIES OCCUPIED BY ISRAEL–LIVING CONDITIONS (Agenda item 11)
E/2010/SR.41

**Holmes, John (UN. Under-Secretary-General for Humanitarian Affairs and Emergency Relief Coordinator)**

HUMANITARIAN ASSISTANCE (Agenda item 5)
E/2010/SR.33; E/2010/SR.34; E/2010/SR.35; E/2010/SR.36

**Hussain, Thilmeeza (Maldives)**

SUSTAINABLE DEVELOPMENT (Agenda item 13a)
E/2010/SR.43

**Hwang, Hyuni (Republic of Korea)**

CRIME PREVENTION (Agenda item 14c)
E/2010/SR.44
REFUGEES (Agenda item 14e)
E/2010/SR.44
WOMEN'S ADVANCEMENT (Agenda item 14a)
E/2010/SR.42

**Immonen, Kaarina (UNDP)**

GENDER EQUALITY (Agenda item 2c)
E/2010/SR.12

**Itoua, Martin (Congo)**

GENDER EQUALITY (Agenda item 2c)
E/2010/SR.18(A)

**Iyer, Akhil (UNICEF)**

HUMANITARIAN ASSISTANCE (Agenda item 5)
E/2010/SR.36

**Iziraren, Tarik (Morocco)**

BRETTON WOODS INSTITUTIONS
E/2010/SR.5

**Ja'afari, Bashar (Syrian Arab Republic)**

PALESTINIANS–TERRITORIES OCCUPIED BY
ISRAEL–LIVING CONDITIONS (Agenda item 11)
E/2010/SR.41

**Jaiswal, Randhir Kumar (India)**

HUMANITARIAN ASSISTANCE (Agenda item 5)
E/2010/SR.36
LEAST DEVELOPED COUNTRIES–INTERNATIONAL
DECADE (2001-2010) (Agenda item 6b)
E/2010/SR.37
POVERTY MITIGATION (Agenda item 4)
E/2010/SR.26
RESOLUTIONS–UN. GENERAL ASSEMBLY–
IMPLEMENTATION (Agenda item 8)
E/2010/SR.26
UN. PERMANENT FORUM ON INDIGENOUS ISSUES
(Agenda item 14h)
E/2010/SR.44
UN CONFERENCES–FOLLOW-UP (Agenda item 6)
E/2010/SR.26
UN POLICY RECOMMENDATIONS–FOLLOW-UP
(Agenda item 3a)
E/2010/SR.31
UNDP/UNFPA (Agenda item 3b)
E/2010/SR.31
UNICEF (Agenda item 3b)
E/2010/SR.31
WORLD FOOD PROGRAMME (Agenda item 3b)
E/2010/SR.31

**Janneh, Abdoulie (UN. ECA. Under-Secretary-General and Executive Secretary)**

REGIONAL COOPERATION–AFRICA (Agenda item 10)
E/2010/SR.20

**Janz, Udo (UNHCR)**

HUMANITARIAN ASSISTANCE (Agenda item 5)
E/2010/SR.36

**Janz, Udo (UNHCR. New York Liaison Office. Director)**

REFUGEES (Agenda item 14e)
E/2010/SR.44

**Jha, Saroj Kumar (Global Facility for Disaster Reduction and Recovery)**

HUMANITARIAN ASSISTANCE (Agenda item 5)
E/2010/SR.35

**Jilani, Marwan (International Federation of Red Cross and Red Crescent Societies)**

EMPOWERMENT OF WOMEN (Agenda item 2d)
E/2010/SR.19(B)
WOMEN'S ADVANCEMENT (Agenda item 14a)
E/2010/SR.19(B)

**Jomo K.S. (Jomo Kwame Sundaram) (UN. Assistant Secretary-General for Economic Development)**

INFORMATICS–INTERNATIONAL COOPERATION
(Agenda item 7c)
E/2010/SR.38
SCIENCE AND TECHNOLOGY–DEVELOPMENT
(Agenda item 13b)
E/2010/SR.38

**Jordan, Stephen (Chamber of Commerce of the United States of America)**

BRETTON WOODS INSTITUTIONS
E/2010/SR.6

**Kalamwina, Christine (Zambia)**

EMPOWERMENT OF WOMEN (Agenda item 2d)
E/2010/SR.19(B)
GENDER EQUALITY (Agenda item 2c)
E/2010/SR.19(B)
HUMANITARIAN ASSISTANCE (Agenda item 5)
E/2010/SR.36
WOMEN IN DEVELOPMENT (Agenda item 13k)
E/2010/SR.19(B)
WOMEN'S ADVANCEMENT (Agenda item 14a)
E/2010/SR.19(B)

**Kalyoncu, Mehmet (Organisation of the Islamic Conference)**

EMPOWERMENT OF WOMEN (Agenda item 2d)
E/2010/SR.19(B)
GENDER EQUALITY (Agenda item 2c)
E/2010/SR.19(B)
WOMEN IN DEVELOPMENT (Agenda item 13k)
E/2010/SR.19(B)
WOMEN'S ADVANCEMENT (Agenda item 14a)
E/2010/SR.19(B)

**Kantrow, Louise (International Chamber of Commerce)**

BRETTON WOODS INSTITUTIONS
E/2010/SR.4

**Karmakar, Sudhangshu (International Committee for Arab-Israeli Reconciliation)**

EMPOWERMENT OF WOMEN (Agenda item 2d)
E/2010/SR.19(B)
GENDER EQUALITY (Agenda item 2c)
E/2010/SR.19(B)

**Kaur, Preneet (India)**

EMPOWERMENT OF WOMEN (Agenda item 2d)
E/2010/SR.19(B)

**Kaur, Preneet (India) (continued)**

GENDER EQUALITY (Agenda item 2c)
E/2010/SR.19(B)
WOMEN IN DEVELOPMENT (Agenda item 13k)
E/2010/SR.19(B)
WOMEN'S ADVANCEMENT (Agenda item 14a)
E/2010/SR.19(B)

**Kavun, Olha (Ukraine)**

CRIME PREVENTION (Agenda item 14c)
E/2010/SR.44
HUMAN RIGHTS (Agenda item 14g)
E/2010/SR.44
NARCOTIC DRUGS (Agenda item 14d)
E/2010/SR.44
POVERTY MITIGATION (Agenda item 4)
E/2010/SR.26
RESOLUTIONS–UN. GENERAL ASSEMBLY–
IMPLEMENTATION (Agenda item 8)
E/2010/SR.26
SOCIAL DEVELOPMENT (Agenda item 14b)
E/2010/SR.44
UN CONFERENCES–FOLLOW-UP (Agenda item 6)
E/2010/SR.26
WOMEN'S ADVANCEMENT (Agenda item 14a)
E/2010/SR.42

**Khalil, Bassem (Egypt)**

PALESTINIANS–TERRITORIES OCCUPIED BY
ISRAEL–LIVING CONDITIONS (Agenda item 11)
E/2010/SR.45

**Khan, Yusra (Indonesia)**

PALESTINIANS–TERRITORIES OCCUPIED BY
ISRAEL–LIVING CONDITIONS (Agenda item 11)
E/2010/SR.41

**Khane, Moncef (UN. Economic and Social Council
(2010 : New York). Secretary)**

HUMANITARIAN ASSISTANCE (Agenda item 5)
E/2010/SR.36

**Khattab, Moushira (Egypt)**

GENDER EQUALITY (Agenda item 2c)
E/2010/SR.11

**Khosa, Sardar Muhammad Latif Khan (Pakistan)**

EMPOWERMENT OF WOMEN (Agenda item 2d)
E/2010/SR.17(B)
GENDER EQUALITY (Agenda item 2c)
E/2010/SR.17(B)
INTERNATIONAL FINANCIAL INSTITUTIONS (Agenda
item 2a)
E/2010/SR.19(A)

**Kim, Bonghyun (Republic of Korea)**

GENDER EQUALITY (Agenda item 2c)
E/2010/SR.17(A)

**Kim, Chang-mo (Republic of Korea)**

INFORMATICS–INTERNATIONAL COOPERATION
(Agenda item 7c)
E/2010/SR.38
LEAST DEVELOPED COUNTRIES–INTERNATIONAL
DECADE (2001-2010) (Agenda item 6b)
E/2010/SR.37
SCIENCE AND TECHNOLOGY–DEVELOPMENT
(Agenda item 13b)
E/2010/SR.38

**Kim, Soo Gwon (Republic of Korea)**

HUMANITARIAN ASSISTANCE (Agenda item 5)
E/2010/SR.33

**Kleib, Hasan (Indonesia)**

BRETTON WOODS INSTITUTIONS
E/2010/SR.4
GENDER EQUALITY (Agenda item 2c)
E/2010/SR.17(A)

**Kleist, Ruediger Wilhelm von (IBRD)**

BRETTON WOODS INSTITUTIONS
E/2010/SR.5

**Klerk, Piet de (Netherlands)**

GENDER EQUALITY (Agenda item 2c)
E/2010/SR.17(A)

**Kmonicek, Hynek (Czech Republic)**

EMPOWERMENT OF WOMEN (Agenda item 2d)
E/2010/SR.17(B)
GENDER EQUALITY (Agenda item 2c)
E/2010/SR.17(B)

**Kodera, Kiyoshi (Development Committee.
Executive Secretary)**

BRETTON WOODS INSTITUTIONS
E/2010/SR.4

**Kononuchenko, Sergei (Russian Federation)**

ENVIRONMENT (Agenda item 13e)
E/2010/SR.43
SUSTAINABLE DEVELOPMENT (Agenda item 13a)
E/2010/SR.43
TAXATION (Agenda item 13h)
E/2010/SR.43

**Korneev, Mikhail (Russian Federation)**

BRETTON WOODS INSTITUTIONS
E/2010/SR.5

**Kotte, Detlef J. (UNCTAD. Division on
Globalization and Development Strategies.
Macroeconomic and Development Policies
Branch)**

BRETTON WOODS INSTITUTIONS
E/2010/SR.7

**Koukku-Ronde, Ritva (Finland)**

GENDER EQUALITY (Agenda item 2c)
E/2010/SR.15(A); E/2010/SR.17(A)

**Kubis, Ján (UN. ECE. Under-Secretary-General and Executive Secretary)**

REGIONAL COOPERATION–EUROPE (Agenda item 10)
E/2010/SR.20

**Kvasov, Alexey (IBRD)**

BRETTON WOODS INSTITUTIONS
E/2010/SR.4; E/2010/SR.6

**Lake, Tony (UNICEF)**

UN POLICY RECOMMENDATIONS–FOLLOW-UP (Agenda item 3a)
E/2010/SR.29
UNICEF (Agenda item 3b)
E/2010/SR.29

**Lallemand Zeller, Loïc (European Union)**

HUMANITARIAN ASSISTANCE (Agenda item 5)
E/2010/SR.35

**Lambert, Thomas (Belgium) (European Union)**

LEAST DEVELOPED COUNTRIES–INTERNATIONAL DECADE (2001-2010) (Agenda item 6b)
E/2010/SR.37

**Laroche, Eric (WHO. Health Action in Crises. Assistant Director-General)**

HUMANITARIAN ASSISTANCE (Agenda item 5)
E/2010/SR.35

**Lazarte, Alfredo (ILO)**

ECONOMIC ASSISTANCE–HAITI (Agenda item 7d)
E/2010/SR.32

**Lear, Judy (HelpAge International)**

EMPOWERMENT OF WOMEN (Agenda item 2d)
E/2010/SR.19(B)
GENDER EQUALITY (Agenda item 2c)
E/2010/SR.19(B)

**Leckomba Loumeto-Pombo, Jeanne Françoise (Congo)**

GENDER EQUALITY (Agenda item 2c)
E/2010/SR.12; E/2010/SR.18(A)

**Lee, So-rie (Republic of Korea)**

HUMANITARIAN ASSISTANCE (Agenda item 5)
E/2010/SR.35
UN POLICY RECOMMENDATIONS–FOLLOW-UP (Agenda item 3a)
E/2010/SR.29
UNDP/UNFPA (Agenda item 3b)
E/2010/SR.29

**Leite, Bruno (Brazil)**

UN POLICY RECOMMENDATIONS–FOLLOW-UP (Agenda item 3a)
E/2010/SR.29

**Leiva Roesch, Jimena (Guatemala)**

SUSTAINABLE DEVELOPMENT (Agenda item 13a)
E/2010/SR.43

**Leroy, Marcus (Belgium)**

BRETTON WOODS INSTITUTIONS
E/2010/SR.5

**Lewis, Jeffrey D. (IBRD. Poverty Reduction and Economic Management)**

BRETTON WOODS INSTITUTIONS
E/2010/SR.5

**Li, Baodong (China)**

BRETTON WOODS INSTITUTIONS
E/2010/SR.4
EMPOWERMENT OF WOMEN (Agenda item 2d)
E/2010/SR.18(B)

**Likwelile, Servacius (United Republic of Tanzania)**

GENDER EQUALITY (Agenda item 2c)
E/2010/SR.15(A)

**Lima, Antonio Pedro Monteiro (Cape Verde)**

GENDER EQUALITY (Agenda item 2c)
E/2010/SR.17(A)

**Lin, Katy (Australia)**

DEVELOPMENT FINANCE–CONFERENCE (2002 : MONTERREY, MEXICO)–FOLLOW-UP (Agenda item 6a)
E/2010/SR.47

**Looz Karageorgiades, Bertrand de (Malta)**

HUMANITARIAN ASSISTANCE (Agenda item 5)
E/2010/SR.36

**Loulichki, Mohammed (Morocco)**

HUMANITARIAN ASSISTANCE (Agenda item 5)
E/2010/SR.36
LEAST DEVELOPED COUNTRIES–INTERNATIONAL DECADE (2001-2010) (Agenda item 6b)
E/2010/SR.37

**Lukiyantsev, Grigory Y. (Russian Federation)**

HUMAN RIGHTS (Agenda item 14g)
E/2010/SR.44
NON-GOVERNMENTAL ORGANIZATIONS (Agenda item 12)
E/2010/SR.39

**Luo, Yang (IMF)**

BRETTON WOODS INSTITUTIONS
E/2010/SR.7

**Maboundou, Raphael Dieudonné (Congo)**

REFUGEES (Agenda item 14e)
E/2010/SR.50

**Macheve, António (Mozambique)**

BRETTON WOODS INSTITUTIONS
E/2010/SR.7

**Madrazo, Elena (Spain) (European Union)**

BRETTON WOODS INSTITUTIONS
E/2010/SR.4

**Mahmood, Jemilah (UNFPA. Humanitarian Response Branch. Chief)**

HUMANITARIAN ASSISTANCE (Agenda item 5)
E/2010/SR.35

**Manyala Keya, Atanas (Kenya)**

EMPOWERMENT OF WOMEN (Agenda item 2d).
E/2010/SR.17(B)
GENDER EQUALITY (Agenda item 2c)
E/2010/SR.17(B)

**Martín Carretero, José Moisés (Spain)**

BRETTON WOODS INSTITUTIONS
E/2010/SR.7

**Marzano, Antonio (International Association of Economic and Social Councils and Similar Institutions)**

EMPOWERMENT OF WOMEN (Agenda item 2d)
E/2010/SR.19(B)
GENDER EQUALITY (Agenda item 2c)
E/2010/SR.19(B)
POVERTY MITIGATION (Agenda item 4)
E/2010/SR.21

**Mawazini, Fyras (NGO Coordination Committee for Iraq)**

HUMANITARIAN ASSISTANCE (Agenda item 5)
E/2010/SR.34

**Mayanja, Rachel N. (UN. Special Adviser to the Secretary-General on Gender Issues and Advancement of Women)**

WOMEN'S ADVANCEMENT (Agenda item 14a)
E/2010/SR.42

**McMullan, Bob (Australia)**

EMPOWERMENT OF WOMEN (Agenda item 2d)
E/2010/SR.17(B)
GENDER EQUALITY (Agenda item 2c)
E/2010/SR.17(B); E/2010/SR.18(A)

**McNee, John (Canada)**

BRETTON WOODS INSTITUTIONS
E/2010/SR.4
ECONOMIC ASSISTANCE–HAITI (Agenda item 7d)
E/2010/SR.32
HUMANITARIAN ASSISTANCE (Agenda item 5)
E/2010/SR.33

**Melon, María Luz (Argentina)**

NON-GOVERNMENTAL ORGANIZATIONS (Agenda item 12)
E/2010/SR.39

**Mercado, Douglas E. (United States)**

HUMANITARIAN ASSISTANCE (Agenda item 5)
E/2010/SR.34; E/2010/SR.36

**Mero, Modest Jonathan (United Republic of Tanzania)**

UN. ECONOMIC AND SOCIAL COUNCIL (2010, SUBSTANTIVE SESS. : NEW YORK)–AGENDA (Agenda item 1)
E/2010/SR.47

**Mérorès, Léo (Haiti) (UN. Economic and Social Council (2010 : New York). President)**

DEVELOPMENT COOPERATION FORUM (Agenda item 2b)
E/2010/SR.16

**Miculescu, Simona Mirela (Romania)**

GENDER EQUALITY (Agenda item 2c)
E/2010/SR.12

**Migiro, Asha-Rose Mtengeti (UN. Deputy Secretary-General)**

COORDINATION AND PROGRAMMES (Agenda item 7)
E/2010/SR.40
POST-CONFLICT RECONSTRUCTION–AFRICA (Agenda item 7f)
E/2010/SR.40

**Migliore, Celestino (Holy See)**

EMPOWERMENT OF WOMEN (Agenda item 2d)
E/2010/SR.18(B)

**Mikec, Neven (Croatia)**

EMPOWERMENT OF WOMEN (Agenda item 2d)
E/2010/SR.18(B)

**Milovanovic, Ivana (WHO)**

HUMANITARIAN ASSISTANCE (Agenda item 5)
E/2010/SR.36

**Mitchell, Andrew (United Kingdom)**

GENDER EQUALITY (Agenda item 2c)
E/2010/SR.11

**Moberg, Mette (Norway)**

GENDER EQUALITY (Agenda item 2c)
E/2010/SR.17(A)

**Moghadam, Reza (IMF. Strategy, Policy and Review Department. Director)**

INTERNATIONAL FINANCIAL INSTITUTIONS (Agenda item 2a)
E/2010/SR.19(A)

**Mogwanja, Martin (UN. Office of the United Nations Humanitarian Coordinator for Pakistan)**

> HUMANITARIAN ASSISTANCE (Agenda item 5)
> E/2010/SR.34

**Mohammed, Ahmed Hameed (Iraq)**

> WOMEN'S ADVANCEMENT (Agenda item 14a)
> E/2010/SR.42

**Momen, Abulkalam Abdul (Bangladesh)**

> HUMANITARIAN ASSISTANCE (Agenda item 5)
> E/2010/SR.36
> UN. PERMANENT FORUM ON INDIGENOUS ISSUES (Agenda item 14h)
> E/2010/SR.44
> UN POLICY RECOMMENDATIONS–FOLLOW-UP (Agenda item 3a)
> E/2010/SR.31
> UNDP/UNFPA (Agenda item 3b)
> E/2010/SR.31
> UNICEF (Agenda item 3b)
> E/2010/SR.31
> WORLD FOOD PROGRAMME (Agenda item 3b)
> E/2010/SR.31

**Monasebian, Simone (UN Office on Drugs and Crime)**

> CRIME PREVENTION (Agenda item 14c)
> E/2010/SR.44
> HUMAN RIGHTS (Agenda item 14g)
> E/2010/SR.44
> NARCOTIC DRUGS (Agenda item 14d)
> E/2010/SR.46

**Montenegro, Mirna (Guatemala)**

> GENDER EQUALITY (Agenda item 2c)
> E/2010/SR.12

**Montilla, Marcos (Dominican Republic)**

> WOMEN'S ADVANCEMENT (Agenda item 14a)
> E/2010/SR.42

**Moorehead, Susanna (IBRD)**

> BRETTON WOODS INSTITUTIONS
> E/2010/SR.4

**Morales, Fabiola (Peru)**

> REGIONAL COOPERATION–LATIN AMERICA AND THE CARIBBEAN (Agenda item 10)
> E/2010/SR.20

**Morrill, Keith (Canada)**

> ECONOMIC ASSISTANCE–HAITI (Agenda item 7d)
> E/2010/SR.44
> HUMAN SETTLEMENTS (Agenda item 13d)
> E/2010/SR.43
> INFORMATICS–INTERNATIONAL COOPERATION (Agenda item 7c)
> E/2010/SR.38
> NON-GOVERNMENTAL ORGANIZATIONS (Agenda item 12)
> E/2010/SR.39

**Morrill, Keith (Canada) (continued)**

> REGIONAL COOPERATION (Agenda item 10)
> E/2010/SR.42
> SCIENCE AND TECHNOLOGY–DEVELOPMENT (Agenda item 13b)
> E/2010/SR.38
> UN. ECONOMIC AND SOCIAL COUNCIL (2010, SUBSTANTIVE SESS. : NEW YORK)–AGENDA (Agenda item 1)
> E/2010/SR.47

**Mosquini, Elyse (International Red Cross)**

> HUMANITARIAN ASSISTANCE (Agenda item 5)
> E/2010/SR.36

**Mporogomyi, Kilontsi (Inter-Parliamentary Union)**

> EMPOWERMENT OF WOMEN (Agenda item 2d)
> E/2010/SR.19(B)
> WOMEN'S ADVANCEMENT (Agenda item 14a)
> E/2010/SR.19(B)

**Muedin, Amy (International Organization for Migration)**

> GENDER EQUALITY (Agenda item 2c)
> E/2010/SR.19(B)
> GENDER MAINSTREAMING–UN SYSTEM (Agenda item 7e)
> E/2010/SR.19(B)
> HUMANITARIAN ASSISTANCE (Agenda item 5)
> E/2010/SR.36

**Murakami, Kenju (Japan)**

> BRETTON WOODS INSTITUTIONS
> E/2010/SR.5

**Nahayo, Adolphe (Burundi)**

> GENDER EQUALITY (Agenda item 2c)
> E/2010/SR.12

**Najam, Adil (UN. Committee for Development Policy)**

> SUSTAINABLE DEVELOPMENT (Agenda item 13a)
> E/2010/SR.43

**Nasir, Arrmanatha (Indonesia)**

> BRETTON WOODS INSTITUTIONS
> E/2010/SR.7

**Navarro Barro, Nadieska (Cuba)**

> BRETTON WOODS INSTITUTIONS
> E/2010/SR.5

**Nebenzia, Vasilii (Russian Federation)**

> HUMANITARIAN ASSISTANCE (Agenda item 5)
> E/2010/SR.33
> POVERTY MITIGATION (Agenda item 4)
> E/2010/SR.23
> RESOLUTIONS–UN. GENERAL ASSEMBLY–IMPLEMENTATION (Agenda item 8)
> E/2010/SR.23

**Nebenzia, Vasilii (Russian Federation) (continued)**

UN CONFERENCES–FOLLOW-UP (Agenda item 6)
E/2010/SR.23

**Nemroff, Courtney (United States)**

INFORMATICS–INTERNATIONAL COOPERATION
(Agenda item 7c)
E/2010/SR.38
SCIENCE AND TECHNOLOGY–DEVELOPMENT
(Agenda item 13b)
E/2010/SR.38

**Ngapi, Cornelie Adou (Congo)**

GENDER EQUALITY (Agenda item 2c)
E/2010/SR.18(A)

**Nihon, Nicolas (Belgium) (European Union)**

WOMEN'S ADVANCEMENT (Agenda item 14a)
E/2010/SR.42

**Ning'ang'a, Eric (Malawi)**

UN POLICY RECOMMENDATIONS–FOLLOW-UP
(Agenda item 3a)
E/2010/SR.29
UNDP/UNFPA (Agenda item 3b)
E/2010/SR.29
UNICEF (Agenda item 3b)
E/2010/SR.29
WORLD FOOD PROGRAMME (Agenda item 3b)
E/2010/SR.29

**Nofukuka, Xolulela Lawrence (South Africa)**

HUMANITARIAN ASSISTANCE (Agenda item 5)
E/2010/SR.36

**Nour, Amr (UN. Regional Commissions New York Office. Director)**

PALESTINIANS–TERRITORIES OCCUPIED BY
ISRAEL–LIVING CONDITIONS (Agenda item 11)
E/2010/SR.41
REGIONAL COOPERATION (Agenda item 10)
E/2010/SR.41

**Novoa, Natalia (Uruguay)**

BRETTON WOODS INSTITUTIONS
E/2010/SR.7

**Nwadinobi, Ezinne (Nigeria)**

EMPOWERMENT OF WOMEN (Agenda item 2d)
E/2010/SR.19(B)
WOMEN IN DEVELOPMENT (Agenda item 13k)
E/2010/SR.19(B)
WOMEN'S ADVANCEMENT (Agenda item 14a)
E/2010/SR.19(B)

**Nyam-Osor, Tuya (Mongolia)**

BRETTON WOODS INSTITUTIONS
E/2010/SR.5

**Obaid, Thoraya (UNFPA. Executive Director)**

UN POLICY RECOMMENDATIONS–FOLLOW-UP
(Agenda item 3a)
E/2010/SR.29
UNDP/UNFPA (Agenda item 3b)
E/2010/SR.29

**Okuda, Norihiro (Japan)**

EMPOWERMENT OF WOMEN (Agenda item 2d)
E/2010/SR.19(B)
GENDER EQUALITY (Agenda item 2c)
E/2010/SR.18(A); E/2010/SR.19(B)
WOMEN IN DEVELOPMENT (Agenda item 13k)
E/2010/SR.19(B)
WOMEN'S ADVANCEMENT (Agenda item 14a)
E/2010/SR.19(B)

**Omer, Afaf (UN. ESCWA. Centre for Women. Chief)**

REGIONAL COOPERATION–WESTERN ASIA (Agenda
item 10)
E/2010/SR.20

**Onambèlè, Joseph (International Chamber of Commerce)**

BRETTON WOODS INSTITUTIONS
E/2010/SR.7

**Oosterhof, Pytrik Dieuwke (International Federation of Red Cross and Red Crescent Societies)**

POVERTY MITIGATION (Agenda item 4)
E/2010/SR.26
UN CONFERENCES–FOLLOW-UP (Agenda item 6)
E/2010/SR.26

**Oppegaard, Svein (Norway)**

GENDER EQUALITY (Agenda item 2c)
E/2010/SR.17(A)

**Oquist, Paul (Nicaragua)**

INTERNATIONAL FINANCIAL INSTITUTIONS (Agenda
item 2a)
E/2010/SR.19(A)

**Ortiz de Urbina, Yera (Spain) (European Union)**

BRETTON WOODS INSTITUTIONS
E/2010/SR.5

**Ovalles-Santos, Víctor Lautaro (Venezuela (Bolivarian Republic of))**

BRETTON WOODS INSTITUTIONS
E/2010/SR.5; E/2010/SR.6; E/2010/SR.7

**Paet, Urmas (Estonia)**

EMPOWERMENT OF WOMEN (Agenda item 2d)
E/2010/SR.17(B)
GENDER EQUALITY (Agenda item 2c)
E/2010/SR.17(B)

**Paik, Hee-Young (Republic of Korea)**

GENDER EQUALITY (Agenda item 2c)
E/2010/SR.17(A)

**Pais, Elza (Portugal)**

GENDER EQUALITY (Agenda item 2c)
E/2010/SR.17(A)

**Panitchpakdi, Supachai (UNCTAD. Secretary-General)**

INTERNATIONAL FINANCIAL INSTITUTIONS (Agenda item 2a)
E/2010/SR.19(A)

**Parham, Philip John (United Kingdom)**

NON-GOVERNMENTAL ORGANIZATIONS (Agenda item 12)
E/2010/SR.39

**Patriota, Guilherme de Aguiar (Brazil)**

BRETTON WOODS INSTITUTIONS
E/2010/SR.5; E/2010/SR.6

**Pavlichenko, Oleksandr (Ukraine)**

SUSTAINABLE DEVELOPMENT (Agenda item 13a)
E/2010/SR.43

**Peña, Belén Muñoz de la (Chile)**

WOMEN'S ADVANCEMENT (Agenda item 14a)
E/2010/SR.42

**Petranto, Ade (Indonesia)**

HUMANITARIAN ASSISTANCE (Agenda item 5)
E/2010/SR.36
POVERTY MITIGATION (Agenda item 4)
E/2010/SR.23
RESOLUTIONS–UN. GENERAL ASSEMBLY–
IMPLEMENTATION (Agenda item 8)
E/2010/SR.23
UN CONFERENCES–FOLLOW-UP (Agenda item 6)
E/2010/SR.23

**Phipps, Laurie Shestack (United States)**

WOMEN'S ADVANCEMENT (Agenda item 14a)
E/2010/SR.42

**Piebalgs, Andris (European Commission)**

DEVELOPMENT COOPERATION FORUM (Agenda item 2b)
E/2010/SR.13

**Piminov, Denis V. (Russian Federation)**

OPERATIONAL ACTIVITIES–UN (Agenda item 3)
E/2010/SR.30

**Pistrinciuk, Vadim (Republic of Moldova)**

GENDER EQUALITY (Agenda item 2c)
E/2010/SR.12

**Pliner, Vivian C. (UN. Economic and Social Council (2010 : New York). Deputy Secretary)**

ECONOMIC ASSISTANCE–HAITI (Agenda item 7d)
E/2010/SR.46
REGIONAL COOPERATION–WESTERN ASIA (Agenda item 10)
E/2010/SR.42

**Poretti, Mattia (Switzerland)**

OPERATIONAL ACTIVITIES–UN (Agenda item 3)
E/2010/SR.30

**Porretti, Eduardo (Argentina)**

HUMANITARIAN ASSISTANCE (Agenda item 5)
E/2010/SR.36

**Prado, Antonio (UN. ECLAC. Under-Secretary-General and Executive Secretary)**

REGIONAL COOPERATION–LATIN AMERICA AND THE CARIBBEAN (Agenda item 10)
E/2010/SR.20

**Priyadarshi, Shishir (World Trade Organization)**

BRETTON WOODS INSTITUTIONS
E/2010/SR.4; E/2010/SR.5; E/2010/SR.6

**Prorok, Hanna V. (Ukraine)**

UNDP/UNFPA (Agenda item 3b)
E/2010/SR.30
UNICEF (Agenda item 3b)
E/2010/SR.30

**Puri, Hardeep Singh (India)**

BRETTON WOODS INSTITUTIONS
E/2010/SR.6

**Rahdiansyah, Danny (Indonesia)**

SUSTAINABLE DEVELOPMENT (Agenda item 13a)
E/2010/SR.43

**Rahman, A.K.M. Mashiur (Bangladesh)**

DEVELOPMENT FINANCE–CONFERENCE (2002 : MONTERREY, MEXICO)–FOLLOW-UP (Agenda item 6a)
E/2010/SR.26
HUMANITARIAN ASSISTANCE (Agenda item 5)
E/2010/SR.35

**Rahman, Nojibur (Bangladesh)**

BRETTON WOODS INSTITUTIONS
E/2010/SR.4
EMPOWERMENT OF WOMEN (Agenda item 2d)
E/2010/SR.19(B)
GENDER EQUALITY (Agenda item 2c)
E/2010/SR.15(A); E/2010/SR.19(B)
LEAST DEVELOPED COUNTRIES–INTERNATIONAL DECADE (2001-2010) (Agenda item 6b)
E/2010/SR.46
UN POLICY RECOMMENDATIONS–FOLLOW-UP (Agenda item 3a)
E/2010/SR.29

**Rahman, Nojibur (Bangladesh) (continued)**

UNDP/UNFPA (Agenda item 3b)
E/2010/SR.29
WOMEN IN DEVELOPMENT (Agenda item 13k)
E/2010/SR.19(B)
WOMEN'S ADVANCEMENT (Agenda item 14a)
E/2010/SR.19(B)
WORLD FOOD PROGRAMME (Agenda item 3b)
E/2010/SR.29

**Rajabi, Ahmad (Iran (Islamic Republic of))**

INFORMATICS–INTERNATIONAL COOPERATION
(Agenda item 7c)
E/2010/SR.38
NARCOTIC DRUGS (Agenda item 14d)
E/2010/SR.44
PALESTINIANS–TERRITORIES OCCUPIED BY
ISRAEL–LIVING CONDITIONS (Agenda item 11)
E/2010/SR.41
SCIENCE AND TECHNOLOGY–DEVELOPMENT
(Agenda item 13b)
E/2010/SR.38

**Rakovskiy, Nikolay S. (Russian Federation)**

SOCIAL DEVELOPMENT (Agenda item 14b)
E/2010/SR.44
WOMEN'S ADVANCEMENT (Agenda item 14a)
E/2010/SR.42

**Ratsifandrihamanana, Lila Hanitra (FAO)**

EMPOWERMENT OF WOMEN (Agenda item 2d)
E/2010/SR.19(B)
GENDER EQUALITY (Agenda item 2c)
E/2010/SR.19(B)
WOMEN IN DEVELOPMENT (Agenda item 13k)
E/2010/SR.19(B)

**Renford, Mazal (Israel)**

EMPOWERMENT OF WOMEN (Agenda item 2d)
E/2010/SR.17(B)
GENDER EQUALITY (Agenda item 2c)
E/2010/SR.12; E/2010/SR.15(A); E/2010/SR.17(B);
E/2010/SR.18(A)
REGIONAL COOPERATION (Agenda item 10)
E/2010/SR.20

**Rodríguez, Roberto (Peru)**

NON-GOVERNMENTAL ORGANIZATIONS (Agenda
item 12)
E/2010/SR.39
WOMEN'S ADVANCEMENT (Agenda item 14a)
E/2010/SR.42

**Rodríguez Pineda, Ana Cristina (Guatemala)**

GENDER EQUALITY (Agenda item 2c)
E/2010/SR.12

**Romero, Moira Méndez (Venezuela (Bolivarian
Republic of))**

NON-GOVERNMENTAL ORGANIZATIONS (Agenda
item 12)
E/2010/SR.39

**Rosenthal, Gert (Guatemala)**

BRETTON WOODS INSTITUTIONS
E/2010/SR.4; E/2010/SR.6; E/2010/SR.7
GENDER EQUALITY (Agenda item 2c)
E/2010/SR.11; E/2010/SR.12; E/2010/SR.15(A);
E/2010/SR.17(A); E/2010/SR.19(B)
GENDER MAINSTREAMING–UN SYSTEM (Agenda
item 7e)
E/2010/SR.19(B)
REGIONAL COOPERATION–LATIN AMERICA AND
THE CARIBBEAN (Agenda item 10)
E/2010/SR.20

**Rovirosa, Socorro (Mexico)**

BRETTON WOODS INSTITUTIONS
E/2010/SR.4

**Rutilo, Gustavo (Argentina)**

GENDER EQUALITY (Agenda item 2c)
E/2010/SR.11

**Sahasrabuddhe, Vinay (Rambhau Mhalgi
Prabodhini (Organization : India))**

GENDER EQUALITY (Agenda item 2c)
E/2010/SR.12; E/2010/SR.15(A)

**Sakoh, Mayumi (World Society for the Protection
of Animals)**

WOMEN IN DEVELOPMENT (Agenda item 13k)
E/2010/SR.19(B)

**Sambili, Edward (Kenya)**

INTERNATIONAL FINANCIAL INSTITUTIONS (Agenda
item 2a)
E/2010/SR.19(A)

**Sammis, John F. (United States)**

BRETTON WOODS INSTITUTIONS
E/2010/SR.4
DECOLONIZATION (Agenda item 9)
E/2010/SR.46

**Sangqu, Baso (South Africa)**

EMPOWERMENT OF WOMEN (Agenda item 2d)
E/2010/SR.18(B)

**Santos Filho, Otavio Canuto dos (IBRD. Poverty
Reduction and Economic Management)**

INTERNATIONAL FINANCIAL INSTITUTIONS (Agenda
item 2a)
E/2010/SR.19(A)

**Sardjana, Agus (Indonesia)**

OPERATIONAL ACTIVITIES–UN (Agenda item 3)
E/2010/SR.30

**Sarlis, Irini (International Alliance of Women)**

EMPOWERMENT OF WOMEN (Agenda item 2d)
E/2010/SR.19(B)
GENDER EQUALITY (Agenda item 2c)
E/2010/SR.19(B)

**Savostianov, Mikhail Y. (Russian Federation)**

UN POLICY RECOMMENDATIONS–FOLLOW-UP
(Agenda item 3a)
E/2010/SR.29

**Sayinzoga, Kampeta (Rwanda)**

EMPOWERMENT OF WOMEN (Agenda item 2d)
E/2010/SR.17(B)
GENDER EQUALITY (Agenda item 2c)
E/2010/SR.17(B)

**Schaper, Herman (Netherlands)**

GENDER EQUALITY (Agenda item 2c)
E/2010/SR.12; E/2010/SR.15(A)

**Sergeev, Sergei (Belarus)**

INFORMATICS–INTERNATIONAL COOPERATION
(Agenda item 7c)
E/2010/SR.38
OPERATIONAL ACTIVITIES–UN (Agenda item 3)
E/2010/SR.30
SCIENCE AND TECHNOLOGY–DEVELOPMENT
(Agenda item 13b)
E/2010/SR.38
SUSTAINABLE DEVELOPMENT (Agenda item 13a)
E/2010/SR.43

**Sergeyev, Yuriy (Ukraine)**

DEVELOPMENT FINANCE–CONFERENCE (2002 :
MONTERREY, MEXICO)–FOLLOW-UP (Agenda item
6a)
E/2010/SR.26
EMPOWERMENT OF WOMEN (Agenda item 2d)
E/2010/SR.18(B)
HUMANITARIAN ASSISTANCE (Agenda item 5)
E/2010/SR.36

**Sha, Zukang (UN. Under-Secretary-General for
Economic and Social Affairs)**

DEVELOPMENT COOPERATION FORUM (Agenda
item 2b)
E/2010/SR.13; E/2010/SR.47
DEVELOPMENT FINANCE–CONFERENCE (2002 :
MONTERREY, MEXICO)–FOLLOW-UP (Agenda item
6a)
E/2010/SR.26
EMPOWERMENT OF WOMEN (Agenda item 2d)
E/2010/SR.15(B); E/2010/SR.47
GENDER EQUALITY (Agenda item 2c)
E/2010/SR.15(A); E/2010/SR.15(B); E/2010/SR.47

**Sha, Zukang (UN. Under-Secretary-General for
Economic and Social Affairs) (continued)**

INTERNATIONAL FINANCIAL INSTITUTIONS (Agenda
item 2a)
E/2010/SR.19(A)
OPERATIONAL ACTIVITIES–UN (Agenda item 3)
E/2010/SR.27; E/2010/SR.47
UN POLICY RECOMMENDATIONS–FOLLOW-UP
(Agenda item 3a)
E/2010/SR.27

**Shaban, Naomi N. (Kenya)**

HUMANITARIAN ASSISTANCE (Agenda item 5)
E/2010/SR.33; E/2010/SR.35

**Shin, Boonam (Republic of Korea)**

BRETTON WOODS INSTITUTIONS
E/2010/SR.5

**Shin, Kak-soo (Republic of Korea)**

EMPOWERMENT OF WOMEN (Agenda item 2d)
E/2010/SR.18(B)

**Sial, Amjad Hussain B. (Pakistan)**

HUMANITARIAN ASSISTANCE (Agenda item 5)
E/2010/SR.33

**Silkalna, Solveiga (Latvia)**

EMPOWERMENT OF WOMEN (Agenda item 2d)
E/2010/SR.17(B)
GENDER EQUALITY (Agenda item 2c)
E/2010/SR.17(B)

**Silva, Ramiro Armando de Oliveira Lopes da
(World Food Programme)**

HUMANITARIAN ASSISTANCE (Agenda item 5)
E/2010/SR.34
UN POLICY RECOMMENDATIONS–FOLLOW-UP
(Agenda item 3a)
E/2010/SR.29
WORLD FOOD PROGRAMME (Agenda item 3b)
E/2010/SR.29

**Simonovic, Ivan (UN. Office of the High
Commissioner for Human Rights. New York Office.
Assistant Secretary-General)**

HUMAN RIGHTS (Agenda item 14g)
E/2010/SR.44

**Sioka, Doreen (Namibia)**

EMPOWERMENT OF WOMEN (Agenda item 2d)
E/2010/SR.17(B)
GENDER EQUALITY (Agenda item 2c)
E/2010/SR.15(A); E/2010/SR.17(B)

**Sirotkina, Marina A. (Russian Federation)**

INFORMATICS–INTERNATIONAL COOPERATION
(Agenda item 7c)
E/2010/SR.38

**Sirotkina, Marina A. (Russian Federation) (continued)**

SCIENCE AND TECHNOLOGY–DEVELOPMENT
(Agenda item 13b)
E/2010/SR.38

**Siwakoti, Gopal Krishna (International Institute for Human Rights, Environment and Development (Kathmandu))**

BRETTON WOODS INSTITUTIONS
E/2010/SR.6

**Skalli, Nouzha (Morocco)**

EMPOWERMENT OF WOMEN (Agenda item 2d)
E/2010/SR.17(B)
GENDER EQUALITY (Agenda item 2c)
E/2010/SR.11; E/2010/SR.15(A); E/2010/SR.17(B)

**Slowing-Umaña, Karin (Guatemala)**

GENDER EQUALITY (Agenda item 2c)
E/2010/SR.12

**Soborun, Somduth (Mauritius) (UN. Economic and Social Council (2010 : New York). Vice-President)**

CRIME PREVENTION (Agenda item 14c)
E/2010/SR.45
EMPOWERMENT OF WOMEN (Agenda item 2d)
E/2010/SR.17(B)
GENDER EQUALITY (Agenda item 2c)
E/2010/SR.17(B)
HUMAN RIGHTS (Agenda item 14g)
E/2010/SR.45
INFORMATICS–INTERNATIONAL COOPERATION
(Agenda item 7c)
E/2010/SR.38
INTERNATIONAL NARCOTICS CONTROL BOARD–
MEMBERS (Agenda item 1)
E/2010/SR.42
NARCOTIC DRUGS (Agenda item 14d)
E/2010/SR.45
REFUGEES (Agenda item 14e)
E/2010/SR.45
REGIONAL COOPERATION–LATIN AMERICA AND
THE CARIBBEAN (Agenda item 10)
E/2010/SR.42
SCIENCE AND TECHNOLOGY–DEVELOPMENT
(Agenda item 13b)
E/2010/SR.38
SOCIAL DEVELOPMENT (Agenda item 14b)
E/2010/SR.45
SUSTAINABLE DEVELOPMENT (Agenda item 13a)
E/2010/SR.45
TOBACCO–HEALTH (Agenda item 7g)
E/2010/SR.45
UN. COMMISSION ON POPULATION AND
DEVELOPMENT–MEMBERS (Agenda item 1)
E/2010/SR.42
UN. COMMITTEE FOR DEVELOPMENT POLICY–
MEMBERS (Agenda item 1)
E/2010/SR.42

**Soborun, Somduth (Mauritius) (UN. Economic and Social Council (2010 : New York). Vice-President) (continued)**

UN. PERMANENT FORUM ON INDIGENOUS ISSUES
(Agenda item 14h)
E/2010/SR.45
UN-HABITAT. GOVERNING COUNCIL–MEMBERS
(Agenda item 1)
E/2010/SR.42

**Spatolisano, Maria (European Union)**

INTERNATIONAL FINANCIAL INSTITUTIONS (Agenda
item 2a)
E/2010/SR.19(A)

**Sportis, Cécile (France)**

GENDER EQUALITY (Agenda item 2c)
E/2010/SR.12; E/2010/SR.15(A); E/2010/SR.18(A)

**St. Aimee, Donatus Keith (Saint Lucia)**

INTERNATIONAL FINANCIAL INSTITUTIONS (Agenda
item 2a)
E/2010/SR.19(A)
NON-GOVERNMENTAL ORGANIZATIONS (Agenda
item 12)
E/2010/SR.39
PALESTINIANS–TERRITORIES OCCUPIED BY
ISRAEL–LIVING CONDITIONS (Agenda item 11)
E/2010/SR.46

**St. Aimee, Donatus Keith (Saint Lucia) (Caribbean Community)**

BRETTON WOODS INSTITUTIONS
E/2010/SR.4; E/2010/SR.7

**St. Aimee, Donatus Keith (Saint Lucia) (SIDSNet)**

SUSTAINABLE DEVELOPMENT (Agenda item 13a)
E/2010/SR.43

**St. Aimee, Donatus Keith (Saint Lucia) (UN. Special Committee of 24. Chairman)**

DECOLONIZATION (Agenda item 9)
E/2010/SR.41

**Starr, Gregory B. (UN. Under-Secretary-General for Safety and Security)**

HUMANITARIAN ASSISTANCE (Agenda item 5)
E/2010/SR.34

**Staur, Carsten (Denmark)**

GENDER EQUALITY (Agenda item 2c)
E/2010/SR.15(A)

**Stelzer, Thomas (UN. Assistant Secretary-General for Policy Coordination and Inter-Agency Affairs)**

COORDINATION–REPORTS (Agenda item 7a)
E/2010/SR.23; E/2010/SR.26
POVERTY MITIGATION (Agenda item 4)
E/2010/SR.21

**Stewart, Frances (UN. Committee for Development Policy)**

GENDER EQUALITY (Agenda item 2c)
E/2010/SR.11

**Stewart, Jane (ILO)**

BRETTON WOODS INSTITUTIONS
E/2010/SR.5

**Stewart-David, Julia (European Union)**

HUMANITARIAN ASSISTANCE (Agenda item 5)
E/2010/SR.34

**Stillhart, Dominik (International Committee of the Red Cross)**

HUMANITARIAN ASSISTANCE (Agenda item 5)
E/2010/SR.34

**Suárez Garzón, Carlos Alberto (Colombia)**

HUMANITARIAN ASSISTANCE (Agenda item 5)
E/2010/SR.34; E/2010/SR.36

**Sumi, Shigeki (Japan)**

BRETTON WOODS INSTITUTIONS
E/2010/SR.4; E/2010/SR.6
HUMANITARIAN ASSISTANCE (Agenda item 5)
E/2010/SR.33

**Sundnes, Trine Lise (Norway)**

GENDER EQUALITY (Agenda item 2c)
E/2010/SR.17(A)

**Tachie-Menson, Henry (Ghana)**

HUMANITARIAN ASSISTANCE (Agenda item 5)
E/2010/SR.34

**Tagle, Jorge (Chile)**

COORDINATION AND PROGRAMMES (Agenda item 7)
E/2010/SR.40
POST-CONFLICT RECONSTRUCTION–AFRICA
(Agenda item 7f)
E/2010/SR.40

**Taracena Secaira, Connie (Guatemala)**

UN. PERMANENT FORUM ON INDIGENOUS ISSUES
(Agenda item 14h)
E/2010/SR.44
WOMEN'S ADVANCEMENT (Agenda item 14a)
E/2010/SR.42

**Thomas, Laurent (FAO. Emergency Operations and Rehabilitation Division. Director)**

HUMANITARIAN ASSISTANCE (Agenda item 5)
E/2010/SR.35; E/2010/SR.35

**Tollefsen, Petter (Norway)**

NON-GOVERNMENTAL ORGANIZATIONS (Agenda item 12)
E/2010/SR.39

**Tommo Monthe, Michel (Cameroon)**

ECONOMIC ASSISTANCE–HAITI (Agenda item 7d)
E/2010/SR.44
REFUGEES (Agenda item 14e)
E/2010/SR.45
REGIONAL COOPERATION–AFRICA (Agenda item 10)
E/2010/SR.20

**Treffers, Rudolf Jan (IBRD)**

BRETTON WOODS INSTITUTIONS
E/2010/SR.6

**Tsymbaliuk, Yevhenii (Ukraine)**

REGIONAL COOPERATION (Agenda item 10)
E/2010/SR.41

**Tugsjargal, Gandi (Mongolia)**

GENDER EQUALITY (Agenda item 2c)
E/2010/SR.18(A)

**Tutuhatunewa, Spica Alphanya (Indonesia)**

CRIME PREVENTION (Agenda item 14c)
E/2010/SR.44
NARCOTIC DRUGS (Agenda item 14d)
E/2010/SR.44

**Urantsooj, Gombosuren (Mongolia)**

GENDER EQUALITY (Agenda item 2c)
E/2010/SR.18(A)

**Valero Briceño, Jorge (Venezuela (Bolivarian Republic of))**

BRETTON WOODS INSTITUTIONS
E/2010/SR.4
PALESTINIANS–TERRITORIES OCCUPIED BY
ISRAEL–LIVING CONDITIONS (Agenda item 11)
E/2010/SR.41

**Van der Velden, Mark (Netherlands)**

PALESTINIANS–TERRITORIES OCCUPIED BY
ISRAEL–LIVING CONDITIONS (Agenda item 11)
E/2010/SR.46

**Vasiliev, Sergey Yu. (Russian Federation)**

BRETTON WOODS INSTITUTIONS
E/2010/SR.7

**Vayrynen, Paavo (Finland)**

DEVELOPMENT COOPERATION FORUM (Agenda item 2b)
E/2010/SR.13

**Velichko, Irina (Belarus)**

CRIME PREVENTION (Agenda item 14c)
E/2010/SR.44
NARCOTIC DRUGS (Agenda item 14d)
E/2010/SR.44
REFUGEES (Agenda item 14e)
E/2010/SR.44

**Velichko, Irina (Belarus) (continued)**

WOMEN'S ADVANCEMENT (Agenda item 14a)
E/2010/SR.42

**Verveer, Melanne (United States)**

GENDER EQUALITY (Agenda item 2c)
E/2010/SR.15(A)

**Vianès, Michèle (France)**

GENDER EQUALITY (Agenda item 2c)
E/2010/SR.15(A)

**Vilovic, Ranko (Croatia)**

HUMAN RIGHTS (Agenda item 14g)
E/2010/SR.44

**Voltaire, Leslie (Haiti)**

ECONOMIC ASSISTANCE–HAITI (Agenda item 7d)
E/2010/SR.32

**Vos, Robert (UN. Department of Economic and Social Affairs. Development Policy Analysis Division. Director)**

BRETTON WOODS INSTITUTIONS
E/2010/SR.5; E/2010/SR.7

**Waffa-Ogoo, Susan (Gambia)**

EMPOWERMENT OF WOMEN (Agenda item 2d)
E/2010/SR.18(B)

**Wahab, Dewi Savitri (Indonesia)**

BRETTON WOODS INSTITUTIONS
E/2010/SR.5; E/2010/SR.6

**Walker, Peter (Feinstein International Center)**

HUMANITARIAN ASSISTANCE (Agenda item 5)
E/2010/SR.35

**Wang, Hongbo (China)**

HUMANITARIAN ASSISTANCE (Agenda item 5)
E/2010/SR.33

**Wang, Min (China)**

LEAST DEVELOPED COUNTRIES–INTERNATIONAL
DECADE (2001-2010) (Agenda item 6b)
E/2010/SR.37
OPERATIONAL ACTIVITIES–UN (Agenda item 3)
E/2010/SR.30
POVERTY MITIGATION (Agenda item 4)
E/2010/SR.23
RESOLUTIONS–UN. GENERAL ASSEMBLY–
IMPLEMENTATION (Agenda item 8)
E/2010/SR.23
UN CONFERENCES–FOLLOW-UP (Agenda item 6)
E/2010/SR.23

**Wang, Qun (China)**

ENVIRONMENT (Agenda item 13e)
E/2010/SR.43

**Wenaweser, Christian (Liechtenstein)**

EMPOWERMENT OF WOMEN (Agenda item 2d)
E/2010/SR.18(B)

**Wetland, Morten (Norway) (UN. Economic and Social Council (2010 : New York). Vice-President)**

POVERTY MITIGATION (Agenda item 4)
E/2010/SR.21

**Windsor, David Anthony (Australia)**

PALESTINIANS–TERRITORIES OCCUPIED BY
ISRAEL–LIVING CONDITIONS (Agenda item 11)
E/2010/SR.46
WOMEN'S ADVANCEMENT (Agenda item 14a)
E/2010/SR.42

**Wittig, Peter (Germany)**

BRETTON WOODS INSTITUTIONS
E/2010/SR.5
EMPOWERMENT OF WOMEN (Agenda item 2d)
E/2010/SR.18(B)
GENDER EQUALITY (Agenda item 2c)
E/2010/SR.12

**Wittig, Peter (UN. Peacebuilding Commission. Chairman)**

COORDINATION AND PROGRAMMES (Agenda item 7)
E/2010/SR.40
POST-CONFLICT RECONSTRUCTION–AFRICA
(Agenda item 7f)
E/2010/SR.40

**Workie, Daniel Yilma (Ethiopia)**

POVERTY MITIGATION (Agenda item 4)
E/2010/SR.23
RESOLUTIONS–UN. GENERAL ASSEMBLY–
IMPLEMENTATION (Agenda item 8)
E/2010/SR.23
UN CONFERENCES–FOLLOW-UP (Agenda item 6)
E/2010/SR.23

**Xu, Jing (China)**

NON-GOVERNMENTAL ORGANIZATIONS (Agenda
item 12)
E/2010/SR.39

**Yakovenko, Alexander V. (Russian Federation)**

EMPOWERMENT OF WOMEN (Agenda item 2d)
E/2010/SR.17(B)
GENDER EQUALITY (Agenda item 2c)
E/2010/SR.17(B)
INTERNATIONAL FINANCIAL INSTITUTIONS (Agenda
item 2a)
E/2010/SR.19(A)
REGIONAL COOPERATION–ASIA AND THE PACIFIC
(Agenda item 10)
E/2010/SR.20
REGIONAL COOPERATION–EUROPE (Agenda item
10)
E/2010/SR.20

**Yamashita, Nozomu (Japan)**

UN POLICY RECOMMENDATIONS–FOLLOW-UP
(Agenda item 3a)
E/2010/SR.31
UNDP/UNFPA (Agenda item 3b)
E/2010/SR.31
UNICEF (Agenda item 3b)
E/2010/SR.31
WORLD FOOD PROGRAMME (Agenda item 3b)
E/2010/SR.31

**Yánez-Barnuevo, Juan Antonio (Spain)**

GENDER EQUALITY (Agenda item 2c)
E/2010/SR.15(A)

**Yarlett, Kathryn (Australia)**

HUMANITARIAN ASSISTANCE (Agenda item 5)
E/2010/SR.34

**Yi, Xiaozhun (China)**

DEVELOPMENT COOPERATION FORUM (Agenda
item 2b)
E/2010/SR.13

**Zainal Abidin, Raja Nushirwan (Malaysia)**

BRETTON WOODS INSTITUTIONS
E/2010/SR.4; E/2010/SR.5

**Zdorov, Denis (Belarus)**

DEVELOPMENT FINANCE–CONFERENCE (2002 :
MONTERREY, MEXICO)–FOLLOW-UP (Agenda item
6a)
E/2010/SR.26
REGIONAL COOPERATION (Agenda item 10)
E/2010/SR.41

**Zeidan, Yousef (Palestine)**

WOMEN'S ADVANCEMENT (Agenda item 14a)
E/2010/SR.42

**Zhang, Dan (China)**

GENDER EQUALITY (Agenda item 2c)
E/2010/SR.18(A)

**Zinsou, Jean-Francis Régis (Benin)**

BRETTON WOODS INSTITUTIONS
E/2010/SR.6
ECONOMIC ASSISTANCE–HAITI (Agenda item 7d)
E/2010/SR.32

## BRETTON WOODS INSTITUTIONS

Association Femmes Soleil d'Haiti
  Edmond, Jean Paul – E/2010/SR.6
Australia
  Davies, Fleur Margaret – E/2010/SR.5; E/2010/SR.6
Bangladesh
  Rahman, Nojibur – E/2010/SR.4
Belgium
  Bassompierre, Christophe de – E/2010/SR.6
  Leroy, Marcus – E/2010/SR.5
Benin
  Zinsou, Jean-Francis Régis – E/2010/SR.6
Brazil
  Dunlop, Regina Maria Cordeiro – E/2010/SR.4
  Patriota, Guilherme de Aguiar – E/2010/SR.5;
    E/2010/SR.6
Canada
  McNee, John – E/2010/SR.4
Caribbean Community
  St. Aimee, Donatus Keith (Saint Lucia) –
    E/2010/SR.4; E/2010/SR.7
Chamber of Commerce of the United States of America
  Jordan, Stephen – E/2010/SR.6
China
  Li, Baodong – E/2010/SR.4
Colombia
  Guerra, María Paula – E/2010/SR.5
Cuba
  Navarro Barro, Nadieska – E/2010/SR.5
Development Committee. Executive Secretary
  Kodera, Kiyoshi – E/2010/SR.4
Egypt
  Edrees, Mohamed Fathi – E/2010/SR.4
El Salvador
  Gallardo Hernández, Carmen María – E/2010/SR.5
European Union
  Madrazo, Elena (Spain) – E/2010/SR.4
  Ortiz de Urbina, Yera (Spain) – E/2010/SR.5
France
  Cormon-Veyssière, Florence – E/2010/SR.7
  Follain, Moncef – E/2010/SR.5; E/2010/SR.6
Germany
  Wittig, Peter – E/2010/SR.5
Group of 77
  Alyemany, Khaled (Yemen) – E/2010/SR.4;
    E/2010/SR.5
Group of Landlocked Developing Countries
  Dos Santos, José Antonio (Paraguay) –
    E/2010/SR.7
Group of Least Developed Countries
  Acharya, Gyan Chandra (Nepal) – E/2010/SR.4
  Acharya, Madhu Raman (Nepal) – E/2010/SR.5
  Aguirre, Patricio (Nepal) – E/2010/SR.6
Guatemala
  Rosenthal, Gert – E/2010/SR.4; E/2010/SR.6;
    E/2010/SR.7

## BRETTON WOODS INSTITUTIONS (continued)

IBRD
  Braga, Carlos Alberto Primo – E/2010/SR.4;
    E/2010/SR.5; E/2010/SR.6
  Brandt, Anna Margaretha – E/2010/SR.4
  Cliffe, Sarah – E/2010/SR.6
  Dib, Sid Ahmed – E/2010/SR.5
  Kleist, Ruediger Wilhelm von – E/2010/SR.5
  Kvasov, Alexey – E/2010/SR.4; E/2010/SR.6
  Moorehead, Susanna – E/2010/SR.4
  Treffers, Rudolf Jan – E/2010/SR.6
IBRD. Poverty Reduction and Economic Management
  Lewis, Jeffrey D. – E/2010/SR.5
ILO
  Stewart, Jane – E/2010/SR.5
IMF
  Barendregt, Ester – E/2010/SR.5; E/2010/SR.7
  Geadah, Sami – E/2010/SR.7
  Luo, Yang – E/2010/SR.7
India
  Puri, Hardeep Singh – E/2010/SR.6
Indonesia
  Kleib, Hasan – E/2010/SR.4
  Nasir, Arrmanatha – E/2010/SR.7
  Wahab, Dewi Savitri – E/2010/SR.5; E/2010/SR.6
International Chamber of Commerce
  Kantrow, Louise – E/2010/SR.4
  Onambèlè, Joseph – E/2010/SR.7
International Institute for Human Rights, Environment
and Development (Kathmandu)
  Siwakoti, Gopal Krishna – E/2010/SR.6
International Monetary and Financial Committee
  Dimian, Hany (Egypt) – E/2010/SR.4
Iran (Islamic Republic of)
  Hassani Nejad Pirkouhi, Mohammad – E/2010/SR.6
Japan
  Murakami, Kenju – E/2010/SR.5
  Sumi, Shigeki – E/2010/SR.4; E/2010/SR.6
Jubilee Campaign
  Hanfstaengl, Eva – E/2010/SR.5
Libyan Arab Jamahiriya
  Alahraf, Mohamed A. A. – E/2010/SR.4
Malaysia
  Zainal Abidin, Raja Nushirwan – E/2010/SR.4;
    E/2010/SR.5
Mexico
  González Segura, Noel – E/2010/SR.6; E/2010/SR.7
  Heller, Claude – E/2010/SR.5
  Rovirosa, Socorro – E/2010/SR.4
Mongolia
  Enkhtsetseg, Ochir – E/2010/SR.6
  Nyam-Osor, Tuya – E/2010/SR.5
Morocco
  Iziraren, Tarik – E/2010/SR.5
Mozambique
  Macheve, António – E/2010/SR.7
New Rules for Global Finance Coalition
  Griesgraber, Jo Marie – E/2010/SR.7
NGO Committee on Financing for Development
  Dance, Kevin – E/2010/SR.4
Norway
  Fiskaa, Ingrid – E/2010/SR.4
Peru
  Chávez, Luis Enrique – E/2010/SR.7

## BRETTON WOODS INSTITUTIONS (continued)

Republic of Korea
Shin, Boonam – E/2010/SR.5
Rio Group
Aguirre, Patricio (Chile) – E/2010/SR.6
Gálvez, Eduardo (Chile) – E/2010/SR.4;
E/2010/SR.5; E/2010/SR.7
Russian Federation
Korneev, Mikhail – E/2010/SR.5
Vasiliev, Sergey Yu. – E/2010/SR.7
Spain
Martín Carretero, José Moisés – E/2010/SR.7
Switzerland
Bachmann, Matthias – E/2010/SR.6
Turkey
Dilekli, Evren – E/2010/SR.5; E/2010/SR.6
UN. Department of Economic and Social Affairs.
Development Policy Analysis Division. Director
Vos, Robert – E/2010/SR.5; E/2010/SR.7
UN. Economic and Social Council (2010 : New York).
President
Ali, Hamidon (Malaysia) – E/2010/SR.4;
E/2010/SR.7
UNCTAD
Gore, Charles – E/2010/SR.6
UNCTAD. Division on Globalization and Development
Strategies. Macroeconomic and Development Policies
Branch
Kotte, Detlef J. – E/2010/SR.7
UNCTAD. Trade and Development Board. President
Feyder, Jean – E/2010/SR.4; E/2010/SR.6
United Kingdom
Dodd, Eleanor – E/2010/SR.5
United States
Barton, Frederick D. – E/2010/SR.5
Sammis, John F. – E/2010/SR.4
Uruguay
Cancela, José Luis – E/2010/SR.5
Novoa, Natalia – E/2010/SR.7
Venezuela (Bolivarian Republic of)
Ovalles-Santos, Víctor Lautaro – E/2010/SR.5;
E/2010/SR.6; E/2010/SR.7
Valero Briceño, Jorge – E/2010/SR.4
Wisconsin Women's Business Initiative Corporation
Baumann, Wendy Katherine – E/2010/SR.5
World Trade Organization
Priyadarshi, Shishir – E/2010/SR.4; E/2010/SR.5;
E/2010/SR.6

## COORDINATION–REPORTS (Agenda item 7a)

Cuba
Cumberbatch Miguén, Jorge – E/2010/SR.26
Russian Federation
Birichevskiy, Dimitry – E/2010/SR.37
UN. Assistant Secretary-General for Policy Coordination
and Inter-Agency Affairs
Stelzer, Thomas – E/2010/SR.23; E/2010/SR.26

## COORDINATION AND PROGRAMMES (Agenda item 7)

Chile
Tagle, Jorge – E/2010/SR.40

## COORDINATION AND PROGRAMMES (Agenda item 7) (continued)

UN. Deputy Secretary-General
Migiro, Asha-Rose Mtengeti – E/2010/SR.40
UN. Economic and Social Council (2010 : New York).
President
Ali, Hamidon (Malaysia) – E/2010/SR.40
UN. Peacebuilding Commission. Chairman
Wittig, Peter – E/2010/SR.40

## CRIME PREVENTION (Agenda item 14c)

Belarus
Velichko, Irina – E/2010/SR.44
Brazil
Andrade, Pedro Aurélio Florencio Cabral de –
E/2010/SR.44
European Union
Geest, Ellen de (Belgium) – E/2010/SR.44
Indonesia
Tutuhatunewa, Spica Alphanya – E/2010/SR.44
Republic of Korea
Hwang, Hyuni – E/2010/SR.44
Ukraine
Kavun, Olha – E/2010/SR.44
UN. Economic and Social Council (2010 : New York).
President
Ali, Hamidon (Malaysia) – E/2010/SR.45
UN. Economic and Social Council (2010 : New York).
Vice-President
Soborun, Somduth (Mauritius) – E/2010/SR.45
UN Office on Drugs and Crime
Monasebian, Simone – E/2010/SR.44

## DECOLONIZATION (Agenda item 9)

Argentina
Díaz Bartolomé, Gerardo – E/2010/SR.46
Cuba
Benítez Versón, Rodolfo Eliseo – E/2010/SR.41
Group of 77
Al-Aud, Awsan Abdullah (Yemen) – E/2010/SR.41
Russian Federation
Alimov, Alexander S. – E/2010/SR.46
UN. Special Committee of 24. Chairman
St. Aimee, Donatus Keith (Saint Lucia) –
E/2010/SR.41
United States
Sammis, John F. – E/2010/SR.46
Venezuela (Bolivarian Republic of)
Anzola Padrón, Mariaelena Margarita –
E/2010/SR.41

## DEVELOPMENT COOPERATION FORUM (Agenda item 2b)

China
Yi, Xiaozhun – E/2010/SR.13
European Commission
Piebalgs, Andris – E/2010/SR.13
Finland
Vayrynen, Paavo – E/2010/SR.13

## DEVELOPMENT COOPERATION FORUM (Agenda item 2b) (continued)

UN. Economic and Social Council (2010 : New York). President
    Ali, Hamidon (Malaysia) – E/2010/SR.11; E/2010/SR.13; E/2010/SR.14; E/2010/SR.47
    Mérorès, Léo (Haiti) – E/2010/SR.16
UN. Under-Secretary-General for Economic and Social Affairs
    Sha, Zukang – E/2010/SR.13; E/2010/SR.47

## DEVELOPMENT FINANCE–CONFERENCE (2002 : MONTERREY, MEXICO)–FOLLOW-UP (Agenda item 6a)

Australia
    Lin, Katy – E/2010/SR.47
Bangladesh
    Rahman, A.K.M. Mashiur – E/2010/SR.26
Belarus
    Zdorov, Denis – E/2010/SR.26
Belgium
    Bassompierre, Christophe de – E/2010/SR.26
Brazil
    Almeida, João Lucas Quental Novaes de – E/2010/SR.46
European Union
    Bassompierre, Christophe de (Belgium) – E/2010/SR.47
Group of 77
    Al Shami, Waheed Abdulwahab Ahmed (Yemen) – E/2010/SR.46
    Al-Aud, Awsan Abdullah (Yemen) – E/2010/SR.47
ILO
    Diop, Assane – E/2010/SR.23
Mexico
    González Segura, Noel – E/2010/SR.26; E/2010/SR.46
Peru
    Gutiérrez, Gonzalo – E/2010/SR.26
Russian Federation
    Birichevskiy, Dimitry – E/2010/SR.26
Ukraine
    Sergeyev, Yuriy – E/2010/SR.26
UN. Under-Secretary-General for Economic and Social Affairs
    Sha, Zukang – E/2010/SR.26
Yemen
    Al-Aud, Awsan Abdullah – E/2010/SR.26

## ECONOMIC ASSISTANCE–HAITI (Agenda item 7d)

Benin
    Zinsou, Jean-Francis Régis – E/2010/SR.32
Brazil
    Dunlop, Regina Maria Cordeiro – E/2010/SR.32
Cameroon
    Tommo Monthe, Michel – E/2010/SR.44
Canada
    McNee, John – E/2010/SR.32
    Morrill, Keith – E/2010/SR.44
Chile
    Errázuriz, Octavio – E/2010/SR.32

## ECONOMIC ASSISTANCE–HAITI (Agenda item 7d) (continued)

Haiti
    Exantus, William – E/2010/SR.46
    Voltaire, Leslie – E/2010/SR.32
ILO
    Lazarte, Alfredo – E/2010/SR.32
Peru
    Gutiérrez, Gonzalo – E/2010/SR.32
UN. Economic and Social Council (2010 : New York). Deputy Secretary
    Pliner, Vivian C. – E/2010/SR.46
UN. Economic and Social Council (2010 : New York). President
    Ali, Hamidon (Malaysia) – E/2010/SR.47

## ECONOMIC, SOCIAL AND CULTURAL RIGHTS–TREATY (1966) (Agenda item 14g)

UN. Economic and Social Council (2010 : New York). Secretary
    De Laurentis, Jennifer – E/2010/SR.51

## EMPOWERMENT OF WOMEN (Agenda item 2d)

Argentina
    Argüello, Jorge – E/2010/SR.18(B)
Australia
    McMullan, Bob – E/2010/SR.17(B)
Austria
    Freudenschuss-Reichl, Irene – E/2010/SR.17(B)
Bahamas
    Bethel, Paulette A. – E/2010/SR.18(B)
Bangladesh
    Rahman, Nojibur – E/2010/SR.19(B)
Belarus
    Dapkiunas, Andrei – E/2010/SR.18(B)
Bolivia (Plurinational State of)
    Daza, Varinia – E/2010/SR.17(B)
Brazil
    Freire, Nilcéa – E/2010/SR.17(B)
Chile
    Errázuriz, Octavio – E/2010/SR.19(B)
China
    Li, Baodong – E/2010/SR.18(B)
Colombia
    Blum, Claudia – E/2010/SR.19(B)
Croatia
    Mikec, Neven – E/2010/SR.18(B)
Cuba
    Benítez Versón, Rodolfo Eliseo – E/2010/SR.18(B)
Czech Republic
    Kmonicek, Hynek – E/2010/SR.17(B)
El Salvador
    García González, Carlos Enrique – E/2010/SR.18(B)
Estonia
    Paet, Urmas – E/2010/SR.17(B)
Ethiopia
    Bame, Aman Hassen – E/2010/SR.18(B)
European Union
    Grauls, Jan (Belgium) – E/2010/SR.17(B)
FAO
    Ratsifandrihamanana, Lila Hanitra – E/2010/SR.19(B)

## EMPOWERMENT OF WOMEN (Agenda item 2d) (continued)

Gambia
    Waffa-Ogoo, Susan – E/2010/SR.18(B)
Germany
    Wittig, Peter – E/2010/SR.18(B)
Ghana
    Christian, Leslie – E/2010/SR.18(B)
Group of 77
    Al Shami, Waheed Abdulwahab Ahmed (Yemen) –
        E/2010/SR.47
    Alsaidi, Abdullah M. (Yemen) – E/2010/SR.17(B)
Group of Least Developed Countries
    Acharya, Gyan Chandra (Nepal) – E/2010/SR.17(B)
HelpAge International
    Lear, Judy – E/2010/SR.19(B)
Holy See
    Migliore, Celestino – E/2010/SR.18(B)
Honduras
    Flores, Mary Elizabeth – E/2010/SR.18(B)
ILO
    Gastaldo, Elena – E/2010/SR.19(B)
India
    Kaur, Preneet – E/2010/SR.19(B)
Inter-Parliamentary Union
    Mporogomyi, Kilontsi – E/2010/SR.19(B)
International Alliance of Women
    Sarlis, Irini – E/2010/SR.19(B)
International Association of Economic and Social
Councils and Similar Institutions
    Marzano, Antonio – E/2010/SR.19(B)
International Committee for Arab-Israeli Reconciliation
    Karmakar, Sudhangshu – E/2010/SR.19(B)
International Federation of Red Cross and Red Crescent
Societies
    Jilani, Marwan – E/2010/SR.19(B)
International Right to Life Federation
    Head, Jeanne – E/2010/SR.17(B)
Iran (Islamic Republic of)
    Farahi, Hossin – E/2010/SR.17(B)
Iraq
    Al Bayati, Hamid – E/2010/SR.19(B)
Israel
    Renford, Mazal – E/2010/SR.17(B)
Italy
    Carfagna, Mara – E/2010/SR.17(B)
Japan
    Okuda, Norihiro – E/2010/SR.19(B)
Kenya
    Manyala Keya, Atanas – E/2010/SR.17(B)
Latvia
    Silkalna, Solveiga – E/2010/SR.17(B)
Liechtenstein
    Wenaweser, Christian – E/2010/SR.18(B)
Lithuania
    Cekuolis, Dalius – E/2010/SR.18(B)
Mexico
    Heller, Claude – E/2010/SR.18(B)
Morocco
    Skalli, Nouzha – E/2010/SR.17(B)
Mozambique
    Abreu, Alcinda Antonio de – E/2010/SR.17(B)

## EMPOWERMENT OF WOMEN (Agenda item 2d) (continued)

Namibia
    Sioka, Doreen – E/2010/SR.17(B)
Nigeria
    Nwadinobi, Ezinne – E/2010/SR.19(B)
Organisation of the Islamic Conference
    Kalyoncu, Mehmet – E/2010/SR.19(B)
Pakistan
    Khosa, Sardar Muhammad Latif Khan –
        E/2010/SR.17(B)
Peru
    Gutiérrez, Gonzalo – E/2010/SR.18(B)
Philippines
    Cabactulan, Libran N. – E/2010/SR.19(B)
Poland
    Fedak, Jolanta – E/2010/SR.17(B)
Republic of Korea
    Shin, Kak-soo – E/2010/SR.18(B)
Russian Federation
    Yakovenko, Alexander V. – E/2010/SR.17(B)
Rwanda
    Sayinzoga, Kampeta – E/2010/SR.17(B)
Saudi Arabia
    Al Nafisee, Khalid Abdalrazaq – E/2010/SR.18(B)
Slovakia
    Algayerová, Olga – E/2010/SR.17(B)
South Africa
    Sangqu, Baso – E/2010/SR.18(B)
Switzerland
    Chave, Olivier – E/2010/SR.17(B)
Turkey
    Apakan, Ertugrul – E/2010/SR.18(B)
Ukraine
    Sergeyev, Yuriy – E/2010/SR.18(B)
UN. Economic and Social Council (2010 : New York).
President
    Ali, Hamidon (Malaysia) – E/2010/SR.47
UN. Economic and Social Council (2010 : New York).
Vice-President
    Soborun, Somduth (Mauritius) – E/2010/SR.17(B)
UN. Under-Secretary-General for Economic and Social
Affairs
    Sha, Zukang – E/2010/SR.15(B); E/2010/SR.47
United States
    Barton, Frederick D. – E/2010/SR.19(B)
Uruguay
    Cancela, José Luis – E/2010/SR.18(B)
Zambia
    Kalamwina, Christine – E/2010/SR.19(B)

## ENVIRONMENT (Agenda item 13e)

China
    Wang, Qun – E/2010/SR.43
European Union
    Delieux, Delphine (Belgium) – E/2010/SR.43
Iraq
    Al Bayati, Hamid – E/2010/SR.43
Russian Federation
    Kononuchenko, Sergei – E/2010/SR.43
UNEP
    Castaño, Juanita – E/2010/SR.43

## GENDER EQUALITY (Agenda item 2c)

Angola
  Chicoty, George – E/2010/SR.11
Argentina
  Rutilo, Gustavo – E/2010/SR.11
Australia
  McMullan, Bob – E/2010/SR.17(B);
    E/2010/SR.18(A)
Austria
  Freudenschuss-Reichl, Irene – E/2010/SR.17(B)
Azerbaijan
  Garayev, Asif – E/2010/SR.12
Bangladesh
  Rahman, Nojibur – E/2010/SR.15(A);
    E/2010/SR.19(B)
Bolivia (Plurinational State of)
  Daza, Varinia – E/2010/SR.17(B)
Brazil
  Freire, Nilcéa – E/2010/SR.11; E/2010/SR.17(B)
Burundi
  Nahayo, Adolphe – E/2010/SR.12
Cape Verde
  Lima, Antonio Pedro Monteiro – E/2010/SR.17(A)
Chile
  Bachelet, Michelle – E/2010/SR.11
  Errázuriz, Octavio – E/2010/SR.17(A);
    E/2010/SR.18(A); E/2010/SR.19(B)
China
  Zhang, Dan – E/2010/SR.18(A)
Colombia
  Blum, Claudia – E/2010/SR.19(B)
Congo
  Itoua, Martin – E/2010/SR.18(A)
  Leckomba Loumeto-Pombo, Jeanne Françoise –
    E/2010/SR.12; E/2010/SR.18(A)
  Ngapi, Cornelie Adou – E/2010/SR.18(A)
Czech Republic
  Kmonicek, Hynek – E/2010/SR.17(B)
Denmark
  Staur, Carsten – E/2010/SR.15(A)
Egypt
  Khattab, Moushira – E/2010/SR.11
Estonia
  Paet, Urmas – E/2010/SR.17(B)
European Union
  Bassompierre, Christophe de (Belgium) –
    E/2010/SR.19(A)
  Grauls, Jan (Belgium) – E/2010/SR.17(B)
FAO
  Ratsifandrihamanana, Lila Hanitra –
    E/2010/SR.19(B)
Finland
  Koukku-Ronde, Ritva – E/2010/SR.15(A);
    E/2010/SR.17(A)
France
  Heyfries, Fabrice – E/2010/SR.15(A)
  Sportis, Cécile – E/2010/SR.12; E/2010/SR.15(A);
    E/2010/SR.18(A)
  Vianès, Michèle – E/2010/SR.15(A)
Geena Davis Institute on Gender in Media
  Davis, Geena – E/2010/SR.11
Germany
  Wittig, Peter – E/2010/SR.12

## GENDER EQUALITY (Agenda item 2c) (continued)

Group of 77
  Al Shami, Waheed Abdulwahab Ahmed (Yemen) –
    E/2010/SR.47
  Alsaidi, Abdullah M. (Yemen) – E/2010/SR.17(B)
Group of Least Developed Countries
  Acharya, Gyan Chandra (Nepal) – E/2010/SR.17(B)
Guatemala
  Argueta de Barillas, Marisol – E/2010/SR.17(A)
  Montenegro, Mirna – E/2010/SR.12
  Rodríguez Pineda, Ana Cristina – E/2010/SR.12
  Rosenthal, Gert – E/2010/SR.11; E/2010/SR.12;
    E/2010/SR.15(A); E/2010/SR.17(A);
    E/2010/SR.19(B)
  Slowing-Umaña, Karin – E/2010/SR.12
HelpAge International
  Lear, Judy – E/2010/SR.19(B)
ILO
  Gastaldo, Elena – E/2010/SR.19(B)
India
  Kaur, Preneet – E/2010/SR.19(B)
Indonesia
  Kleib, Hasan – E/2010/SR.17(A)
International Alliance of Women
  Sarlis, Irini – E/2010/SR.19(B)
International Association of Economic and Social
Councils and Similar Institutions
  Marzano, Antonio – E/2010/SR.19(B)
International Committee for Arab-Israeli Reconciliation
  Karmakar, Sudhangshu – E/2010/SR.19(B)
International Olympic Committee
  DeFrantz, Anita L. – E/2010/SR.19(B)
International Organization for Migration
  Muedin, Amy – E/2010/SR.19(B)
International Right to Life Federation
  Head, Jeanne – E/2010/SR.17(B)
Iran (Islamic Republic of)
  Farahi, Hossin – E/2010/SR.17(B)
Iraq
  Al Bayati, Hamid – E/2010/SR.19(B)
Israel
  Renford, Mazal – E/2010/SR.12; E/2010/SR.15(A);
    E/2010/SR.17(B); E/2010/SR.18(A)
Italy
  Carfagna, Mara – E/2010/SR.17(B)
Japan
  Okuda, Norihiro – E/2010/SR.18(A);
    E/2010/SR.19(B)
Kenya
  Manyala Keya, Atanas – E/2010/SR.17(B)
Latvia
  Silkalna, Solveiga – E/2010/SR.17(B)
Liberia
  Chenoweth, Florence – E/2010/SR.11
Mexico
  Carreño, Aida – E/2010/SR.12
  García Gaytán, Maria del Rocio – E/2010/SR.11
Mongolia
  Enkhnasan, Nasan-Ulzii – E/2010/SR.18(A)
  Tugsjargal, Gandi – E/2010/SR.18(A)
  Urantsooj, Gombosuren – E/2010/SR.18(A)
Morocco
  Skalli, Nouzha – E/2010/SR.11; E/2010/SR.15(A);
    E/2010/SR.17(B)

## GENDER EQUALITY (Agenda item 2c) (continued)

Mozambique
Abreu, Alcinda Antonio de – E/2010/SR.17(B)
Namibia
Chirawu, Tapera O. – E/2010/SR.15(A)
Sioka, Doreen – E/2010/SR.15(A); E/2010/SR.17(B)
Netherlands
Dijksterhuis, Robert – E/2010/SR.12
Klerk, Piet de – E/2010/SR.17(A)
Schaper, Herman – E/2010/SR.12; E/2010/SR.15(A)
Norway
Fiskaa, Ingrid – E/2010/SR.17(A)
Moberg, Mette – E/2010/SR.17(A)
Oppegaard, Svein – E/2010/SR.17(A)
Sundnes, Trine Lise – E/2010/SR.17(A)
Organisation of the Islamic Conference
Kalyoncu, Mehmet – E/2010/SR.19(B)
Pakistan
Khosa, Sardar Muhammad Latif Khan –
E/2010/SR.17(B)
Papua New Guinea
Aisi, Robert Guba – E/2010/SR.18(A)
Poland
Fedak, Jolanta – E/2010/SR.17(B)
Portugal
Cravinho, Joao Gomes – E/2010/SR.17(A);
E/2010/SR.18(A)
Pais, Elza – E/2010/SR.17(A)
Rambhau Mhalgi Prabodhini (Organization : India)
Sahasrabuddhe, Vinay – E/2010/SR.12;
E/2010/SR.15(A)
Republic of Korea
Kim, Bonghyun – E/2010/SR.17(A)
Paik, Hee-Young – E/2010/SR.17(A)
Republic of Moldova
Bodiu, Victor – E/2010/SR.12
Bodrug-Lungu, Valentina – E/2010/SR.12
Pistrinciuk, Vadim – E/2010/SR.12
Romania
Miculescu, Simona Mirela – E/2010/SR.12
Russian Federation
Yakovenko, Alexander V. – E/2010/SR.17(B)
Rwanda
Sayinzoga, Kampeta – E/2010/SR.17(B)
Senegal
Diop, Maymouna – E/2010/SR.11
Slovakia
Algayerová, Olga – E/2010/SR.17(B)
South Africa
Dzivhani, Mbangiseni – E/2010/SR.15(A)
Spain
Yánez-Barnuevo, Juan Antonio – E/2010/SR.15(A)
Sweden
Grunditz, Marten – E/2010/SR.17(A)
Switzerland
Chave, Olivier – E/2010/SR.17(B)
Timor-Leste
Borges, Sofia – E/2010/SR.18(A)
UN. Committee for Development Policy
Stewart, Frances – E/2010/SR.11
UN. Economic and Social Council (2010 : New York).
President
Ali, Hamidon (Malaysia) – E/2010/SR.19(A);
E/2010/SR.47

## GENDER EQUALITY (Agenda item 2c) (continued)

UN. Economic and Social Council (2010 : New York).
Vice-President
Soborun, Somduth (Mauritius) – E/2010/SR.17(B)
UN. Under-Secretary-General for Economic and Social
Affairs
Sha, Zukang – E/2010/SR.15(A); E/2010/SR.15(B);
E/2010/SR.47
UNDP
Immonen, Kaarina – E/2010/SR.12
United Kingdom
Mitchell, Andrew – E/2010/SR.11
United Republic of Tanzania
Likwelile, Servacius – E/2010/SR.15(A)
United States
Barton, Frederick D. – E/2010/SR.11; E/2010/SR.12;
E/2010/SR.19(B)
Fulgham, Alonzo – E/2010/SR.15(A)
Verveer, Melanne – E/2010/SR.15(A)
Venezuela (Bolivarian Republic of)
Escalona Ojeda, Julio Rafael – E/2010/SR.19(B)
WMO
Batjargal, Zamba – E/2010/SR.18(A)
Yemen
Al Shami, Waheed Abdulwahab Ahmed –
E/2010/SR.19(A)
Zambia
Kalamwina, Christine – E/2010/SR.19(B)

## GENDER MAINSTREAMING–UN SYSTEM (Agenda item 7e)

Chile
Errázuriz, Octavio – E/2010/SR.47
Guatemala
Rosenthal, Gert – E/2010/SR.19(B)
International Organization for Migration
Muedin, Amy – E/2010/SR.19(B)

## GENETIC PRIVACY–DISCRIMINATION (Agenda item 14i)

Russian Federation
Birichevskiy, Dimitry – E/2010/SR.37
Unesco
Alfsen-Norodom, Christine – E/2010/SR.37

## HUMAN RIGHTS (Agenda item 14g)

Croatia
Vilovic, Ranko – E/2010/SR.44
Iraq
Al-Obaidi, Yahya Ibraheem Fadhil – E/2010/SR.44
Russian Federation
Lukiyantsev, Grigory Y. – E/2010/SR.44
Ukraine
Kavun, Olha – E/2010/SR.44
UN. Economic and Social Council (2010 : New York).
President
Ali, Hamidon (Malaysia) – E/2010/SR.45
UN. Economic and Social Council (2010 : New York).
Vice-President
Soborun, Somduth (Mauritius) – E/2010/SR.45

## HUMAN RIGHTS (Agenda item 14g) (continued)

UN. Office of the High Commissioner for Human Rights.
New York Office. Assistant Secretary-General
Simonovic, Ivan – E/2010/SR.44
UN Office on Drugs and Crime
Monasebian, Simone – E/2010/SR.44

## HUMAN SETTLEMENTS (Agenda item 13d)

Brazil
Farias, Fábio Moreira Carbonell – E/2010/SR.43
Canada
Morrill, Keith – E/2010/SR.43
European Union
Delieux, Delphine (Belgium) – E/2010/SR.43
UN-HABITAT
Djacta, Yamina – E/2010/SR.43
United States
Farrell, Sita – E/2010/SR.43

## HUMANITARIAN ASSISTANCE (Agenda item 5)

Argentina
Porretti, Eduardo – E/2010/SR.36
Australia
Yarlett, Kathryn – E/2010/SR.34
Bahamas
Bethel, Paulette A. – E/2010/SR.36
Bangladesh
Momen, Abulkalam Abdul – E/2010/SR.36
Rahman, A.K.M. Mashiur – E/2010/SR.35
Brazil
Dunlop, Regina Maria Cordeiro – E/2010/SR.33
Canada
Bonser, Michael – E/2010/SR.35
McNee, John – E/2010/SR.33
Chile
Errázuriz, Octavio – E/2010/SR.47
Gálvez, Eduardo – E/2010/SR.33
China
Wang, Hongbo – E/2010/SR.33
Colombia
Suárez Garzón, Carlos Alberto – E/2010/SR.34;
E/2010/SR.36
Cuba
Benítez Versón, Rodolfo Eliseo – E/2010/SR.33
Ethiopia
Bame, Aman Hassen – E/2010/SR.33
European Union
Grauls, Jan (Belgium) – E/2010/SR.33
Lallemand Zeller, Loïc – E/2010/SR.35
Stewart-David, Julia – E/2010/SR.34
FAO. Emergency Operations and Rehabilitation Division.
Director
Thomas, Laurent – E/2010/SR.35; E/2010/SR.35
Feinstein International Center
Walker, Peter – E/2010/SR.35
Ghana
Christian, Leslie – E/2010/SR.33
Tachie-Menson, Henry – E/2010/SR.34
Global Facility for Disaster Reduction and Recovery
Jha, Saroj Kumar – E/2010/SR.35
Group of 77
Al Shami, Waheed Abdulwahab Ahmed (Yemen) –
E/2010/SR.33

## HUMANITARIAN ASSISTANCE (Agenda item 5) (continued)

Guatemala
Del Águila-Castillo, María José – E/2010/SR.36
Holy See
Bharanikulangara, Kuriakose – E/2010/SR.36
India
Jaiswal, Randhir Kumar – E/2010/SR.36
Indonesia
Petranto, Ade – E/2010/SR.36
International Committee of the Red Cross
Stillhart, Dominik – E/2010/SR.34
International Organization for Migration
Muedin, Amy – E/2010/SR.36
International Red Cross
Mosquini, Elyse – E/2010/SR.36
Iraq
Al Bayati, Hamid – E/2010/SR.36
Al-Seedi, Razzaq Khleef Mansoor – E/2010/SR.34
Japan
Sumi, Shigeki – E/2010/SR.33
Kenya
Shaban, Naomi N. – E/2010/SR.33; E/2010/SR.35
Liechtenstein
Dornig, Swen – E/2010/SR.36
Malta
Looz Karageorgiades, Bertrand de – E/2010/SR.36
Mexico
Heller, Claude – E/2010/SR.36
Morocco
Loulichki, Mohammed – E/2010/SR.36
NGO Coordination Committee for Iraq
Mawazini, Fyras – E/2010/SR.34
Norway
Eckey, Susan – E/2010/SR.33; E/2010/SR.34
Organisation of the Islamic Conference
Gokcen, Ufuk – E/2010/SR.36
Pakistan
Sial, Amjad Hussain B. – E/2010/SR.33
Republic of Korea
Kim, Soo Gwon – E/2010/SR.33
Lee, So-rie – E/2010/SR.35
Russian Federation
Nebenzia, Vasilii – E/2010/SR.33
South Africa
Nofukuka, Xolulela Lawrence – E/2010/SR.36
Sweden
Byman, Per – E/2010/SR.35
Switzerland
Frisch, Toni – E/2010/SR.33
Ukraine
Sergeyev, Yuriy – E/2010/SR.36
UN. Deputy High Commissioner for Refugees
Aleinikoff, Thomas Alexander – E/2010/SR.34
UN. Economic and Social Council (2010 : New York).
President
Ali, Hamidon (Malaysia) – E/2010/SR.47
UN. Economic and Social Council (2010 : New York).
Secretary
Khane, Moncef – E/2010/SR.36
UN. Economic and Social Council (2010 : New York).
Vice-President
Errázuriz, Octavio (Chile) – E/2010/SR.33

## HUMANITARIAN ASSISTANCE (Agenda item 5) (continued)

UN. Office of the United Nations Humanitarian Coordinator for Pakistan
    Mogwanja, Martin – E/2010/SR.34
UN. Under-Secretary-General for Humanitarian Affairs and Emergency Relief Coordinator
    Holmes, John – E/2010/SR.33; E/2010/SR.34; E/2010/SR.35; E/2010/SR.36
UN. Under-Secretary-General for Safety and Security
    Starr, Gregory B. – E/2010/SR.34
Unesco
    Falatar, Boris – E/2010/SR.36
UNFPA. Humanitarian Response Branch. Chief
    Mahmood, Jemilah – E/2010/SR.35
UNHCR
    Janz, Udo – E/2010/SR.36
UNICEF
    Iyer, Akhil – E/2010/SR.36
United States
    Mercado, Douglas E. – E/2010/SR.34; E/2010/SR.36
Uruguay
    Cancela, José Luis – E/2010/SR.33
WHO
    Milovanovic, Ivana – E/2010/SR.36
WHO. Health Action in Crises. Assistant Director-General
    Laroche, Eric – E/2010/SR.35
World Food Programme
    Silva, Ramiro Armando de Oliveira Lopes da – E/2010/SR.34
Zambia
    Kalamwina, Christine – E/2010/SR.36

## INFORMATICS–INTERNATIONAL COOPERATION (Agenda item 7c)

Belarus
    Sergeev, Sergei – E/2010/SR.38
Belgium
    Bassompierre, Christophe de – E/2010/SR.52
Brazil
    Farias, Fábio Moreira Carbonell – E/2010/SR.38
Canada
    Morrill, Keith – E/2010/SR.38
China
    Chen, Yin – E/2010/SR.38
Egypt
    Hassan, Yasser – E/2010/SR.38
European Union
    Bassompierre, Christophe de (Belgium) – E/2010/SR.38
Group of 77
    Al-Aud, Awsan Abdullah (Yemen) – E/2010/SR.38
Iran (Islamic Republic of)
    Rajabi, Ahmad – E/2010/SR.38
Iraq
    Al Bayati, Hamid – E/2010/SR.38
Republic of Korea
    Kim, Chang-mo – E/2010/SR.38
Russian Federation
    Sirotkina, Marina A. – E/2010/SR.38

## INFORMATICS–INTERNATIONAL COOPERATION (Agenda item 7c) (continued)

UN. Assistant Secretary-General for Economic Development
    Jomo K.S. (Jomo Kwame Sundaram) – E/2010/SR.38
UN. Economic and Social Council (2010 : New York). Vice-President
    Soborun, Somduth (Mauritius) – E/2010/SR.38
UN. Information Technology Services Division. Director
    Blinder, Eduardo – E/2010/SR.38
UNCTAD. Division on Technology and Logistics. Science, Technology and ICT Branch
    Hamdi, Mongi – E/2010/SR.38
Unesco
    Alfsen-Norodom, Christine – E/2010/SR.38
United States
    Nemroff, Courtney – E/2010/SR.38

## INTERNATIONAL FINANCIAL INSTITUTIONS (Agenda item 2a)

Brazil
    Dunlop, Regina Maria Cordeiro – E/2010/SR.19(A)
European Union
    Spatolisano, Maria – E/2010/SR.19(A)
IBRD. Poverty Reduction and Economic Management
    Santos Filho, Otavio Canuto dos – E/2010/SR.19(A)
IMF. Strategy, Policy and Review Department. Director
    Moghadam, Reza – E/2010/SR.19(A)
Indonesia
    Herawan, Cecep – E/2010/SR.19(A)
International Trade Centre UNCTAD/WTO. Executive Director
    Francis, Patricia – E/2010/SR.19(A)
Kenya
    Sambili, Edward – E/2010/SR.19(A)
Nicaragua
    Oquist, Paul – E/2010/SR.19(A)
Pakistan
    Khosa, Sardar Muhammad Latif Khan – E/2010/SR.19(A)
Peru
    Gutiérrez, Gonzalo – E/2010/SR.19(A)
Russian Federation
    Yakovenko, Alexander V. – E/2010/SR.19(A)
Saint Lucia
    St. Aimee, Donatus Keith – E/2010/SR.19(A)
UN. Under-Secretary-General for Economic and Social Affairs
    Sha, Zukang – E/2010/SR.19(A)
UNCTAD. Secretary-General
    Panitchpakdi, Supachai – E/2010/SR.19(A)
World Trade Organization
    Boonekamp, Clemens – E/2010/SR.19(A)

## INTERNATIONAL NARCOTICS CONTROL BOARD– MEMBERS (Agenda item 1)

UN. Economic and Social Council (2010 : New York). Vice-President
    Soborun, Somduth (Mauritius) – E/2010/SR.42

## LEAST DEVELOPED COUNTRIES–INTERNATIONAL DECADE (2001-2010) (Agenda item 6b)

Bangladesh
Rahman, Nojibur – E/2010/SR.46
Brazil
Farias, Fábio Moreira Carbonell – E/2010/SR.37
China
Wang, Min – E/2010/SR.37
European Union
Lambert, Thomas (Belgium) – E/2010/SR.37
Group of 77
Al-Aud, Awsan Abdullah (Yemen) – E/2010/SR.37;
E/2010/SR.41
Group of Least Developed Countries
Acharya, Gyan Chandra (Nepal) – E/2010/SR.37;
E/2010/SR.46
India
Jaiswal, Randhir Kumar – E/2010/SR.37
Morocco
Loulichki, Mohammed – E/2010/SR.37
Republic of Korea
Kim, Chang-mo – E/2010/SR.37
Solomon Islands
Beck, Collin D. – E/2010/SR.37
Turkey
Corman, Fazli – E/2010/SR.37
UN. High Representative of the Secretary-General for
the Least Developed Countries, Landlocked Developing
Countries and Small Island Developing States
Diarra, Cheick Sidi – E/2010/SR.37

## NARCOTIC DRUGS (Agenda item 14d)

Belarus
Velichko, Irina – E/2010/SR.44
European Union
Geest, Ellen de (Belgium) – E/2010/SR.44
Indonesia
Tutuhatunewa, Spica Alphanya – E/2010/SR.44
International Narcotics Control Board. President
Ghodse, Hamid A. – E/2010/SR.44
Iran (Islamic Republic of)
Rajabi, Ahmad – E/2010/SR.44
Ukraine
Kavun, Olha – E/2010/SR.44
UN. Economic and Social Council (2010 : New York).
President
Ali, Hamidon (Malaysia) – E/2010/SR.45
UN. Economic and Social Council (2010 : New York).
Vice-President
Soborun, Somduth (Mauritius) – E/2010/SR.45
UN Office on Drugs and Crime
Monasebian, Simone – E/2010/SR.46

## NON-GOVERNMENTAL ORGANIZATIONS (Agenda item 12)

Argentina
Melon, María Luz – E/2010/SR.39
Australia
Goledzinowski, Andrew – E/2010/SR.39
Canada
Morrill, Keith – E/2010/SR.39

## NON-GOVERNMENTAL ORGANIZATIONS (Agenda item 12) (continued)

China
Xu, Jing – E/2010/SR.39
Egypt
Abdelaziz, Maged Abdelfattah – E/2010/SR.39
European Union
Grauls, Jan (Belgium) – E/2010/SR.39
Israel
Carmon, Daniel – E/2010/SR.39
Japan
Fujimoto, Shoko – E/2010/SR.39
Norway
Tollefsen, Petter – E/2010/SR.39
Peru
Rodríguez, Roberto – E/2010/SR.39
Russian Federation
Lukiyantsev, Grigory Y. – E/2010/SR.39
Saint Lucia
St. Aimee, Donatus Keith – E/2010/SR.39
Saudi Arabia
Al Nafisee, Khalid Abdalrazaq – E/2010/SR.39
UN. Economic and Social Council (2010 : New York).
Secretary
Gustafik, Otto – E/2010/SR.39
United Kingdom
Parham, Philip John – E/2010/SR.39
United States
DiCarlo, Rosemary A. – E/2010/SR.39
Uruguay
Alvarez, Gustavo – E/2010/SR.39
Venezuela (Bolivarian Republic of)
Romero, Moira Méndez – E/2010/SR.39

## OPERATIONAL ACTIVITIES–UN (Agenda item 3)

Belarus
Sergeev, Sergei – E/2010/SR.30
Brazil
Dunlop, Regina Maria Cordeiro – E/2010/SR.30
China
Wang, Min – E/2010/SR.30
European Union
Grauls, Jan (Belgium) – E/2010/SR.30
Group of 77
Alsaidi, Abdullah M. (Yemen) – E/2010/SR.30
Indonesia
Sardjana, Agus – E/2010/SR.30
Russian Federation
Piminov, Denis V. – E/2010/SR.30
Switzerland
Poretti, Mattia – E/2010/SR.30
UN. Economic and Social Council (2010 : New York).
President
Ali, Hamidon (Malaysia) – E/2010/SR.47
UN. Economic and Social Council (2010 : New York).
Vice-President
Cujba, Alexandru (Republic of Moldova) –
E/2010/SR.27
UN. Under-Secretary-General for Economic and Social
Affairs
Sha, Zukang – E/2010/SR.27; E/2010/SR.47

## PALESTINIANS–TERRITORIES OCCUPIED BY ISRAEL–LIVING CONDITIONS (Agenda item 11)

Australia
> Windsor, David Anthony – E/2010/SR.46

Cuba
> Benítez Versón, Rodolfo Eliseo – E/2010/SR.41

Egypt
> Khalil, Bassem – E/2010/SR.45

Group of 77
> Al-Aud, Awsan Abdullah (Yemen) – E/2010/SR.41

Indonesia
> Khan, Yusra – E/2010/SR.41

Iran (Islamic Republic of)
> Rajabi, Ahmad – E/2010/SR.41

Israel
> Davidovich, Shulamit Yona – E/2010/SR.41; E/2010/SR.46

Netherlands
> Van der Velden, Mark – E/2010/SR.46

Palestine
> Barghouti, Somaia – E/2010/SR.46
> Hijazi, Ammar M.B. – E/2010/SR.41

Saint Lucia
> St. Aimee, Donatus Keith – E/2010/SR.46

Syrian Arab Republic
> Ja'afari, Bashar – E/2010/SR.41

UN. Regional Commissions New York Office. Director
> Nour, Amr – E/2010/SR.41

Venezuela (Bolivarian Republic of)
> Valero Briceño, Jorge – E/2010/SR.41

## POST-CONFLICT RECONSTRUCTION–AFRICA (Agenda item 7f)

Chile
> Tagle, Jorge – E/2010/SR.40

UN. Deputy Secretary-General
> Migiro, Asha-Rose Mtengeti – E/2010/SR.40

UN. Economic and Social Council (2010 : New York). President
> Ali, Hamidon (Malaysia) – E/2010/SR.40

UN. Peacebuilding Commission. Chairman
> Wittig, Peter – E/2010/SR.40

## POVERTY MITIGATION (Agenda item 4)

Bahamas
> Bethel, Paulette A. – E/2010/SR.26

Brazil
> Almeida, João Lucas Quental Novaes de – E/2010/SR.23

China
> Wang, Min – E/2010/SR.23

Congo
> Fila, Jean-Lezin – E/2010/SR.26

Cuba
> Cumberbatch Miguén, Jorge – E/2010/SR.26

Ethiopia
> Workie, Daniel Yilma – E/2010/SR.23

European Union
> Bassompierre, Christophe de (Belgium) – E/2010/SR.23

Group of 77
> Alsaidi, Abdullah M. (Yemen) – E/2010/SR.23

## POVERTY MITIGATION (Agenda item 4) (continued)

India
> Gómez Durán, Rosa Delia – E/2010/SR.26
> Jaiswal, Randhir Kumar – E/2010/SR.26

Indonesia
> Petranto, Ade – E/2010/SR.23

International Association of Economic and Social Councils and Similar Institutions
> Marzano, Antonio – E/2010/SR.21

International Federation of Red Cross and Red Crescent Societies
> Oosterhof, Pytrik Dieuwke – E/2010/SR.26

Israel
> Fluss, Ilan Simon – E/2010/SR.26

Peru
> Gutiérrez, Gonzalo – E/2010/SR.23

Russian Federation
> Nebenzia, Vasilii – E/2010/SR.23

Switzerland
> Chave, Olivier – E/2010/SR.26

Ukraine
> Kavun, Olha – E/2010/SR.26

UN. Assistant Secretary-General for Policy Coordination and Inter-Agency Affairs
> Stelzer, Thomas – E/2010/SR.21

UN. Economic and Social Council (2010 : New York). Vice-President
> Wetland, Morten (Norway) – E/2010/SR.21

## REFUGEES (Agenda item 14e)

Belarus
> Velichko, Irina – E/2010/SR.44

Cameroon
> Tommo Monthe, Michel – E/2010/SR.45

Congo
> Maboundou, Raphael Dieudonné – E/2010/SR.50

Republic of Korea
> Hwang, Hyuni – E/2010/SR.44

UN. Economic and Social Council (2010 : New York). President
> Ali, Hamidon (Malaysia) – E/2010/SR.45

UN. Economic and Social Council (2010 : New York). Vice-President
> Soborun, Somduth (Mauritius) – E/2010/SR.45

UNHCR. New York Liaison Office. Director
> Janz, Udo – E/2010/SR.44

## REGIONAL COOPERATION (Agenda item 10)

Belarus
> Zdorov, Denis – E/2010/SR.41

Canada
> Morrill, Keith – E/2010/SR.42

Group of 77
> Al-Aud, Awsan Abdullah (Yemen) – E/2010/SR.41

Indonesia
> Herawan, Cecep – E/2010/SR.20

Iraq
> Al-Seedi, Razzaq Khleef Mansoor – E/2010/SR.20

Israel
> Renford, Mazal – E/2010/SR.20

## REGIONAL COOPERATION (Agenda item 10) (continued)

National Right to Life Educational Trust Fund (United States)
Head, Jeanne – E/2010/SR.20
Ukraine
Tsymbaliuk, Yevhenii – E/2010/SR.41
UN. Regional Commissions New York Office. Director
Nour, Amr – E/2010/SR.41

## REGIONAL COOPERATION–AFRICA (Agenda item 10)

Cameroon
Tommo Monthe, Michel – E/2010/SR.20
Congo
Bidounga, Ruffin – E/2010/SR.20
UN. ECA. Under-Secretary-General and Executive Secretary
Janneh, Abdoulie – E/2010/SR.20

## REGIONAL COOPERATION–ASIA AND THE PACIFIC (Agenda item 10)

Russian Federation
Yakovenko, Alexander V. – E/2010/SR.20
UN. ESCAP. Under-Secretary-General and Executive Secretary
Heyzer, Noeleen – E/2010/SR.20

## REGIONAL COOPERATION–EUROPE (Agenda item 10)

Russian Federation
Yakovenko, Alexander V. – E/2010/SR.20
UN. ECE. Under-Secretary-General and Executive Secretary
Kubis, Ján – E/2010/SR.20

## REGIONAL COOPERATION–LATIN AMERICA AND THE CARIBBEAN (Agenda item 10)

Brazil
Brichta, Daniella Poppius – E/2010/SR.20
Guatemala
Rosenthal, Gert – E/2010/SR.20
Peru
Morales, Fabiola – E/2010/SR.20
UN. ECLAC. Under-Secretary-General and Executive Secretary
Prado, Antonio – E/2010/SR.20
UN. Economic and Social Council (2010 : New York). Vice-President
Soborun, Somduth (Mauritius) – E/2010/SR.42

## REGIONAL COOPERATION–WESTERN ASIA (Agenda item 10)

UN. Economic and Social Council (2010 : New York). Deputy Secretary
Pliner, Vivian C. – E/2010/SR.42
UN. ESCWA. Centre for Women. Chief
Omer, Afaf – E/2010/SR.20

## RESOLUTIONS–UN. GENERAL ASSEMBLY–IMPLEMENTATION (Agenda item 8)

Bahamas
Bethel, Paulette A. – E/2010/SR.26
Brazil
Almeida, João Lucas Quental Novaes de – E/2010/SR.23
China
Wang, Min – E/2010/SR.23
Congo
Fila, Jean-Lezin – E/2010/SR.26
Cuba
Cumberbatch Miguén, Jorge – E/2010/SR.26
Ethiopia
Workie, Daniel Yilma – E/2010/SR.23
European Union
Bassompierre, Christophe de (Belgium) – E/2010/SR.23
Group of 77
Alsaidi, Abdullah M. (Yemen) – E/2010/SR.23
India
Gómez Durán, Rosa Delia – E/2010/SR.26
Jaiswal, Randhir Kumar – E/2010/SR.26
Indonesia
Petranto, Ade – E/2010/SR.23
Israel
Fluss, Ilan Simon – E/2010/SR.26
Peru
Gutiérrez, Gonzalo – E/2010/SR.23
Russian Federation
Nebenzia, Vasilii – E/2010/SR.23
Switzerland
Chave, Olivier – E/2010/SR.26
Ukraine
Kavun, Olha – E/2010/SR.26

## SCIENCE AND TECHNOLOGY–DEVELOPMENT (Agenda item 13b)

Belarus
Sergeev, Sergei – E/2010/SR.38
Brazil
Farias, Fábio Moreira Carbonell – E/2010/SR.38
Canada
Morrill, Keith – E/2010/SR.38
China
Chen, Yin – E/2010/SR.38
Egypt
Hassan, Yasser – E/2010/SR.38
European Union
Bassompierre, Christophe de (Belgium) – E/2010/SR.38
Group of 77
Al-Aud, Awsan Abdullah (Yemen) – E/2010/SR.38
Iran (Islamic Republic of)
Rajabi, Ahmad – E/2010/SR.38
Iraq
Al Bayati, Hamid – E/2010/SR.38
Republic of Korea
Kim, Chang-mo – E/2010/SR.38
Russian Federation
Sirotkina, Marina A. – E/2010/SR.38

## SCIENCE AND TECHNOLOGY–DEVELOPMENT (Agenda item 13b) (continued)

UN. Assistant Secretary-General for Economic Development
    Jomo K.S. (Jomo Kwame Sundaram) – E/2010/SR.38
UN. Economic and Social Council (2010 : New York). Vice-President
    Soborun, Somduth (Mauritius) – E/2010/SR.38
UNCTAD. Division on Technology and Logistics. Science, Technology and ICT Branch
    Hamdi, Mongi – E/2010/SR.38
Unesco
    Alfsen-Norodom, Christine – E/2010/SR.38
United States
    Nemroff, Courtney – E/2010/SR.38

## SOCIAL DEVELOPMENT (Agenda item 14b)

European Union
    Geest, Ellen de (Belgium) – E/2010/SR.44
Ius Primi Viri International Association
    Filiotis, Georgia – E/2010/SR.44
Russian Federation
    Rakovskiy, Nikolay S. – E/2010/SR.44
Ukraine
    Kavun, Olha – E/2010/SR.44
UN. Economic and Social Council (2010 : New York). President
    Ali, Hamidon (Malaysia) – E/2010/SR.11; E/2010/SR.45
UN. Economic and Social Council (2010 : New York). Vice-President
    Soborun, Somduth (Mauritius) – E/2010/SR.45
UN. Secretary-General
    Ban, Ki-moon, 1944- – E/2010/SR.11

## SUSTAINABLE DEVELOPMENT (Agenda item 13a)

Belarus
    Sergeev, Sergei – E/2010/SR.43
European Union
    Delieux, Delphine (Belgium) – E/2010/SR.43
FAO. Committee on World Food Security. Chair
    De Luna, Noel – E/2010/SR.43
Guatemala
    Leiva Roesch, Jimena – E/2010/SR.43
Indonesia
    Rahdiansyah, Danny – E/2010/SR.43
Iraq
    Al Bayati, Hamid – E/2010/SR.43
Maldives
    Hussain, Thilmeeza – E/2010/SR.43
Russian Federation
    Kononuchenko, Sergei – E/2010/SR.43
SIDSNet
    St. Aimee, Donatus Keith (Saint Lucia) – E/2010/SR.43
Ukraine
    Pavlichenko, Oleksandr – E/2010/SR.43
UN. Committee for Development Policy
    Najam, Adil – E/2010/SR.43
UN. Economic and Social Council (2010 : New York). President
    Ali, Hamidon (Malaysia) – E/2010/SR.45

## SUSTAINABLE DEVELOPMENT (Agenda item 13a) (continued)

UN. Economic and Social Council (2010 : New York). Vice-President
    Soborun, Somduth (Mauritius) – E/2010/SR.45

## TAXATION (Agenda item 13h)

Bahamas
    Bethel, Paulette A. – E/2010/SR.43
European Union
    Bassompierre, Christophe de (Belgium) – E/2010/SR.43
Russian Federation
    Kononuchenko, Sergei – E/2010/SR.43

## TOBACCO–HEALTH (Agenda item 7g)

Group of 77
    Al-Aud, Awsan Abdullah (Yemen) – E/2010/SR.38
Morocco
    Belakhel, Latifa – E/2010/SR.37
Russian Federation
    Birichevskiy, Dimitry – E/2010/SR.37
UN. Economic and Social Council (2010 : New York). President
    Ali, Hamidon (Malaysia) – E/2010/SR.45
UN. Economic and Social Council (2010 : New York). Vice-President
    Soborun, Somduth (Mauritius) – E/2010/SR.45
WHO
    Bettcher, Douglas – E/2010/SR.37

## UN. COMMISSION ON POPULATION AND DEVELOPMENT–MEMBERS (Agenda item 1)

UN. Economic and Social Council (2010 : New York). Vice-President
    Soborun, Somduth (Mauritius) – E/2010/SR.42

## UN. COMMITTEE FOR DEVELOPMENT POLICY–MEMBERS (Agenda item 1)

UN. Economic and Social Council (2010 : New York). Vice-President
    Soborun, Somduth (Mauritius) – E/2010/SR.42

## UN. COMMITTEE OF EXPERTS ON INTERNATIONAL COOPERATION IN TAX MATTERS–MEMBERS (Agenda item 1)

UN. Economic and Social Council (2010 : New York). President
    Ali, Hamidon (Malaysia) – E/2010/SR.49

## UN. ECONOMIC AND SOCIAL COUNCIL (2010, SUBSTANTIVE SESS. : NEW YORK)–AGENDA (Agenda item 1)

Canada
    Morrill, Keith – E/2010/SR.47
United Republic of Tanzania
    Mero, Modest Jonathan – E/2010/SR.47

## UN. PERMANENT FORUM ON INDIGENOUS ISSUES (Agenda item 14h)

Bangladesh
Momen, Abulkalam Abdul – E/2010/SR.44
Guatemala
Taracena Secaira, Connie – E/2010/SR.44
India
Jaiswal, Randhir Kumar – E/2010/SR.44
UN. Economic and Social Council (2010 : New York). President
Ali, Hamidon (Malaysia) – E/2010/SR.45
UN. Economic and Social Council (2010 : New York). Vice-President
Soborun, Somduth (Mauritius) – E/2010/SR.45

## UN. SUBCOMMITTEE OF EXPERTS ON THE TRANSPORT OF DANGEROUS GOODS– MEMBERS (Agenda item 1)

UN. Economic and Social Council (2010 : New York). President
Ali, Hamidon (Malaysia) – E/2010/SR.49

## UN CONFERENCES–FOLLOW-UP (Agenda item 6)

Bahamas
Bethel, Paulette A. – E/2010/SR.26
Brazil
Almeida, João Lucas Quental Novaes de – E/2010/SR.23
China
Wang, Min – E/2010/SR.23
Congo
Fila, Jean-Lezin – E/2010/SR.26
Cuba
Cumberbatch Miguén, Jorge – E/2010/SR.26
Ethiopia
Workie, Daniel Yilma – E/2010/SR.23
European Union
Bassompierre, Christophe de (Belgium) – E/2010/SR.23
Group of 77
Alsaidi, Abdullah M. (Yemen) – E/2010/SR.23
India
Gómez Durán, Rosa Delia – E/2010/SR.26
Jaiswal, Randhir Kumar – E/2010/SR.26
Indonesia
Petranto, Ade – E/2010/SR.23
International Federation of Red Cross and Red Crescent Societies
Oosterhof, Pytrik Dieuwke – E/2010/SR.26
Israel
Fluss, Ilan Simon – E/2010/SR.26
Peru
Gutiérrez, Gonzalo – E/2010/SR.23
Russian Federation
Nebenzia, Vasilii – E/2010/SR.23
Switzerland
Chave, Olivier – E/2010/SR.26
Ukraine
Kavun, Olha – E/2010/SR.26

## UN POLICY RECOMMENDATIONS–FOLLOW-UP (Agenda item 3a)

Australia
Cohen, Nathalie – E/2010/SR.29; E/2010/SR.31
Bangladesh
Momen, Abulkalam Abdul – E/2010/SR.31
Rahman, Nojibur – E/2010/SR.29
Brazil
Leite, Bruno – E/2010/SR.29
Cuba
Cumberbatch Miguén, Jorge – E/2010/SR.29; E/2010/SR.31
Egypt
Elshaar, Hussein – E/2010/SR.29
European Union
Charlier, Pierre (Belgium) – E/2010/SR.29; E/2010/SR.46
India
Jaiswal, Randhir Kumar – E/2010/SR.31
International Labour Office
Amorim, Anita – E/2010/SR.31
Israel
Fluss, Ilan Simon – E/2010/SR.29; E/2010/SR.31
Japan
Yamashita, Nozomu – E/2010/SR.31
Malawi
Ning'ang'a, Eric – E/2010/SR.29
Norway
Ajamay, Astrid Helle – E/2010/SR.29; E/2010/SR.31
Republic of Korea
Lee, So-rie – E/2010/SR.29
Russian Federation
Savostianov, Mikhail Y. – E/2010/SR.29
UN. Economic and Social Council (2010 : New York). Vice-President
Cujba, Alexandru (Republic of Moldova) – E/2010/SR.27; E/2010/SR.31
UN. Under-Secretary-General for Economic and Social Affairs
Sha, Zukang – E/2010/SR.27
UNDP. Administrator
Clark, Helen – E/2010/SR.29
UNFPA. Executive Director
Obaid, Thoraya – E/2010/SR.29
UNICEF
Lake, Tony – E/2010/SR.29
United States
Barton, Frederick D. – E/2010/SR.29
World Food Programme
Silva, Ramiro Armando de Oliveira Lopes da – E/2010/SR.29

## UN-HABITAT. GOVERNING COUNCIL–MEMBERS (Agenda item 1)

UN. Economic and Social Council (2010 : New York). Vice-President
Soborun, Somduth (Mauritius) – E/2010/SR.42

## UN-WOMEN. EXECUTIVE BOARD–MEMBERS (Agenda item 1)

UN. Economic and Social Council (2010 : New York).
President
    Ali, Hamidon (Malaysia) – E/2010/SR.48;
      E/2010/SR.49; E/2010/SR.50
UN. Economic and Social Council (2010 : New York).
Secretary
    De Laurentis, Jennifer – E/2010/SR.50

## UNDP/UNFPA (Agenda item 3b)

Australia
    Cohen, Nathalie – E/2010/SR.31
Bangladesh
    Momen, Abulkalam Abdul – E/2010/SR.31
    Rahman, Nojibur – E/2010/SR.29
Cuba
    Cumberbatch Miguén, Jorge – E/2010/SR.29;
      E/2010/SR.31
European Union
    Charlier, Pierre (Belgium) – E/2010/SR.29
India
    Jaiswal, Randhir Kumar – E/2010/SR.31
International Labour Office
    Amorim, Anita – E/2010/SR.31
Israel
    Fluss, Ilan Simon – E/2010/SR.31
Japan
    Yamashita, Nozomu – E/2010/SR.31
Malawi
    Ning'ang'a, Eric – E/2010/SR.29
Norway
    Ajamay, Astrid Helle – E/2010/SR.29; E/2010/SR.31
Republic of Korea
    Lee, So-rie – E/2010/SR.29
Ukraine
    Prorok, Hanna V. – E/2010/SR.30
UN. Economic and Social Council (2010 : New York).
Vice-President
    Cujba, Alexandru (Republic of Moldova) –
      E/2010/SR.31
UNDP. Administrator
    Clark, Helen – E/2010/SR.29
UNFPA. Executive Director
    Obaid, Thoraya – E/2010/SR.29

## UNICEF (Agenda item 3b)

Australia
    Cohen, Nathalie – E/2010/SR.31
Bangladesh
    Momen, Abulkalam Abdul – E/2010/SR.31
Cuba
    Cumberbatch Miguén, Jorge – E/2010/SR.31
European Union
    Charlier, Pierre (Belgium) – E/2010/SR.29
India
    Jaiswal, Randhir Kumar – E/2010/SR.31
International Labour Office
    Amorim, Anita – E/2010/SR.31
Israel
    Fluss, Ilan Simon – E/2010/SR.31
Japan
    Yamashita, Nozomu – E/2010/SR.31

## UNICEF (Agenda item 3b) (continued)

Malawi
    Ning'ang'a, Eric – E/2010/SR.29
Norway
    Ajamay, Astrid Helle – E/2010/SR.29; E/2010/SR.31
Ukraine
    Prorok, Hanna V. – E/2010/SR.30
UN. Economic and Social Council (2010 : New York).
Vice-President
    Cujba, Alexandru (Republic of Moldova) –
      E/2010/SR.31
UNDP. Administrator
    Clark, Helen – E/2010/SR.29
UNICEF
    Lake, Tony – E/2010/SR.29

## WOMEN IN DEVELOPMENT (Agenda item 13k)

Bangladesh
    Rahman, Nojibur – E/2010/SR.19(B)
Chile
    Errázuriz, Octavio – E/2010/SR.19(B)
Colombia
    Blum, Claudia – E/2010/SR.19(B)
FAO
    Ratsifandrihamanana, Lila Hanitra –
      E/2010/SR.19(B)
India
    Kaur, Preneet – E/2010/SR.19(B)
Iraq
    Al Bayati, Hamid – E/2010/SR.19(B)
Japan
    Okuda, Norihiro – E/2010/SR.19(B)
Nigeria
    Nwadinobi, Ezinne – E/2010/SR.19(B)
Organisation of the Islamic Conference
    Kalyoncu, Mehmet – E/2010/SR.19(B)
Philippines
    Cabactulan, Libran N. – E/2010/SR.19(B)
UN. Economic and Social Council (2010 : New York).
President
    Ali, Hamidon (Malaysia) – E/2010/SR.11
UN. Secretary-General
    Ban, Ki-moon, 1944- – E/2010/SR.11
United States
    Barton, Frederick D. – E/2010/SR.19(B)
World Society for the Protection of Animals
    Sakoh, Mayumi – E/2010/SR.19(B)
Zambia
    Kalamwina, Christine – E/2010/SR.19(B)

## WOMEN'S ADVANCEMENT (Agenda item 14a)

Australia
    Windsor, David Anthony – E/2010/SR.42
Bangladesh
    Rahman, Nojibur – E/2010/SR.19(B)
Belarus
    Velichko, Irina – E/2010/SR.42
Chile
    Errázuriz, Octavio – E/2010/SR.19(B)
    Peña, Belén Muñoz de la – E/2010/SR.42
Colombia
    Blum, Claudia – E/2010/SR.19(B)

## WOMEN'S ADVANCEMENT (Agenda item 14a) (continued)

Dominican Republic
Montilla, Marcos – E/2010/SR.42
European Union
Nihon, Nicolas (Belgium) – E/2010/SR.42
Guatemala
Taracena Secaira, Connie – E/2010/SR.42
India
Kaur, Preneet – E/2010/SR.19(B)
Inter-Parliamentary Union
Mporogomyi, Kilontsi – E/2010/SR.19(B)
International Federation of Red Cross and Red Crescent
Societies
Jilani, Marwan – E/2010/SR.19(B)
Iraq
Al Bayati, Hamid – E/2010/SR.19(B)
Mohammed, Ahmed Hameed – E/2010/SR.42
Israel
Davidovich, Shulamit Yona – E/2010/SR.42
Japan
Okuda, Norihiro – E/2010/SR.19(B)
Nigeria
Nwadinobi, Ezinne – E/2010/SR.19(B)
Organisation of the Islamic Conference
Kalyoncu, Mehmet – E/2010/SR.19(B)
Palestine
Zeidan, Yousef – E/2010/SR.42
Peru
Rodríguez, Roberto – E/2010/SR.42
Philippines
Cabactulan, Libran N. – E/2010/SR.19(B)
Republic of Korea
Hwang, Hyuni – E/2010/SR.42
Russian Federation
Rakovskiy, Nikolay S. – E/2010/SR.42
Ukraine
Kavun, Olha – E/2010/SR.42
UN. Economic and Social Council (2010 : New York).
President
Ali, Hamidon (Malaysia) – E/2010/SR.11
UN. Secretary-General
Ban, Ki-moon, 1944- – E/2010/SR.11
UN. Special Adviser to the Secretary-General on Gender
Issues and Advancement of Women
Mayanja, Rachel N. – E/2010/SR.42
United States
Barton, Frederick D. – E/2010/SR.19(B)
Phipps, Laurie Shestack – E/2010/SR.42
Venezuela (Bolivarian Republic of)
Escalona Ojeda, Julio Rafael – E/2010/SR.19(B)
Zambia
Kalamwina, Christine – E/2010/SR.19(B)

## WORLD FOOD PROGRAMME (Agenda item 3b)

Australia
Cohen, Nathalie – E/2010/SR.31
Bangladesh
Momen, Abulkalam Abdul – E/2010/SR.31
Rahman, Nojibur – E/2010/SR.29
Cuba
Cumberbatch Miguén, Jorge – E/2010/SR.31

## WORLD FOOD PROGRAMME (Agenda item 3b) (continued)

European Union
Charlier, Pierre (Belgium) – E/2010/SR.29
India
Jaiswal, Randhir Kumar – E/2010/SR.31
International Labour Office
Amorim, Anita – E/2010/SR.31
Israel
Fluss, Ilan Simon – E/2010/SR.31
Japan
Yamashita, Nozomu – E/2010/SR.31
Malawi
Ning'ang'a, Eric – E/2010/SR.29
Norway
Ajamay, Astrid Helle – E/2010/SR.29; E/2010/SR.31
UN. Economic and Social Council (2010 : New York).
Vice-President
Cujba, Alexandru (Republic of Moldova) –
E/2010/SR.31
World Food Programme
Silva, Ramiro Armando de Oliveira Lopes da –
E/2010/SR.29

# LIST OF RESOLUTIONS

*Vote reads Yes-No-Abstain*

| E/RES/2010/ | Title | Meeting / Date, 2010 (E/2010/SR.-) | A.I. No. | Vote |
|---|---|---|---|---|
| 1 | Strengthening of the coordination of emergency humanitarian assistance of the United Nations | 36 / 15 July 10 | 5 | without vote |
| 2 | Assessment of the progress made in the implementation of and follow-up to the outcomes of the World Summit on the Information Society | 39 / 19 July 10 | 13b | without vote |
| 3 | Science and technology for development | 39 / 19 July 10 | 13b | without vote |
| 4 | Venue of the 34th session of the Economic Commission for Latin America and the Caribbean | 42 / 20 July 10 | 10 | without vote |
| 5 | Establishment of the Economic and Social Commission for Western Asia Technology Centre | 42 / 20 July 10 | 10 | without vote |
| 6 | Situation of and assistance to Palestinian women | 42 / 20 July 10 | 14a | 24-3-15 |
| 7 | Strengthening the institutional arrangements for support of gender equality and the empowerment of women | 42 / 20 July 10 | 14a | without vote |
| 8 | Tobacco use and maternal and child health | 45 / 22 July 10 | 7g | without vote |
| 9 | Report of the Committee for Development Policy on its 12th session | 45 / 22 July 10 | 13a | without vote |
| 10 | Future organization and methods of work of the Commission for Social Development | 45 / 22 July 10 | 14b | without vote |
| 11 | Social dimensions of the New Partnership for Africa's Development | 45 / 22 July 10 | 14b | without vote |
| 12 | Promoting social integration | 45 / 22 July 10 | 14b | without vote |
| 13 | Mainstreaming disability in the development agenda | 45 / 22 July 10 | 14b | without vote |
| 14 | Future implementation of the Madrid International Plan of Action on Ageing, 2002 | 45 / 22 July 10 | 14b | without vote |
| 15 | Strengthening crime prevention and criminal justice responses to violence against women | 45 / 22 July 10 | 14c | without vote |
| 16 | United Nations Rules for the Treatment of Women Prisoners and Non-custodial Measures for Women Offenders (the Bangkok Rules) | 45 / 22 July 10 | 14c | without vote |
| 17 | Realignment of the functions of the United Nations Office on Drugs and Crime and changes to the strategic framework | 45 / 22 July 10 | 14c | without vote |
| 18 | Twelfth United Nations Congress on Crime Prevention and Criminal Justice | 45 / 22 July 10 | 14c | without vote |
| 19 | Crime prevention and criminal justice responses to protect cultural property, especially with regard to its trafficking | 45 / 22 July 10 | 14c | without vote |
| 20 | Support for the development and implementation of an integrated approach to programme development at the United Nations Office on Drugs and Crime | 45 / 22 July 10 | 14c | without vote |
| 21 | Realignment of the functions of the United Nations Office on Drugs and Crime and changes to the strategic framework | 45 / 22 July 10 | 14d | without vote |
| 22 | Progress in the implementation of General Assembly resolution 62/208 on the triennial comprehensive policy review of operational activities for development of the United Nations system | 46 / 23 July 10 | 3a | without vote |
| 23 | Renaming of the title of the Executive Board of the United Nations Development Programme and the United Nations Population Fund to include the United Nations Office for Project Services | 46 / 23 July 10 | 3b | without vote |
| 24 | The role of the United Nations system in implementing the ministerial declaration on the internationally agreed goals and commitments in regard to global public health adopted at the high-level segment of the 2009 substantive session of the Economic and Social Council | 46 / 23 July 10 | 4 | without vote |
| 25 | Recovering from the world financial and economic crisis : a Global Jobs Pact | 46 / 23 July 10 | 6a | without vote |
| 26 | Follow-up to the International Conference on Financing for Development and the 2008 Review Conference | 46 / 23 July 10 | 6a | without vote |

# LIST OF RESOLUTIONS

| E/RES/2010/ | Title | Meeting / Date, 2010 (E/2010/SR.-) | A.I. No. | Vote |
|---|---|---|---|---|
| 27 | Implementation of the Programme of Action for the Least Developed Countries for the Decade 2001-2010 | 46 / 23 July 10 | 6b | without vote |
| 28 | Ad Hoc Advisory Group on Haiti | 46 / 23 July 10 | 7d | without vote |
| 29 | Mainstreaming a gender perspective into all policies and programmes in the United Nations system | 46 / 23 July 10 | 7e | without vote |
| 30 | Support to Non-Self-Governing Territories by the specialized agencies and international institutions associated with the United Nations | 46 / 23 July 10 | 9 | 26-0-26 |
| 31 | Economic and social repercussions of the Israeli occupation on the living conditions of the Palestinian people in the Occupied Palestinian Territory, including East Jerusalem, and the Arab population in the occupied Syrian Golan | 46 / 23 July 10 | 11 | 45-3-3 |
| 32 | Consolidated List of Products Whose Consumption and / or Sale Have Been Banned, Withdrawn, Severely Restricted or Not Approved by Governments | 46 / 23 July 10 | 13e | without vote |
| 33 | Committee of Experts on International Cooperation in Tax Matters | 46 / 23 July 10 | 13h | without vote |
| 34 | Review of United Nations support for small island developing States | 47 / 23 July 10 | 13a | without vote |
| 35 | Procedures for the election of the members of the Executive Board of the United Nations Entity for Gender Equality and the Empowerment of Women | 49 / 25 Oct. 10 | 1 | without vote |
| 36 | Membership of the Economic and Social Council in the Organizational Committee of the Peacebuilding Commission | 51 / 14 Dec. 10 | 1 | without vote |
| 37 | Report of the Committee on Economic, Social and Cultural Rights on its 42nd and 43rd sessions | 51 / 14 Dec. 10 | 14g | without vote |
| 38 | The need to harmonize and improve United Nations informatics systems for optimal utilization and accessibility by all States | 52 / 15 Dec. 10 | 7c | without vote |

# LIST OF DOCUMENTS

NOTE: Languages of corrigenda are indicated only when corrigenda are not issued in all six languages. Documents issued as Supplements to the Official Records of the Economic and Social Council, 2010 are also indicated. The information provided below is current as of the date this Index is submitted for publication.

**General series**

E/2010/1
E/2010/2 + Corr.1
E/2010/2/Add.1
E/2010/3 (A/64/578)
E/2010/4 (E/CN.6/2010/2)
E/2010/5
E/2010/6 (E/ICEF/2010/3)
E/2010/7
E/2010/8 (A/64/649)
E/2010/9 + Add.1-22
E/2010/10
E/2010/11
E/2010/12 (A/65/64)
E/2010/13 (A/65/72)
E/2010/14
E/2010/15 + Add.1
E/2010/16
E/2010/17
E/2010/18
E/2010/19
E/2010/20
E/2010/21 *Symbol not used*
E/2010/22 (E/C.12/2009/3) (ESCOR, 2010, Suppl. no. 2)
E/2010/23 *Symbol not used*
E/2010/24 (E/CN.3/2010/34) (ESCOR, 2010, Suppl. no. 4)
E/2010/25 (E/CN.9/2010/9) (ESCOR, 2010, Suppl. no. 5)
E/2010/26 (E/CN.5/2010/9) (ESCOR, 2010, Suppl. no. 6)
E/2010/27 + Corr.1 (E/CN.6/2010/11 + Corr.1) (ESCOR, 2010, Suppl. no. 7)
E/2010/28 (E/CN.7/2010/18) (ESCOR, 2010, Suppl. no. 8)
E/2010/28/Add.1 (E/CN.7/2010/18/Add.1) (ESCOR, 2010, Suppl. no. 8A)
E/2010/29 (E/CN.17/2010/15) (ESCOR, 2010, Suppl. no. 9)
E/2010/30 (E/CN.15/2010/20) (ESCOR, 2010, Suppl. no. 10)
E/2010/30/Add.1 (E/CN.15/2010/20/Add.1) (ESCOR, 2010, Suppl. no. 10A
E/2010/31 (E/CN.16/2010/5) (ESCOR, 2010, Suppl. no. 11)
E/2010/32(PartI)
E/2010/32(PartII)
E/2010/33 (ESCOR, 2010, Suppl. no. 13)
E/2010/34/Rev.1 (E/ICEF/2010/7/Rev.1) (ESCOR, 2010, Suppl. no. 14)
E/2010/34(PartI) + Add.1 (E/ICEF/2010/7(PartI) + Add.1)
E/2010/34(PartII) + Corr.1 (E/ICEF/2010/7(PartII) + Corr.1)
E/2010/35 (ESCOR, 2010, Suppl. no. 15)
E/2010/36 (ESCOR, 2010, Suppl. no. 16)
E/2010/37 *Symbol not used*
E/2010/38 *Symbol not used*
E/2010/39 (E/ESCAP/66/27) (ESCOR, 2010, Suppl. no. 19)
E/2010/40 *Symbol not used*
E/2010/41 (E/ESCWA/26/9/Report) (ESCOR, 2010, Suppl. no. 21)
E/2010/42 *Symbol not used*
E/2010/43 (E/C.19/2010/15) (ESCOR, 2010, Suppl. no. 23)
E/2010/44 (E/C.16/2010/5) (ESCOR, 2010, Suppl. no. 24)

**General series**

E/2010/45 (E/C.18/2010/7) (ESCOR, 2010, Suppl. no. 25)
E/2010/46 *Symbol not used*
E/2010/47
E/2010/48
E/2010/49
E/2010/50
E/2010/50/Rev.1 (ST/ESA/330)
E/2010/51 (A/65/73)
E/2010/52
E/2010/53
E/2010/54 + Add.1
E/2010/55 + Corr.1
E/2010/56 (A/65/77)
E/2010/57
E/2010/58
E/2010/59
E/2010/60
E/2010/61
E/2010/62
E/2010/63
E/2010/64
E/2010/65
E/2010/66
E/2010/67
E/2010/68 (A/65/78)
E/2010/69
E/2010/70
E/2010/71
E/2010/72
E/2010/73
E/2010/74
E/2010/75
E/2010/76 (A/65/79)
E/2010/77 (A/65/80)
E/2010/78
E/2010/79
E/2010/80
E/2010/81
E/2010/82
E/2010/83 (A/65/81)
E/2010/84
E/2010/85
E/2010/86
E/2010/87
E/2010/88 (A/65/82)
E/2010/89
E/2010/90 (A/65/84)
E/2010/91 (A/64/803)
E/2010/92
E/2010/93
E/2010/94
E/2010/95
E/2010/96
E/2010/97
E/2010/98
E/2010/99 (ESCOR, 2010, Suppl. no. 1)

# LIST OF DOCUMENTS

## General series

E/2010/100
E/2010/101 (A/64/852)
E/2010/102 + Corr.1
E/2010/103
E/2010/104

## Information series

E/2010/INF/1
E/2010/INF/2 + Add.1-2 (To be issued in ESCOR, 2010,
  Suppl. no. 1)
E/2010/INF/3-4

## Limited series

E/2010/L.1-8
E/2010/L.9 + Rev.1
E/2010/L.10-11
E/2010/L.12 + Rev.1
E/2010/L.13-44

## Non-governmental organizations series

E/2010/NGO/1-90

## Summary records

E/2010/SR.1-14
E/2010/SR.15(A)
E/2010/SR.15(B)
E/2010/SR.16
E/2010/SR.17(A)
E/2010/SR.17(B)
E/2010/SR.18(A)
E/2010/SR.18(B)
E/2010/SR.19(A)
E/2010/SR.19(B)
E/2010/SR.20-52

## Miscellaneous documents

E/2010/CRP.1-5

## Other documents considered by the Council

A/65/16 (GAOR, 65th sess., Suppl. no. 16)
A/65/25 (GAOR, 65th sess., Suppl. no. 25)
A/65/41 (GAOR, 65th sess., Suppl. no. 41)
A/65/61 + Corr.1
E/2009/28/Add.1 (E/CN.7/2009/12/Add.1) (ESCOR, 2009,
  Suppl. no. 8A)
E/2009/30/Add.1 (E/CN.15/2009/20/Add.1) (ESCOR, 2009,
  Suppl. no. 10A)
E/2009/35 (ESCOR, 2009, Suppl. no. 15)
E/2009/92
E/CONF.99/3
E/CONF.100/9
E/INCB/2009/1

## Resolutions and Decisions

E/2010/99 (ESCOR, 2010, Suppl.1) Resolutions and
decisions of the Economic and Social Council : organizational
session for 2010, New York, 19 January, 9 and 12 February
2010; resumed organizational session for 2010, New York, 28
April and 21 May 2010; substantive session of 2010, New
York, 28 June-23 July 2010; resumed substantive session of
2010, New York, 9 September, 25 October, 10 November
and 14-15 December 2010

# LIST OF DOCUMENTS

## Supplements to Official Records

**No. 1** E/2010/99
Resolutions and decisions of the Economic and
Social Council : organizational session for 2010,
New York, 19 January, 9 and 12 February 2010;
resumed organizational session for 2010, New
York, 28 April and 21 May 2010; substantive
session of 2010, New York, 28 June-23 July 2010;
resumed substantive session of 2010, New York, 9
September, 25 October, 10 November and 14-15
December 2010. - New York : UN, 2011.
    198 p. - (ESCOR, 2010, Suppl. no. 1).

**No. 2** E/2010/22 (E/C.12/2009/3)
Committee on Economic, Social and Cultural
Rights : report on the 42nd and 43rd sessions, 4-
22 May 2009, 2-20 November 2009. - New York ;
Geneva : UN, 2010.
    v, 158 p. - (ESCOR, 2010, Suppl. no. 2).

**No. 3** *Symbol not used.*

**No. 4** E/2010/24 (E/CN.3/2010/34)
Statistical Commission : report on the 41st session
(23 to 26 February 2009). - New York : UN, 2010.
    iv, 39 p. - (ESCOR, 2010, Suppl. no. 4).

**No. 5** E/2010/25 (E/CN.9/2010/9)
Commission on Population and Development :
report on the 43rd session (3 April 2009 and 12-16
April 2010). - New York : UN, 2010.
    vi, 21 p. - (ESCOR, 2010, Suppl. no. 5).

**No. 6** E/2010/26 (E/CN.5/2010/9)
Commission for Social Development : report on
the 48th session (13 February 2009 and 3-12 and
19 February 2010). - New York : UN, 2010.
    iv, 32 p. - (ESCOR, 2010, Suppl. no. 6).

**No. 7** E/2010/27 + Corr.1 (E/CN.6/2010/11)
Commission on the Status of Women : report on
the 54th session (13 March and 14 October 2009
and 1-12 March 2010). - New York : UN, 2010.
    iv, 97 p. - (ESCOR, 2010, Suppl. no. 7).

**No. 8** E/2010/28 (E/CN.7/2010/18)
Commission on Narcotic Drugs : report on the
53rd session (2 December 2009 and 8-12 March
2010). - New York : UN, 2010.
    vi, 118 p. : table. - (ESCOR, 2010, Suppl. no.
8).

**No. 8A** E/2010/28/Add.1 (E/CN.7/2010/18/Add.1)
Commission on Narcotic Drugs : report on the
reconvened 53rd session (2 December 2010). -
New York : UN, 2010.
    iii, 15 p. - (ESCOR, 2010, Suppl. no. 8A).

**No. 9** E/2010/29 (E/CN.17/2010/15)
Commission on Sustainable Development : report
on the 18th session (15 May 2009 and 3-14 May
2010). - New York : UN, 2010.
    iii, 66 p. - (ESCOR, 2010, Suppl. no. 9).

**No. 10** E/2010/30 (E/CN.15/2010/20)
Commission on Crime Prevention and Criminal
Justice : report on the 19th session (4 December
2009 and 17-21 May 2010). - New York : UN,
2010.
    v, 136 p. - (ESCOR, 2010, Suppl. no. 10).

**No. 10A** E/2010/30/Add.1 (E/CN.15/2010/20/Add.1)
Commission on Crime Prevention and Criminal
Justice : report on the reconvened 19th session (3
December 2010). - New York : UN, 2010.
    iii, 5-19 p. - (ESCOR, 2010, Suppl. no. 10A).

**No. 11** E/2010/31 (E/CN.16/2010/5)
Commission on Science and Technology for
Development : report on the 13th session (17-21
May 2010). - New York : UN, 2010.
    vii, 27 p. : table. - (ESCOR, 2010, Suppl. no.
11).

**No. 12** *Symbol not used.*

**No. 13** E/2010/33
Committee for Development Policy : report on the
12th session (22-26 March 2010). - New York :
UN, 2010.
    iv, 28 p. - (ESCOR, 2010, Suppl. no. 13).

**No. 14** E/2010/34/Rev.1 (E/ICEF/2010/7/Rev.1)
Executive Board of the United Nations Children's
Fund : report on the 1st and 2nd regular sessions
and annual session of 2010. - New York UN, 2010.
    v, 92 p. : tables. - (ESCOR, 2010, Suppl. no.
14).

**No. 15** E/2010/35
Executive Board of the United Nations
Development Programme/United Nations
Population Fund : report of the Executive Board on
its work during 2010. - New York : UN, 2010.
    v, 113 p. - (ESCOR, 2010, Suppl. no. 15).

**No. 16** E/2010/36
Executive Board of the World Food Programme :
report on the 1st and 2nd regular sessions and
annual session of 2009. - New York : UN, 2010.
    iii, 59 p. - (ESCOR, 2010, Suppl. no. 16).

**No. 17** *Symbol not used.*

**No. 18** *Symbol not used.*

**No. 19** E/2010/39 (E/ESCAP/66/27)
Economic and Social Commission for Asia and the
Pacific : annual report, 30 April 2009-19 May 2010.
- New York : UN, 2010.
    vi, 55 p. - (ESCOR, 2010, Suppl. no. 19).

**No. 20** *Symbol not used.*

**No. 21** E/2010/41 (E/ESCWA/26/9/Report)
Economic and Social Commission for Western
Asia : report on the 26th session, 17-20 May 2010.
- New York : UN, 2010.
    44 p. - (ESCOR, 2010, Suppl. no. 21).

# LIST OF DOCUMENTS

## Supplements to Official Records

**No. 22**   *Symbol not used.*

**No. 23**   E/2010/43 (E/C.19/2010/15)
Permanent Forum on Indigenous Issues : report
on the 9th session (19-30 April 2010). - New York :
UN, 2010.
    iii, 44 p. - (ESCOR, 2010, Suppl. no. 23).

**No. 24**   E/2010/44 (E/C.16/2010/5)
Committee of Experts on Public Administration :
report on the 9th session (19-23 April 2010). - New
York : UN, 2010.
    iv, 21 p. - (ESCOR, 2010, Suppl. no. 24).

**No. 25**   E/2010/45 (E/C.18/2010/7)
Committee of Experts on International Cooperation
in Tax Matters : report on the 6th session (18-22
October 2010). - New York : UN, 2011.
    iv, 25 p. - (ESCOR, 2010, Suppl. no. 25).